*Baptists in America*

*The Columbia Contemporary American Religion Series*

**Columbia Contemporary American Religion Series**

The spiritual landscape of contemporary America is as varied and complex as that of any country in the world. The books in this new series, written by leading scholars for students and general readers alike, fall into two categories: Some titles are portraits of the country's major religious groups. They describe and explain particular religious practices and rituals, beliefs, and major challenges facing a given community today. Others explore current themes and topics in American religion that cut across denominational lines. The texts are supplemented with carefully selected photographs and artwork, and annotated bibliographies.

—

*Roman Catholicism in America*
CHESTER GILLIS

*Islam in America*
JANE I. SMITH

*Buddhism in America*
RICHARD HUGHES SEAGER

*Protestantism in America*
RANDALL BALMER AND LAUREN F. WINNER

*Judaism in America*
MARC LEE RAPHAEL

*The Quakers in America*
THOMAS D. HAMM

*New Age and Neopagans in America*
SARAH PIKE

# BAPTISTS

## *in America*

**Bill J. Leonard**

COLUMBIA UNIVERSITY PRESS

NEW YORK

COLUMBIA UNIVERSITY PRESS
*Publishers Since 1893*
New York    Chichester, West Sussex

ISBN: 0-231-12702-2

Library of Congress Cataloging-in-Publication Data are on file
with the Library of Congress

Columbia University Press books are printed on
permanent and durable acid-free paper.

Printed in the United States of America
c 10 9 8 7 6 5 4 3 2 1

To Thomas K. Hearn, President
Wake Forest University
and
James Dunn, Professor of Religion and Public Policy
Wake Forest University
and to the memory of
Alice Wonders, Professor of Religion
Texas Wesleyan University
Mentors of Faith and Freedom

# CONTENTS

# PREFACE

I grew up going to Baptist churches. I was baptized at the age of eight in the First Baptist Church of Decatur, Wise County, Texas. The odds on my being a Baptist were considerable, since until recently there were more Baptists in Texas than any other religious group. (Roman Catholics recently beat them out numerically.) First Baptist was affiliated with the Southern Baptist Convention, but I often went to revival meetings and other services with my grandmother Frankie Henton, who attended the Fundamental Baptist Church of Decatur. It was an Independent Baptist congregation with a big neon anchor outside the church that flashed JESUS SAVES twenty-four hours a day, attracting at least half a million crickets on a hot summer night. People got saved (converted) "hard" at the Fundamental Baptist Church, and I always thought their method for evaluating the effectiveness of the preacher was rather simple: "He don't sweat, we don't listen."

I stayed with the Southern Baptists for a long time, attending one of their seminaries before heading off to Boston University for doctoral work in American religious studies. My first teaching position was at the Southern Baptist Theological Seminary, Louisville, Kentucky, which was the first of the SBC seminaries, founded in 1859. I taught there some sixteen years, carried along by some of the finest students and friends I have ever known. But the school, like its denomination, took a hard turn to the theological and political right, and it was time for me to move elsewhere. Fortunately, Samford University in Birmingham, Alabama, invited me to teach in its religion department, and it was there that my family joined the Sixth Avenue Baptist Church, one of the largest African American Baptist churches in the state. At that point I moved from the SBC to the National Baptist Convention, Inc., and began to learn anew what it means to be a Baptist. Moving to Wake Forest University in Winston-Salem, North Carolina, in 1996, we joined the First Baptist Church, Highland Avenue, the oldest African American Baptist congregation in town. It is affiliated with the American Baptist Churches in the USA. So I am in my third Baptist denomination in twelve years. These shifts have taught me a great deal about diversity in the Baptist house, as has extensive research on Baptist history, much of it done while working on *Baptist Ways: A History*, a survey of Baptist history worldwide, published in 2003. This book, *Baptists in America*, allowed me to build on that earlier investigation, with greater attention to more detailed and contemporary Baptist experiences in the United States.

These experiences keep me a Baptist, ever persuaded by those portions of the tradition that long for uncoerced faith and believers' churches, radical dissent and religious liberty, biblical authority and biblical audacity, and the unceasing power of baptismal immersion (and occasional foot-washings) within a community of faith.

In this endeavor I am grateful for the help of JoAnne Trethaway and Laura Jane Kist, my administrative associates at the Wake Forest University Divinity School; Ryan Parker, my research assistant there; and my faculty colleagues who encourage and bless amid the ordeal and excitement of beginning a new divinity school. As always, I am indebted to my spouse, Dr. Candyce C. Leonard, and our daughter, Stephanie, both of whom bear with me and bear me through these endeavors.

Bill J. Leonard
The Divinity School
Wake Forest University

*Baptists in America*

## CHAPTER ONE

# Introduction

Members of the Little Dove Old Regular Baptist Church, up a hollow in the Appalachian Mountains, contend that their "old-timey" ways validate their claim to be a New Testament community of faith. Services at Little Dove are conducted once or twice a month, attended by no more than twenty to twenty-five people, with preaching by an unpaid, bi-vocational elder (males only). They use no musical instruments, and sing in chant-like plain-song the "shaped-note" hymns of their faith.[1] The preacher holds forth for more than an hour, often abandoning the "sacred desk" (pulpit) to mingle with the worshipers, shaking hands and weeping. Some Baptists exult in their traditionalism.

Others retain traditional accoutrements but reflect new possibilities. At first glance, the Wolf Creek Baptist Church, a rural congregation off a Kentucky state highway, looks like the traditional Southern Baptist Church in its churchly observances and denominational program. Its members sing hymns, welcome "gospel quartets," await the minister's sermon, and call people to be "born again." Yet before the twentieth century's end the church ordained a woman, copastor Cindy Harp Johnson, to the Baptist ministry, a radical action for many similar churches.[2]

Other churches are radically different from past Baptist communions. At Saddleback Valley Church in Lake Forest, California, there are multiple services, conducted in a "worship center" that accommodates at least 5,000 people in each service. Hymns appear on wide-screen projectors across the church. Dressed casually, the minister, nationally known religious leader Rick Warren, preaches sermons that emphasize conversion and practical

Christian living. Skits, film clips, and other visual aids punctuate the service in an effort to attract "seekers" who are turned off by traditional religious rituals. Begun in 1980, Saddleback Valley Church has more than 15,000 members. Some 18,000 people attend its weekly services. The church retains its Baptist connections, but with a decidedly nondenominational ambience.[3]

Salem Baptist Church is one of Chicago's largest African American congregations, with more than 17,000 members. Its pastor, James Meeks, is an Illinois state senator and executive vice president of Rainbow/PUSH (People United to Serve Humanity), and is the chosen successor to Jesse Jackson, the organization's president. However, unlike Jackson, Meeks opposes abortion rights and gay rights as well. An evangelical in theology, Meeks works for spiritual and political equality in racial matters. His church anticipates a $32 million construction program involving a 10,000-seat sanctuary "combined with a seven thousand seat sports arena" in inner-city Chicago.[4] Meeks and his church may reflect old/new Baptist traditions.

Jerry Falwell is a Baptist. So is Jesse Jackson. And don't forget Billy Graham. Their assessments of the state of the American Union are often radically dissimilar.[5] Bill Clinton is a Baptist. So is Jesse Helms. American political life has hardly known two more different public figures. Martin Luther King Jr. was a Baptist. So was Strom Thurman. In symbol and substance those two individuals personified the American conflict over race and civil rights. Tim LaHaye is a Baptist. So is Maya Angelou. Their books are best sellers; their approaches to life essentially antithetical. Baptists are a diverse lot, claiming common and contradictory beliefs and practices. This book documents the faith, practice, and variety of Baptist churches and individuals.

### Baptists in America: A Sectarian Establishment

There are more than thirty million Baptists in the United States of America.[6] They represent the largest Anglo-Saxon and African American Protestant denominations in the nation. And, as historian Walter Shurden wrote decades ago, they are "not a silent people."[7] Baptists do not hesitate to make their theological and ethical opinions known in their churches and in the world at large. Indeed, Baptists often seem the quintessential American dissenters, challenging the moral, ecclesiastical, and political status quo, making their opinions known in pulpits, sit-ins, and on *Larry King Live*. In their rhetoric and public presence, whether supporting civil rights or opposing abortion rights, Baptists sound unceasingly sectarian in their efforts to maintain distinctive theological and moral boundaries.

At the same time, Baptists may appear to be a de facto religious establishment, dominating large segments of the religious landscape with their considerable numbers, their defense of the status quo, and their efforts to achieve a kind evangelistic hegemony that "conquers the nation for Christ." They are at once the "culture despisers" and the "culture promoters," ever critiquing and appropriating selected segments of American society. Baptist churches and denominations represent varying degrees of sectarian and establishment tendencies in American life.

In theology and practice they are a study in contrasts. At first glance, Baptist theology seems classically Protestant in its emphasis on doctrines of the Trinity, the incarnation of Jesus Christ, the authority of Scripture, salvation by faith alone, the priesthood of believers, an ordained ministry, baptism by immersion and the observance of the Lord's Supper, all held together in a congregational form of church government. Yet the interpretation and implementation of these beliefs have made Baptists one of the most fragmented denominations in America, often characterized as a people who "multiply by dividing." For example, Baptist *interpretations* of Protestant orthodoxy cover a broad spectrum from Arminian to Calvinist, from free will to predestination. Arminian or Free Will Baptists believe that Christ died for the whole world (general atonement), that all persons have the free will to choose or reject salvation, and that salvation can be secured by repentance and faith. It is also possible for Christians to turn away from salvation by "falling from grace." Calvinist Baptists, on the other hand, insist that Christ died for only an "elect" chosen by God before the foundation of the world and that the saved will persevere in faith to the end. Still other Baptists combine elements of both of these traditions. Baptist worship practices also reflect great diversity, extending from rural meetinghouses to cathedral-like "sanctuaries" to megachurch "worship centers." While some Baptist ministers have advanced academic degrees, others have little formal education. Some receive salaries in full-time positions, while others are "bi-vocational," working in the secular world on weekdays and serving a church on Sundays. Baptist polity runs the gamut from congregational autonomy to elaborate denominational cooperation and connection, from rabid individualism to a powerful sense of community.

Socially and politically, the contrasts are dramatic. During the early twentieth century, Baptists were at the forefront of both the modernist and the fundamentalist movements. Some Baptists promoted the Social Gospel movement while others vehemently opposed it. The civil rights movement began in African American Baptist churches, only to be opposed by Anglo-Saxon Baptists, particularly in the South. While Baptists have long been outspoken supporters of religious liberty and the separation of church and state, many are advocates of prayer in schools, the public display of the Ten Commandments, funding for private school vouchers, and other forms of government aid to "faith-based" communities. Some are strong supporters of the ordination of women to the ministry, while others resist such actions as a violation of basic biblical teachings.

There are certain commonalities, however. Indeed, in many parts of the United States growing up Baptist once seemed relatively easy. For much of the twentieth century, a variety of Baptists north and south, black and white, carried out "common programs [that] created a surprising uniformity among an otherwise diverse and highly individualistic constituency."[8] On any given Sunday, members set out for church armed with the three great symbols of Baptist faith: A King James Version (KJV) of the Bible (zipper edition), a Sunday school "Quarterly" outlining the standard Bible lesson, and an offering envelope containing the weekly "tithe."[9] The envelope required that individuals "check off" boxes delineating their faithfulness, with points given for attendance, being on time, preparing the lesson, bringing a Bible, giving an offering, and attending worship. The best Christians were those whose box scores totaled 100 percent each week.

Varying styles of worship reflected the diversity, however. Some "pipe organ churches" developed more elaborate "orders of worship," with robed choirs, anthems, and ministers who offered erudite sermons energetically but tastefully presented. Others included livelier "special music" from gospel choirs or quartets, in services where self-taught preachers belted out brimstone, sweating as if they had been to hell that morning and had come back to tell about it.

Growing up Baptist often meant (and in some cases still means) adherence to a clearly defined moral code that forbade dancing, card playing, immodest dress, movies, and other "worldly" practices. Churches frequently held annual revivals, at which traveling evangelists preached dramatic sermons aimed at bringing people to faith in Christ. Baptisms were conducted in creeks and rivers, or in heated baptismal pools (baptisteries) inside the church buildings. It was a rather clear-cut identity with well-established theological and practical boundaries.

As the twenty-first century got under way, many Baptist churches kept continuity with their past. Indeed, certain rural or county-seat Baptist churches in the United States may seem like a time warp, maintaining traditional practices in worship and overall church life.

This is a good time to publish a book on Baptists in America, for a number of reasons. First, Baptists have been exceedingly public in American life during the last twenty years. Internal controversies among Southern and African American Baptists, Baptists' participation in both the Religious Right and the civil rights movement, and debates over the ordination of women and gays have brought Baptists to the attention of the broader American culture. Second, Baptists themselves are experiencing a time of permanent transition in their own sense of churchly and denominational identity. As old denominational systems change, even break down, Baptist churches and individuals are struggling with the foundations of their historical and theological distinctiveness. Many men and women who join Baptist churches have little or no knowledge of Baptist history and beliefs and no particular desire to call themselves Baptist. Some congregations have dropped or distanced themselves from the name "Baptist" in order to attract a constituency including those who are suspicious of or bored with denominational ties. Third, this book offers an opportunity not only to describe Baptist history and beliefs but also to examine the relationship of Baptist groups and individuals to a variety of issues confronting the larger American culture. Because of their numbers and their diversity, Baptists may well offer an intriguing case study in the interaction of religion and culture in the recent history of the United States. The issues discussed in this book are representative rather than definitive or all-inclusive. While every effort is made to identify as many Baptist subgroups as possible, the work of many of those groups is not explored in great detail. Rather, the book traces the basic history of the denomination and then explores specific topics that have galvanized Baptist churches and individuals in the latter third of the twentieth century. Chapters 2 and 3 detail historical developments from the beginning of the movement in seventeenth-century Holland and England through much of the last century. Chapter 4 provides a survey of Baptist doctrines and theologies, with particular attention to various confessions of faith used by churches and denominations in England and the United States. Chapter 5 offers an overview of many of the Baptist denominations or fellowships found in the United States. Chapter 6 explores some of Baptists' most enduring internal debates, including biblical authority, the ordinances (baptism and the Lord's Supper), and their congregational forms of church government.

Chapter 7 examines ideas and controversies related to Baptists and religious liberty, one of the most enduring concerns of the Baptist tradition.

Chapter 8 gives some attention to ethnic and racial responses and tensions in Baptist life. Chapter 9 looks at the role(s) of women in Baptist churches and the responses of various Baptist traditions to women's activities in church and home. Chapter 10 pursues the varying ways in which Baptists relate to certain aspects of American culture.

Baptists in America may declare that this world is not their home, they are just passing through, but any survey of their history illustrates that Baptists are a right worldly community of Christians. Their long-term commitments may be in heaven, but they are ever trying to change the state of things in this world as well. And, through it all, the diversity, unity, and overall messiness of the people called Baptists seem evident, past, present, and future.

# CHAPTER TWO

# *Baptist Beginnings*

Amid multiple theories of origin, Baptist beginnings are relatively easy to discern. The movement was born of the upheavals that descended on the British church during the seventeenth century and the accession of the Stuart monarchy, which began with the reign of James I in 1603. The first identifiable Baptist group began in 1608/1609 with a band of Puritan Separatists exiled in Amsterdam. Led by John Smyth (ca. 1570–1612) and Thomas Helwys (ca.1550–1615), this band of dissenters originated in England among those Puritans who were convinced that the Church of England had been completely corrupted by Romanist and establishmentarian tendencies. They insisted that Anglicanism could not be reformed and that true believers should separate from it.

These separatist sentiments were present in various "conventicles" that were "gathered" throughout England, one of which was served by John Smyth in the town of Gainsborough. Increasing persecution forced a portion of the members to move to Scrooby under the leadership of John Robinson (1572–1625). Some later moved to Holland, first to Amsterdam and then to Leyden. In 1620, led by William Bradford and William Brewster, they boarded the *Mayflower* for America. These "Pilgrims" arrived at Plymouth, founding the first Separatist congregation (not Baptist) in the New World.[1]

## Early Baptist Groups

### *General Baptists*

John Smyth and Thomas Helwys took another faction from the Gainsborough church to Amsterdam to escape persecution by the Stuart monarchy. As Separatists they were committed to a church of believers, gathered around a covenant with God and one another. In Amsterdam they became convinced that baptism should be administered only to those who could testify to a work of grace in their lives and that infant baptism had no precedent in the New Testament church.

John Smyth led the little band in repudiating their previous (infant) baptism in the Church of England and accepting a new baptism administered after each individual professed faith in Christ. They united on the basis of a covenant, an agreement that they would walk circumspectly with God and one another in faith, fellowship, and discipline. One source describes the momentous event:

> Pastor and deacons laid down their office, the church disbanded or avowed itself no church and all stood as private individuals, unbaptized. All being equal Smyth proposed that Helwys their social leader should baptize them, but he deferred to his spiritual leader. Smyth therefore baptized himself, then baptized Helwys and the others.[2]

Smyth thus performed a se-baptism (self-baptism) and then administered the rite to Helwys and the others. The world's first Baptist church was constituted around a confession of personal faith, believers' baptism, and a covenant that united the members to God and with one another. The group met in a bake-house in Amsterdam, wrote a confession of faith that delineated their basic beliefs, and gave themselves to the continued study of the Bible. The mode of their baptism was trine affusion, pouring water on the head three times in the name of the Father, the Son, and the Holy Spirit. This method was used until at least 1641, when immersion became the norm for all Baptist groups.

The first Baptists were Puritan Separatists in their response to Anglicanism and Arminians in their theological orientation. In accepting the teachings of the Dutch theologian Jacob Arminius (d. 1609), these Baptists believed that Christ died for the entire world, not simply for an elect chosen before the world's foundation. This "general" atonement meant that all persons were potentially elected to salvation and needed only to implement repentance and faith to realize it. Individual free will "cooperated" with divine grace to make salvation possible. Yet those who had the free will to choose faith also had the freedom to reject it; thus "falling away" from salvation. Because of their belief in general atonement, these believers were known as General Baptists.

Smyth's restless quest for the true church apparently led him to the Waterlander Mennonites, a historic Anabaptist community in Amsterdam that had practiced believers' baptism since the sixteenth century. Convinced that the Mennonites had a more valid baptismal tradition, he sought membership with them. This action led to Baptists' first schism as Smyth led a group toward the Mennonites while Helwys took the remaining Baptists back to England. Smyth died, probably in 1612, before he could be admitted. Helwys and the others established a church in Spitalfields, just outside the walls of the city of London, the first Baptist church on English soil. Soon other General Baptist churches were organized around the country.

### Particular Baptists

A second company of Baptists began during the 1630s, this one in London as an outgrowth of another Puritan communion located in Southwark and known as the Jacob-Lathrop-Jessey Church, named for its first three pastors: Henry Jacob (1563–1624), John Lathrop (d.1653), and Henry Jessey (1601–1663). While the group was generally independent, it appears that some of its members were Separatists while others were non-separatists who still hoped to purify the Anglican church of its Romanist "corruptions."[3]

By 1638, and perhaps as early as 1633, a group led by Samuel Eaton and Mark Luker had separated from the Jessey church, constituting themselves as a separate congregation. In 1641 they began the practice of immersion baptism as required of all members following a profession of their faith in Christ. Immersion involved the dipping of the entire body in water, the mode of baptism that they believed Jesus received from John the Baptizer in the river Jordan. This practice was probably modeled after that of the Collegiant Mennonites in the Netherlands. Before long, full immersion (or dipping) became the normative mode of baptism in Baptist churches. It remains the baptismal method used by Baptists worldwide.

Theologically, these seventeenth-century Baptists were Calvinists whose beliefs were based on the Bible as interpreted by John Calvin (1509–1664), the reformer of Geneva, Switzerland, whose monumental work, *The Institutes of the Christian Religion*, first published in 1536, set the standard for Baptist support of Reformed theology. They were known as Particular Baptists because of their belief that Christ died for a particular group of people, the elect, chosen out of God's mercy before the foundation of the world. As these Baptists understood the gospel, all persons were born in total depravity, worthy only of complete damnation by a just and righteous God. Yet God in mercy had "elected" some individuals to salvation unconditionally, a result of God's sovereign choice, not because of any merit in the individual believer. All the elect would ultimately be saved through God's irresistible grace and would persevere in Christian discipleship until the end. Christ's death on the cross was therefore "particular" to the elect and did not apply to the entire human race. Thus, by the 1640s there were two distinguishable and diverse groups of Baptists in England, each claiming a commonality of practices while presenting contradictory theological ideals.

## Seventh Day Baptists

By the 1650s another group of Baptists had appeared in England, convinced that certain teachings of the Hebrew Bible were mandated for the Christian church. These Seventh Day Baptists insisted that Saturday was the divinely ordained Sabbath and should continue to be observed by Christians everywhere. Some also retained certain Old Testament dietary practices. Seventh Day Baptists retained basic Baptist practices, and many remained members of General Baptist congregations until their own churches took shape.

## A Dissenting Community

Like other dissenters of the period, many Baptist communions experienced varying degrees of persecution from the English state and its Anglican establishment. Dissenting movements were frequently targeted for punitive action as a result of their refusal to conform to laws regulating religious groups. These included Puritans of various stripes; Levellers, who desired a more democratic approach to government; Diggers, who wanted the common or public lands opened for use by the lower classes; Ranters, who believed that they received the direct inspiration of the Holy Spirit for new revelations and enthusiasms; and Seekers, who insisted that all traditional beliefs should be abolished or held in abeyance until God provided a new source of authority. The Society of Friends, also known as Quakers, founded by George Fox

(1624–1691), offered revelations inspired by the Inner Light of Christ that lay dormant within every individual, waiting to be awakened.

Persecution leveled against these and other dissenting groups was often severe. Many Baptists, clergy and laity alike, were fined or jailed, among them Thomas Helwys, who apparently died in prison around 1616. In response to this harassment, Helwys wrote a treatise on religious liberty addressed to King James I. Titled *The Mystery of Iniquity* (1612), it was the first such publication in English to call for complete religious freedom for the heretic and the atheist alike.

This penchant for radical religious liberty characterized large segments of Baptist life into the twenty-first century. It suggested that God alone was judge of conscience, and therefore no establishment, whether vested in church or in state, could dictate belief or punish unbelief. Individuals were responsible to God alone for the choices they did or did not make. Among the Baptists imprisoned during the mid-seventeenth century was John Bunyan, Bedford Baptist pastor and author of such well-known works as *Pilgrims Progress*. Persecution continued until the overthrow of the Stuart monarchy in the "Glorious Revolution" that brought William and Mary from the Netherlands to the English throne in 1688. A year later the Act of Toleration ended some persecution of dissenting communions but did not give them full freedom.

## *Baptist Church Life*

In addition to their belief in religious liberty, the early Baptists valued the autonomy and uniqueness of the local congregation. Indeed, the first confession of the General Baptists in Amsterdam (1612) declared:

> That as one congregation hath CHRIST, so hath all. 2.cor.10.7. and that the Word of GOD cometh not out from any one, neither to any one congregation in particular. I. Cor. 14.36. But unto every particular Church, as it doth unto all the world. Coll. 1.5.6. And therefore no church ought not challenge any prerogative over any other.[4]

Congregations received their authority directly from Christ and mediated that authority through the community of believers. Each congregation was responsible to God for its mission and ministry.

This emphasis on autonomy did not keep them from developing inter-church relationships, gatherings of congregations for fellowship, discipline, and mutual encouragement. Associations thus became an early form of Baptist denominationalism, linking churches in particular sections of England. The General Baptists were especially sympathetic to associational relationships. New associations were formed by Baptists in the north and south of England. Representatives of churches joined together periodically to affirm their common beliefs and actions, encourage one another in the faith, and respond to questions that were apt to divide the multitudes. These meetings often produced "Circular Letters" that dealt with specific issues confronting the churches. These letters reported on the actions of the associational meeting, addressed doctrinal issues, and responded to practical questions raised by church representatives. When churches experienced controversy they sometimes sought associational mediation. They were not bound to accept the rulings of the association, but to take its recommendations under advisement.

The covenantal agreement meant that churches did not hesitate to dispense discipline to recalcitrant members. Such discipline was administered for sins of lust and drunkenness, infidelity and "harlotry." It included lapses in church attendance, spiritual negligence, and participation in non-Baptist communions. Marriage with non-Baptists was also grounds for disciplinary action. Disciplined members could be excluded from receiving communion or from attending worship services altogether. Repentance was encouraged and behavior monitored. Church leaders insisted that discipline was intended to be redemptive and to protect the reputation of the church in the larger community.[5]

## British Baptists: The Eighteenth Century

Although Baptists remained a distinct sectarian minority among English religious groups, they experienced numerical and organizational growth in the seventeenth century. Schools were begun in Bristol in the south and in Stepney near London. A new Baptist denomination, known as New Connection Baptists, was born in the 1750s out of the influence of the Wesleyan revivals. Its founder, Dan Taylor (1738–1816), was converted under the preaching of John and Charles Wesley. He soon accepted Baptist views and led a movement to rejuvenate the General Baptists and revive their churches. General Baptist hesitancy about this "enthusiastical" movement led to a schism and the formation of the New Connection Baptists.

Funds for support of pastors were established, and the Baptist Missionary Society was founded in 1793. It raised the money to send William Carey

(1761–1834) and his family as missionaries to India, an event that marked the beginnings of a renewed mission effort for British and American Protestants, including Baptists. Carey and his colleagues found themselves surrounded by multitudes of "Hindoos" and "Mussulmans," from which they sought to make converts to Christianity. They were the first of a missionary task force sent out by Baptists in Britain and the United States.

These early missionaries and those who came after them were concerned with presenting the claims of the Christian faith in "foreign" lands. They translated and published the Bible into native languages, preached the gospel, founded schools, and organized churches. Converts were a long time coming, and missionaries were vulnerable to a variety of diseases that were rampant in native cultures. Many Baptist missionaries, their spouses, and their children died soon after their arrival in the mission field. Carey and the others were also concerned with bringing various aspects of Christian "civilization" to the cultures in which they worked; this was particularly true with regard to the Indian practice of suttee, the requirement that a wife throw herself on the funeral pyre of her husband. The missionaries hoped that Christianity would help end this practice. Andrew Fuller (1754–1815), one of the founders of the Baptist Missionary Society, noted this concern to export Christianity and "civilization," writing of their mission:

> The object of this society is to evangelize the poor, dark, idolatrous Heathen, by sending missionaries into different parts of the world where the glorious gospel of Christ is not at present published, to preach the glad tidings of salvation by the blood of the Lamb. . . . Were these ignorant immortals but thoroughly instructed in the doctrines and precepts of Christianity, their civilization would naturally follow.[6]

Nineteenth-century British Baptists expanded their missionary work into Africa, China, and the Caribbean. They formed the Baptist Union in 1832, and in 1873 it became the Baptist Union of Great Britain and Ireland. It established links among many but not all Baptist churches in those regions.

## Baptist Beginnings in America

Religious liberty was a factor in the founding of the first Baptist church in the American colonies. In 1631 Roger Williams (1603?–1683), another Englishman of Puritan sentiment, made his way to Massachusetts, accompanied by his wife, Mary (b. 1609). Educated at Pembroke College, Oxford, he received Anglican ordination after graduation in 1627. By 1629 he had turned to Puritan Separatism, a position that kept him from accepting a position as teacher in the church in Boston, which was more moderate in its views toward the Church of England.

Brilliant and argumentative, Williams served congregations in Plymouth and Salem. Ultimately his radical theological and political views brought him into conflict with representatives of the New England Way, the prevailing religious establishment of the day. These Puritans sought a place to practice their views but hesitated to extend religious liberty to colonial sects lest heretical religion gain the upper hand in the new land.

From the perspective of the Puritan establishment, Williams's views were a double fault. First, he suggested that the Native Americans and not the English king were the real owners of the American land and should be justly compensated for it. Second, like Thomas Helwys in England, Williams declared that God alone was judge of the conscience and each individual was responsible to God for the religious decisions he or she made. There were no Christian nations; there were only Christian believers who practiced their faith without the need for approval from the governmental powers of this world.

These ideas led to Williams's exile from Massachusetts in the winter of 1635. Sent out into a "howling wilderness," he was befriended by the Narragansett Indians, bought land from them, and established Providence Plantation, as "a shelter for persons distressed of conscience."[7] Providence soon became the center of a new colony, Rhode Island, whose charter granted religious liberty to all who settled there. It was in Providence, probably in 1638, that Williams and others founded the first Baptist church in America. Soon afterward, another Baptist congregation was begun at Newport, under the leadership of Dr. John Clarke (1609–1676), a physician. Clarke was instrumental in founding the Newport colony, organizing a Baptist church there, and securing a charter from the English crown in 1663.

Baptist ideas soon spread to other segments of New England. The First Baptist Church of Boston was founded in 1665 by a group led by Thomas Goold (d. 1675), an oft-persecuted minister. The church was continuously under scrutiny by the state, and its facilities were often boarded up or otherwise closed down. By 1682 there was a Baptist church in Kittery, Maine, founded by William Screven (1629–1713). Some of its members moved southward, settling in Charleston, South Carolina, by the late 1690s and marking the beginnings of the Baptist movement in the South, the region in which it would thrive most extensively. The First Baptist Church of Charleston dates its origins from this period.

Like their British counterparts, New England Baptists were early advocates of religious liberty. Isaac Backus (1724–1806), converted in the Great Awakening, moved from Congregationalism to the Baptists in 1756. After serving as pastor of a church in Middleborough, Massachusetts, from 1756 to 1806, he was appointed representative of the Warren Association of New England Baptists to the Continental Congress and thus became one of the first people to lobby formally in behalf of religious liberty. Backus was an institution in American Baptist life, writing one of the earliest histories of Baptists in New England, preaching widely, and working on behalf of Baptist concerns for liberty of conscience and freedom of worship. Of his efforts, Backus wrote:

> Nothing can be true religion but a voluntary obedience unto God's revealed will, of which each rational soul has an actual right to judge for itself; every person has an inalienable right to act in all religious affairs according to the full persuasion of his own mind, where others are not injured thereby.[8]

By the eighteenth century, Baptist churches in Virginia and other parts of the South had confronted an often antagonistic Anglican establishment that closed churches, jailed ministers, and required nonconformist preachers to secure a license from the state. Many Baptist ministers refused to secure state authorization and were subsequently imprisoned. One of those preachers was John "Swearing Jack" Waller (1741–1802), converted under the preaching of Baptist Lewis Craig (1741–1824) and thereafter incarcerated in multiple Virginia jails for his stubborn refusal to secure the necessary license. These Baptists were a versatile lot. Lewis Craig's brother, Elijah (1743–1808), also a Baptist preacher, immigrated to Kentucky, where he discovered the secret for aging whiskey in a way that produced bourbon, a liquor named for the French royal family. Frontier Baptists were indeed an anomaly.

One of the most prominent Virginia Baptists of this period was John Leland (1754–1841), pastor and political activist. Leland, a friend of Thomas Jefferson and James Madison, was an outspoken proponent of religious liberty, highly influenced by the Enlightenment. He wrote unashamedly of the need for freedom of religion and was a leading Virginia lobbyist during the Constitutional period. He wrote:

> Uninspired, fallible men make their own opinions tests of orthodoxy, and use their own systems, as Procrustes used his iron bedstead, to stretch and measure the consciences of all others by. Where no tolera-

tion is granted to non-conformists, either ignorance and superstition prevail, or persecution rages.[9]

Early Baptists in America soon fell into various theological camps, similar to those of their English counterparts. A large number were Particular Baptists, who promoted Reformed theology and its emphasis on total depravity, election, and predestination. Others were General Baptists, affirming Arminian beliefs, with an emphasis on free will and human cooperation in the salvific process. Still others were Seventh Day Baptists, who insisted that Christ's coming had informed but not repudiated aspects of the original command, especially concerning Saturday as the divinely ordained day of worship. These groups all used various confessions of faith, most of them written by British Baptists.

In 1688 English Calvinist Baptists revised an earlier confession that had been written in London. This *Second London Confession* was a lengthy document that delineated the beliefs and practices of Particular Baptists. Much of it is taken directly from the *Westminster Confession of Faith* written in the 1640s, a central doctrinal statement of Reformed theology and Presbyterian polity. The *Second London Confession* contains statements on the authority of Scripture, election and salvation, the need for individual repentance, believer's baptism by immersion, and other dogmas.

By the eighteenth century Reformed Baptists in America had appropriated the *Second London Confession;* they added only two articles to create the *Philadelphia Confession.* The first permitted the singing of hymns, along with the traditional Psalms. The second made optional the laying on of hands at baptism. The *Philadelphia Confession* is an important doctrinal statement for Calvinist Baptists in America, with influence extending into the twenty-first century.

These Baptists also took up the cause of religious liberty. In so doing they anticipated and promoted a response of religious pluralism that would later come to characterize American life as articulated in the Constitution and the Bill of Rights. At the same time, most Baptists desired the conversion of people of no religion or of non-Christian religions to the Christian faith.

### Baptists and the First Great Awakening

The so called Great Awakening has been variously evaluated by scholars of American religion. Some viewed it as a "watershed" of religious and political identity, a precursor of colonial efforts to unite a new nation and form an independent Republic. Others suggested that it was a time of widespread religious fervor that drew people to faith and into colonial churches, a sign that Americans could be spiritually awakened by powerful preaching and divine grace. Still others saw it as one sign of religious enthusiasm among various forms of faith with which colonial citizens experimented, perhaps not nearly so extensive as previously thought. The Great Awakening has long provided a frame of reference for evaluating and examining the nature of Protestant religious life at a formative period of American life.

Traditional analysts point to the beginnings of religious fervor in the work of certain preachers, including George Whitefield (1715–1770), Gilbert Tennent (1703–1764), Jonathan Edwards (1703–1758), and others, none of whom were Baptists. Whitefield, a colleague of John and Charles Wesley, the founders of Methodism, first traveled to the colonies in 1738 and founded an orphanage in Savannah, Georgia. Whitefield traversed the colonies on seven different visits, often preaching to large crowds as the grand itinerant, linking awakenings in various locations. Gilbert Tennent, son of a prominent evangelical family, was widely known in the Raritan Valley of Pennsylvania for his revival enthusiasm and his call for personal conversion for all sinners, including "unconverted ministers."

Jonathan Edwards is perhaps the most famous of the company, known for his extensive theological writings, his description of the revivals that took place in his church in Northampton, Massachusetts, and his famous sermon preached in 1741 at Enfield, Connecticut, taught to generations of American students as "Sinners in the Hands of an Angry God." Edwards's views on "the work of redemption" influenced many who went out with the early mission boards.

The awakenings represented by these and other preachers began in the Calvinistic churches with the conviction that God desired a renewal of the original covenant of grace and redemption. A direct experience of a work of divine grace was the central element of awakening theology as preachers called church members and non–church members alike to repentance and reconciliation with God. As good Calvinists, these religious leaders believed that salvation could come only to the elect, awakened by the preaching of the gospel. Likewise, the church was to be composed only of those who could confess faith in Christ as evidence of a radical transformation of life and belief.

Most Baptists came late to the revival, in part because it began in those churches associated with the New England establishment. Indeed, revival enthusiasm was often brought by non-Baptists converted or awakened in the revivals and then drawn to the Baptist ideal of believer's baptism. This was true of two pivotal figures, Shubal Stearns (1706–1771) and Daniel Marshall (1706–1784), both of whom came to Baptist ranks by way of Congregational revivals. In 1755 Stearns and Marshall and their families ventured into North Carolina territory, where they founded the Sandy Creek Baptist Church, the first Baptist congregation in that region. It became the mother church for some forty additional churches in the Southeast.

The Regular Baptists who came to Charleston in the 1690s were staid and somewhat formal, given to orderly worship, an educated ministry, and Calvinism in their theology. The Separate Baptists, personified by Stearns and Marshall, were "hot gospellers" who preferred spontaneity in worship and were often suspicious of an educated or "hireling" ministry.[10] Their suspicion of educated ministers stemmed from their fear that formal education might squelch the spirit. They sang spiritual songs and hymns, not simply the Psalms, as preferred by the Regulars. While both groups urged people to experience conversion (given that they were among the elect), the Separate Baptists got saved "hard," through religious experiences marked by "enthusiastical" outbursts. Such emotionalism was often viewed as suspect by the Regular Baptists, who warned that God was not the "author of confusion" in spiritual matters. Separates were undaunted in their insistence that conversion was a life-changing, dramatic event that readily affected the whole person, emotions and all.

The Separate Baptists were particularly important to the Baptist witness on the American frontier and the migration of vast numbers of persons to the land west of the Alleghenies. They were willing participants in the camp meetings and "protracted" revivals that characterized certain aspects of religious life on the frontier. Indeed, Baptists flourished in the West, participating in ecumenical revival meetings, founding churches in the wake of mass conversions, and ultimately competing with other denominations for the loyalty of revival converts.

Baptists were present at the great Cane Ridge camp meeting called in August 1801 by the Presbyterian pastor Barton Warren Stone (1772–1844) at his log church not far from Lexington, Kentucky. Some estimate that upwards of ten to twenty thousand people attended the meeting, which was characterized by emotional "exercises" evidenced by shaking, jerking, laughing, running, and shouting. Many Baptist churches in central Kentucky trace their origins to the influence of that pivotal revivalistic event.

Many (though not all) Baptists adapted to the frontier and used revivals to proclaim an evangelical message that called sinners to conversion and baptism. Their conversionist zeal and congregational polity meant that new be-lievers could form new churches without asking permission of any other ec-clesiastical tribunal.

## A National Denomination

As noted, Baptists often sought to balance the autonomy of each congrega-tion with cooperation through associations of local churches. Since local churches generally had limited financial resources, extended ministry and mission efforts required interchurch cooperation and support. Thus, by the late eighteenth and early nineteenth centuries Baptists had begun to form so-cieties aimed at accomplishing specific missionary, benevolent, evangelical, or educational tasks. These organizations were both regional and national in character. As autonomous societies, they were charged with accomplishing specific missions. Churches, individuals, or other associations could choose to participate if they wished. In this way Baptists sought to protect congre-gational autonomy while facilitating broader (voluntary) cooperation.

As Baptists increased in number, particular individuals called churches to unite in certain common tasks, particularly in missionary endeavors. The Philadelphia Association, the first permanent Baptist association in the colonies, was established in 1707, and others soon followed. Regional mis-sionary societies were established before a national organization took shape. Many of these societies were founded through the leadership and energy of women. Mary Webb (1779–1861) of Boston led the founding of the Boston Female Missionary Society in 1800, the first American woman's missionary society. It enlisted Baptist and Congregational women in pledging their "mites" (small amounts of money) to missionary endeavors. Webb, a person of significant physical disabilities, was unable to "go out to the field" herself but felt called to raise the funds to make it possible for others to do so. The society ultimately became one of the first missionary agencies to provide fi-nancial support for single females who went to the mission field. Numerous urban and regional mission societies were founded in the early 1800s, each providing funds and education for various projects.

The Second Great Awakening on the frontier and elsewhere influenced the development of missionary enterprises among American denominations, and Baptists were no exception. The American Board of Commissioners for Foreign Missions (Congregational) was founded by the Congregationalists in 1810 as a means of spreading the gospel to the "ends of the earth." Fueled by the revivals and an expanded ability to traverse the globe on trading ships, many denominations became convinced that it was their "duty" to declare the good news of Christ to people everywhere. This was essentially a "modified Calvinism" set forth by Jonathan Edwards and others, who declared that it was the "obligation" of Christians to preach the gospel widely in order that God might use such preaching to awaken the hearts of the elect. While insisting that they remained proponents of Calvinism, these evangelicals linked missionary endeavor with the church's imperative to spread the word to all lands.

In 1812 the Congregationalist Board sent three missionaries—Adoniram Judson (1788–1850), Ann Hasseltine Judson (1789–1826), and Luther Rice (1783–1836)—to India. While aboard the ship, the three became convinced that the New Testament knew nothing of the baptism of infants and that baptism was to be administered by immersion to those who made a profession of faith in Christ. On arrival in India they became Baptists and received immersion at the hands of a British Baptist missionary. In a letter dated September 7, 1812, Ann Hasseltine Judson wrote to a friend:

> Can you, my dear Nancy, still love me, still desire to hear from me, when I tell you I have become a Baptist? . . . You may, perhaps, think this change very sudden, as I have said nothing of it before; but, my dear girl, this alteration hath not been the work of an hour, a day, or a month. The subject has been maturely, candidly, and, I hope, prayerfully examined for months.[11]

No longer able to receive Congregationalist funds, the Judsons sent Rice back to the United States to petition the Baptists for assistance. Their appeal hastened the founding in 1814 of the General Missionary Convention of the Baptist Denomination in the United States for Foreign Missions, the first national Baptist body in America. Known as the Triennial Convention because it met every three years, it was a society charged with collecting funds from Baptist individuals and groups to support foreign missions.

The Judsons soon moved to Burma, where they established new work and confronted significant challenges of culture, disease, and theology. Like many nineteenth-century missionaries, they lost children and colleagues to illnesses against which they had little or no immunity. Many missionaries died, often barely after they had disembarked. Ann Hasseltine Judson illustrated the devotion and difficulties of missionary women. She lost children, tended to her husband when he was imprisoned for preaching, learned various dialects, and helped translate the Bible into the Burmese vernacular. After her death Adoniram married Sarah Boardman (1803–1845), with whom he had seven children. When she died he married Emily Chubbuck (1817–1854), who also preceded him in death. The Triennial Convention soon sent out missionaries to China, Africa, and South America. Its work raised a denominational consciousness among American Baptists north and south, though the slavery controversy divided the movement and created two new denominations.

The development of a national society highlights the development of other connections regionally and locally for Baptist churches. State Baptist conventions were also formed in the early to mid-nineteenth century. They permitted churches in a given region to work together in common tasks of ministry and mission. The Baptist General Tract Society was founded in 1824 to provide evangelical witness in public venues and to encourage conversion in the broader American society. Colporteurs, special ministers who dispersed tracts and gave personal witness, traveled widely, giving particular attention to train passengers. In 1841 the organization became the American Baptist Tract and Sunday School Society.

A concern for missionary activity at home, particularly among Native or immigrant populations on the American frontier, led to the formation of the American Baptist Home Missionary Society in 1832 under the leadership of Luther Rice. The society raised funds to send missionaries to particular tribes of Native Americans as well as to "plant churches" in areas of the country that were developing as more people moved west. In the Southeast, missionaries such as Isaac McCoy (1784–1846) and Jesse Bushyhead (1804–1844) worked with the Cherokees. Others such as Almon C. Balcone, himself a Native American, worked with Native peoples in the Southwest, especially in Oklahoma, Texas, and New Mexico.

## Anti-Mission Baptists

Not all Baptists supported the mission movement and agenda. Some were convinced that it was an unbiblical effort of human beings to usurp the power of salvation that belonged to God alone. They opposed the founding of mission boards and the denominational organizations necessary to facilitate missionary endeavors.

Certain indigenous mountain Baptist groups developed out of schisms of one sort or another. Primitive Baptists, particularly prominent in the central and southern Appalachian region, began as a result of controversies re-

garding Baptist support of missionary endeavors and other denominationalizing activities. In 1832 a group of Particular Baptists approved the "Black
Rock Address," which delineated the dangers of denominationalism and missionary activity. These concerns included a rejection of tract societies and
Sunday schools because, while well intended, they were false means of bringing sinners to faith. These "arrogant pretensions" were abandoned because

> they are grounded in the notion that conversion or regeneration is pro-
> duced by impressions made upon the natural mind by means of religious
> sentiments instilled into it; and if the Holy Ghost is allowed to be at all
> concerned in the thing, it is in a way which implies his being somehow
> blended with the instruction, or necessarily attendant upon it; all of
> which we know to be wrong.[12]

Mission societies were also unacceptable because they had no precedent in
the New Testament, and the instruction of children in "the letter of Scripture" was condemned because such a practice "made hypocrites of the Jews"
and would doubtless have the same effect on children.[13]

While acknowledging the "duty" of Christians to preach the gospel to
"the destitute," the "Black Rock Address" questioned missionary movements in the church, suggested that these methods were not found in the New
Testament, and confessed: "Our hearts really sicken at this state of things."[14]

The address warned against the development of Christian colleges and
theological schools, not because education was evil but because Christian
schools should have no connection to "human sciences, a principle we cannot
permit." Likewise, it concluded that "we decidedly object to persons, after
professing to have been called of the Lord to preach his gospel, going to a
college or academy to fit themselves for that service." If God called an individual, then God would provide the necessary training.[15]

Underneath these ideas was the basic belief that God was the sole agent
of salvation and that missionary activity, revivals, schools, and other human
"means" were outside the boundaries of genuine faith. The address concluded that "regeneration . . . is exclusively the work of the Holy ghost, performed by his divine power, at his own sovereign pleasure, according to the
provisions of the everlasting covenant."[16] Human efforts implied that there
was something sinners could do in achieving salvation. That kind of "works
righteousness" was anathema to these Calvinist Baptists. Their ideas are retained in Primitive and Old Regular Baptist communions and other strongly
Reformed congregations.

Daniel Parker (1781–1844) was one of the best-known anti-mission Baptists of the nineteenth century. Parker believed that at birth each individual possessed one of two seeds that determined election or damnation as predetermined by God. He wrote: "It is evident that there are the two seeds, one of the Serpent, the other of the woman; and they appear plain in Cain and Abel, and in their offerings."[17] The predestination of people to salvation was established by divine fiat and could not be changed by missionary efforts that implied that all could potentially come to salvation. The seeds of good and evil were planted by God, and no transplanting was allowed!

### Baptists and Education

Baptists have often maintained a love-hate relationship with formal education. On the one hand, they were at the forefront of efforts to establish religiously based higher education throughout the new nation, founding a variety of colleges and universities to train Baptist youth. On the other hand, many Baptists feared that education would prove detrimental to faith and "heart religion." Baptist educational institutions often found themselves in conflict with constituents over curriculum and other elements of academic life.

The first of the Baptist schools, the College of Rhode Island, founded in 1764 and located in Providence, later became Brown University. A second effort, the establishment of Columbian College in Washington, DC, was initiated in 1821. Plagued by funding problems from the beginning, the school struggled to secure a national identity for Baptists in the new nation. In 1825 its theological department moved to Massachusetts to become Newton Theological Institute, one of the country's first theological schools. After numerous mergers it was renamed George Washington University in 1903 and relinquished all Baptist connections.

By the nineteenth century Baptists north and south had established a variety of academies and colleges that continue to the present day. These include Colgate University, Bucknell University, the University of Richmond, Wake Forest University, Mercer University, Samford University, Mississippi College, Louisiana College, Baylor University, Franklin College, Bates College, Eastern College, Shaw University, Ottawa University, Morehouse College, and many more. Most of these schools were established to provide education for Baptist ministers and to improve the educational and economic status of Baptist youth. Many of them antedated state colleges and universities. Controversies over curriculum in Baptist schools, particularly related to studies in religion and science, continue to divide supporters of Baptist higher education today.

## Denominational Competition

With conversions came competition: Whose church shall the saved join? Much of nineteenth-century Baptist life was distinguished by efforts of various American denominations to establish themselves as the true church, or at least the truest of the true over against other communions. Baptists were no exception. They entered the fray with vigor, challenging a broad array of religious groups, from Roman Catholics to Methodists to Restorationists. The interdenominational rhetoric could be volatile. As Peter Cartwright, a Methodist circuit rider, wrote of the Methodist/Baptist interaction in the early to mid-nineteenth century:

> It was the order of the day, (though I am sorry to say it) that we were constantly followed by a certain set of proselyting Baptist preachers. These new and wicked settlements were seldom visited by these Baptist preachers until the Methodist preachers entered them; then, when a revival was gotten up, or the work of God revived, these Baptist preachers came rushing in, and they generally sung their sermons; and when they struck the *long roll*, or their sing-song mode of preaching, in substance it was "water!" "water!" "you must follow your blessed Lord down to the water!". . . Indeed, they made so much ado about baptism by immersion that the uninformed would suppose that heaven was an island, and there was no way to get there but by *diving* or *swimming*![18]

Competition came in many forms. In responding to the Methodists, Baptists were confronting another upstart denomination like themselves that was flourishing on the frontier. In 1776 Baptists and Methodists were small sectarian movements in colonial American life. By the 1840s they had become the two largest denominations in the country. Methodist and Baptist preachers frequently debated one another over infant baptism and falling from grace. Presbyterian and Baptist ministers debated predestination, free will, church government (Presbyterian or Congregational), and, of course, infant baptism.

Perhaps no group frustrated and invigorated Baptists like the Restorationists, those who were related to the thought and work of Barton W. Stone and Alexander Campbell (1788–1866). Stone came from the Presbyterians and Campbell from the Baptists to challenge the denominationalizing of American religion. While differing on style and substance, Stone and Campbell agreed that the true church had been lost in the din of denominational voices and the hegemony of Roman Catholic dominance. Their concern was to return the church to its New Testament roots, a community of "Christians only" adhering only to the teachings and actions of the primitive community and rejecting the "traditions of men."

Baptists responded by insisting that they did not need to restore anything, since they had kept the true church alive since the time of the apostles. In that effort, a movement known as Old Landmarkism was born. "Landmarkists" took their appellation from Proverbs 2:28: "Remove not the ancient landmark which thy fathers hath set." In the 1850s J. R. Graves (1820–1893), pastor of First Baptist Church, Nashville, Tennessee, and J. M. Pendleton (1811–1891), pastor of First Baptist Church, Bowling Green, Kentucky, issued a challenge to Baptists to claim their heritage as the only true church, possessing the "landmarks" of the New Testament community. In treatises such as *An Old Landmark Reset* (Pendleton) and *Old Landmarkism: What Is It?* (Graves), they sought to prove that a variety of evangelical and sectarian groups throughout the church's history—Novatianists, Donatists, Cathari, Waldenses, Anabaptists, and others—were Baptist in everything but name, preserving orthodoxy from the First (Baptist) Church of Jerusalem in the first century, to the First Baptist Church of Nashville nineteen hundred years later. Graves's "marks" of the true church included regenerate church membership, immersion baptism, congregational autonomy, and closed communion. The last practice meant that only members of the specific congregation where the Lord's Supper was celebrated could receive the bread and the cup. Landmarkists also denied the validity of "alien immersion," the immersion of believers in churches other than Baptist churches. This meant that "Campbellite" baptism was invalid and that those who sought membership in Baptist churches from certain non-churchly "societies" were re-immersed in "appropriate" Landmark Baptist communions. Landmark exegesis of Scripture led to their insistence that the Greek word *ecclesia* should be interpreted not simply as *church*, but as *local church*. Thus, the single congregation was the chief (some suggest the only) expression of Baptist organization and authority.

Landmarkism created many controversies for Baptists. For example, Landmarkists were infuriated in the 1890s when William H. Whitsitt (1841–1911), president and church history professor at Southern Baptist Theological Seminary in Louisville, Kentucky, produced research indicating that Baptists did not begin the practice of immersion until 1641, some thirty years after their beginnings in Amsterdam. Whitsitt noted that the earliest Baptists had practiced trine affusion, a form of baptism that involved the pouring of water three times on the head of the new believer. Immersion, or "dipping," was first introduced among the London Particular Baptists around the year 1641, after contact with the Dutch Collegiant Mennonites. Although his research was correct, the Landmark influence was so powerful that Whitsitt was forced to resign and leave the seminary.

Landmarkism continued to affect Baptist polity (government) and practice throughout the twentieth century, particularly with regard to questions of open and closed communion, "alien immersion," and support of missionaries through mission societies. Some Independent Baptist churches, congregations affiliated with the American Baptist Association (ABA), and the Primitive Baptists continue to affirm and promote Landmark views.

Some Baptist groups, particularly in the North and the Midwest, had little or no contact with Landmarkism. Others, while not explicitly Landmark in orientation, were nonetheless influenced by certain Landmark-related agendas. For example, while many Baptist churches now practice open communion, they continue to require the immersion, therefore re-baptism, of those who join Baptist churches from other Christian traditions. Individuals whose Christian experience began in Methodist, Presbyterian, Lutheran, Anglican, or other traditions in which infant baptism is the norm are required to receive immersion if they join certain Baptist churches. This legacy of Landmarkism affects even those who have never heard of the specific movement.

### Baptists and Racial Issues

African Americans have been active in Baptist life since the late eighteenth century. With the decision of many Protestant denominations to seek to evangelize slaves, Baptists made concerted efforts to convert blacks and admit them—often as second-class citizens—to their churches. As noted, slaves attended the camp meetings and experienced dramatic conversions. While blacks were admitted to membership in churches, they were usually compelled to sit in slave galleries (the balcony) or other designated areas during worship. Black preachers often accompanied white evangelists, many serving as "exhorters" who preached alongside their white counterparts. Other self-ordained black preachers were leaders of informal gatherings of slaves, often in secret societies known as "hush arbors" because their activities were conducted away from the watchful eye of the masters.

Nat Turner (1800–1831) was such a person. Born into slavery, Turner was converted under the preaching of Baptists. He was struck by a series of ecstatic experiences—visions, voices, and other manifestations—that convinced him of a divine mandate to destroy slavery. In 1830 he led an uprising of slaves in Virginia that caused the death of certain whites, including the family of his owners. Turner was subsequently arrested and hanged for his actions, but the event struck fear into the slaveholding population, especially since Turner was the slave of Christians who sought to follow "biblical admonitions" in the proper treatment of those they held in bondage.

While the antebellum Baptist population brought together blacks and whites in the same churches, other congregations were established by and for African Americans. Early leaders of black Baptists included George Liele (ca. 1750–1820), Lott Carey (ca. 1780–1828), and David George (ca. 1742–1810). Liele, ordained as a minister to slaves, was instrumental in the conversion of David George. After receiving his freedom in 1784, Liele began work in Jamaica, thus becoming the first African American to go to the mission field. David George helped to found the Silver Bluff Baptist Church in South Carolina sometime between 1773 and 1775, now viewed as the first African American Baptist church in the United States. African American churches were also established in the North. Some of the earliest included the Joy Street Baptist Church in Boston (1804), the Abyssinian Baptist Church in New York City (1808), and the African Baptist Church in Philadelphia (1809).[19]

Following the Civil War, many black Baptists left white churches, in part because of the developing segregationist sentiments in the dominant society and also because blacks resisted the second-class status given them even in the North. Many of these congregations were instrumental in founding of African American Baptist denominations in the South and throughout the nation. Baptists in the North also worked to establish schools aimed primarily at educating the newly freed slaves. In the South these included Spellman Seminary (Georgia, 1881), Shaw University (North Carolina, 1865), Virginia Union University (1865), and Bishop College (Texas, 1881).[20]

The denominationalization of African American churches took many forms as numerous regional and missionary groups took shape. Many early missionary societies evolved into African American denominations or at least contributed to a growing organizational connectionalism among black churches. Early denominations frequently merged into later ones. These included the American Baptist Missionary Convention (1840), the Consolidated American Baptist Missionary Convention (1866), the American National Baptist Convention (1886), the Foreign Mission Convention (1880), and the National Baptist Convention of America (1895).

The Lott Carey Baptist Foreign Mission Convention was founded in 1897 in Washington, DC, by African Americans who were concerned about the directions of the National Baptist Convention, and this agency later came to bridge many African American denominations in securing support for its mission activities, most of which were in Africa and the Caribbean.

## Schism: North and South

By the mid-nineteenth century, the question of human slavery forced Baptists and the rest of the American nation to choose institutional union or schism. Slavery essentially came to the colonies in 1619 with a group of Africans brought as indentured servants to Jamestown, Virginia. Over the next two centuries it became a cultural and political issue debated throughout the nation and the Western world. Limited attention was given to the Christianization of slaves until the late eighteenth century, when missionaries from the Anglican Church sought to provide slaves with baptism and Christian instruction. Slaves often attended and were converted in the camp meetings and revivals of the Second Great Awakening. Many churches, North and South, had biracial congregations. This was true even in the slave states. Many slave owners hesitated, but soon other denominations, Baptists included, were encouraging such actions. Generally speaking, before the 1830s public opinion in the North and in certain areas of the South opposed slavery in principle and supported the gradual manumission of the enslaved blacks. The American Colonization Society was founded in 1814 by various "liberal" or "progressive" individuals in the naïve belief that they could ship younger blacks "back to Africa," let the old ones die off, and be done with the problem. In the meantime, opinions for and against slavery were hardened by economic, political, and religious attitudes and actions. For example, the invention of the cotton gin, with its ability to pluck seeds from cotton, made the production of cotton much more economically feasible, and slaves were seen as essential to the production of the South's great "money crop."

Slave rebellions led by Denmark Vesey (ca. 1767–1822) in 1822 and Nat Turner in 1830 created fear among Southerners that the seemingly docile slave population would rise up to wreak havoc upon them. Likewise, the founding of the American Abolition Society in 1830 and the growth of antislavery literature such as William L. Garrison's *Public Liberator* accelerated the call for an immediate end to the South's Peculiar Institution. Southerners themselves did not hesitate to speak out about the matter. In 1822, Richard Furman, pastor of the First Baptist Church, Charleston, South Carolina, and first president of the Triennial Convention, issued a defense of slavery that became a popular argument for the Southern cause. In it he asserted that since the Bible did not explicitly forbid slavery but admonished slave owners toward the "Christian" treatment of slaves, it was not a moral evil in the church or in the world. On the other side, antislavery Baptists in Kentucky, a border state with Southern inclinations, formed the Baptized Licking-Locust Association, Friends of Humanity, an organization that promoted manumission among Baptists and other Christians.

## The Southern Baptist Convention Founded

These issues came to a head when Southerners nominated James Reeve (1784–1858), a known slaveholder, as a candidate for home missionary service. The Georgia Baptist Convention requested that the American Baptist Home Mission Society grant him appointment, knowing that this would be a test case for the application of slavery as a criterion for missionary service. When the society refused the selection, the Southerners bolted and called a meeting of Baptists in the Southern states in May 1845 at First Baptist Church, Augusta, Georgia. Representatives to that meeting formed a new denomination, the Southern Baptist Convention, insisting that their primary aim was to promote the cause of Christian missions, a cause interrupted by the Northerners who had added an extraneous issue to the terms of missionary appointment. The resulting schism between Baptists in the North and the South anticipated the national dissolution and the Civil War. Baptists in both regions gave support for the fray to their respective regions, sending chaplains, soldiers, and funds.

While Northerners retained the society method as their primary organizational structure, the Southerners introduced a convention system that was much more connectional. Agencies had some autonomy but were not independent. Rather they were connected inside the overall convention organization in which agencies, boards, and other denominational entities were more directly related. Local churches, associations, and state conventions re-tained their individual autonomy but had closer connections to each other.

## Immigrant Baptist Churches

Other new Baptist denominations and churches appeared on the scene dur-ing the nineteenth century. Some were related directly to immigration. Bap-tists from Norway, Sweden, Denmark, and Germany came to the United States and established denominational connections. These groups, discussed in greater detail in a later chapter, often maintained their ethnic and linguis-tic identities well into the twentieth century. The Midwest of the United States was fertile ground for Norwegian, German, and Swedish Baptist churches. These congregations began in Europe among fledgling Baptist communities and were brought to America with the immigrants.

## A Social Gospel

As the nineteenth century drew to a close, some Baptists became increasingly concerned about the rise of urban poverty and the economic and communal inequities fostered by the industrial revolution. This effort, known as the So-cial Gospel movement, sought to apply Jesus' teaching in ways that would "Christianize the social order." While Americans from many denominations were involved in the Social Gospel, Baptists such as Walter Rauschenbusch (1861–1918) were among the early leaders. Raised in a German Baptist home, Rauschenbusch confronted the realities of urban life firsthand as the pastor of a church in a section of midtown New York City known as Hell's Kitchen. Later, as a professor of church history at Rochester Theological Seminary, he wrote extensively on the need to transform society according to the man-dates of Jesus. His great influence on the subject led to his being designated the "father of the Social Gospel." For Rauschenbusch, the Social Gospel was simply the reorganization of society according to the teachings of Jesus. This Kingdom of God was humanity in conformity to the will and rule of God. He wrote:

> The Kingdom means individual men and women who freely do the will of God, and who therefore live rightly with their fellowmen. . . . But the Kingdom also means a growing perfection in the collective life of hu-

manity, in our laws, in the customs of society, in the institutions for education, and for the administration of mercy.[21]

The Social Gospel was in part a response to the so-called Gospel of Wealth, the belief fostered by certain clergy and laity, including the industrialist and philanthropist Andrew Carnegie, that God had chosen certain people to make large amounts of money as a means of benefiting the entire society. Since only a few people actually knew how to secure and utilize wealth appropriately, it would be the responsibility of these chosen ones to use their means to improve the lot of those who were not able to do so. Social Gospel proponents challenged this idea and insisted that such attitudes contributed to economic cycles that kept people poor and destroyed family life.

Baptists themselves were divided over the role of the Social Gospel movement. Some saw it as a distraction from the church's primary responsibility to convert individuals to Christ and ensure their salvation in heaven. Certain individuals even suggested that since the world was essentially the abode of Satan, it was futile to try to change social structures without first converting individuals, who would then change the society. Rauschenbusch was among those Baptists who valued the importance of individual conversion but thought that Christians should work together to transform the society in ways that would ultimately benefit all persons, Christians and non-Christians alike. The debate over the relationship between evangelism and social action continued to divide Baptists into the twenty-first century.

Controversies over the nature of human society were affected by diverse views on eschatology and the Second Coming of Christ. Many colonial Baptists and other Protestants were postmillennialists who believed that Jesus would return at the end of a thousand-year period of peace and religious enthusiasm led by a renewed Christian church. They viewed the awakenings that descended on America as evidence of that Golden Age of religious devotion that would culminate in Christ's return. By the mid-nineteenth century other Baptists were among those Protestants who believed that the Second Coming would be a premillennial event in which Christ himself would inaugurate a cataclysmic reign of a thousand years. William Miller (1782–1849), a Baptist preacher in western New York, was at the forefront of the premillennialist movement. During the 1820s Miller developed an elaborate series of mathematical calculations based on his reading of the Old and New Testaments that led him to conclude that Jesus would return "sometime" between March 1843 and March 1844. He published his views in a document titled *Evidence from Scripture and History concerning the Second Coming of*

*Christ About the Year 1843*. The book created a surprisingly widespread public response, and soon "Millerite" gatherings of persons from various Protestant denominations were being held throughout the East. Periodicals such as *Midnight Cry* and *Signs of the Times* also helped to circulate Miller's calculations and increase the enthusiasm. Miller traveled widely, preaching his views and urging sinners to accept Christ into their hearts before it was too late. When the forecast return did not occur, Miller and others recalculated and insisted that the moment would take place on October 22, 1834. After the "Second Great Disappointment" Miller returned to his farm a broken man and died soon thereafter. Segments of his movement continued, however, represented in Seventh Day Adventism and other Adventist traditions in America.

Baptists in America have never agreed on one single theory of Christ's Second Coming. While premillennialism remains popular among many Baptists, some continue to affirm a postmillennial approach. Still others would consider themselves amillennialists, those who think that millennial language is highly symbolic and therefore not to be applied literally to the details of God's ultimate activity in bringing history to an end.

Baptists confronted the twentieth century with enthusiasm and concern, some wedded to progressivism and the hope that the Kingdom of God would be manifest on earth, brought in by human agents in a Golden Age. Others were more skeptical, finding in modernity the corruptions that were sure signs that the end of the world and the Second Coming of Christ were at hand. Controversies over biblical authority, morality, church order, and theology that were present at the beginning of the twentieth century continued to divide Baptists as the twenty-first century got under way.

## CHAPTER THREE

# Baptists in the Twentieth Century

Baptists in America entered the twentieth century with hope and hesitancy. Progressives like Walter Rauschenbusch looked to the new era as the opportunity for "Christianizing the social order." Missions-oriented leaders such as Henry Morehouse anticipated a global religious awakening that could produce "the evangelization of the world in our generation." Fundamentalists like J. Frank Norris understood the moral compromises and doctrinal distortions of modernity as evidence that the return of Jesus Christ was imminent. African American Baptists such as William J. Simmons wondered if the new century would bring liberation or continued discrimination against his race. As the century progressed, Baptists joined other Protestants in debates over war and peace, faith and reason, race and gender, doctrine and practice.

New Baptist denominations and congregations were born of evangelical fervor and theological disputes. Throughout the century, Baptists divided over issues of theology and ethics that characterized fundamentalist-liberal confrontations. Theological debates created multiple schisms inside the Northern Baptist Convention (later the American Baptist Convention, USA), from which a new denomination, the Conservative Baptist Convention, was born. During the latter twentieth century, Southern Baptist doctrinal disputes led to the formation of the Alliance of Baptists and the Cooperative Baptist Fellowship (CBF). Independent Baptists, a quasi-denominational movement, took up the banner of fundamentalism and established some of the largest (and most argumentative) churches in the United States. Many of those churches came out of the Northern and Southern Baptist Conventions. The Progressive National Baptist Convention (PNBC) began as a result of schism in the National Baptist Convention, Inc.

Ironically, many Baptists found themselves on opposite sides of issues related to the civil rights movement, with African Americans (and a minority of Anglo-Saxons) supporting integration and an end to "separate but equal" apartheid laws, while many white Baptists vehemently opposed such changes. By the late twentieth century, debates raged within Baptist churches and denominations over a wide variety of social issues, including abortion, creationism, school prayer, homosexuality, the ordination of women, and the relationship of church and state. Questions as to what it means to be a Baptist were no less volatile in the year 2000 than they were a century earlier. Indeed, the diversity of Baptist groups and their theological orientations means that many debates remain unresolved and are as intense as they were in 1900.

As the twentieth century got under way, Methodists and Baptists were the two largest religious groups in the United States. By century's end, they were America's largest Protestant denomination, second only to Roman Catholics in number. Southern Baptists and African American Baptists represent the largest segments of the Baptist family in the United States. In 2000 Southern Baptists claimed there were some 17 million Southern Baptists in approximately 35,000 churches. African American Baptists number at least 12 million members in four major denominations. American Baptist Churches, USA claim at least 1.5 million members. Independent Baptist churches, some connected to various "fellowships" of ministers, have many large churches, but their exact membership is difficult to calculate.

## Denominational Developments

Like other Protestant groups, some twentieth-century Baptist denominations expanded their organizational systems, often with structures that mirrored those of American corporations. Many appointed executive secretaries (directors) to oversee the annual administration of the denomination and created elaborate bureaucracies for carrying out national and international ministries. Some were highly centralized in conventions connecting agencies and boards, while others retained the society method, by which denominational organizations retained significant autonomy.

Organized in 1845, the Southern Baptist Convention formed a connectional system linking agencies but funding them as if each board was a self-supporting society. Early on, membership in the denomination was extended to churches, associations, and individuals that contributed to the convention's financial support. Even in 1900 "there were still no standing committees, no commissions, no general secretary, and no headquarters" within the convention system.[1] In a sense, the convention itself was publicly constituted for only a few days each year at its annual meeting. Local churches maintained direct membership in associations, state conventions, and the national convention.

Growth in programs and membership required institutional change in the SBC. In 1917 the denomination appointed its first executive committee, a group charged with coordinating and administrating the work of convention agencies, boards, and related groups more directly. An executive secretary was elected for the first time in 1925, the same year that the Cooperative Program, a collective funding mechanism, was established. Through that program churches contributed funds to their respective state conventions, a portion of which went to the national denomination. In 1931 the official representatives to the annual SBC, known as messengers, were limited to those who came from churches that contributed to the financial support of the denomination.[2] As the twentieth century progressed, the SBC refined and expanded its denominational system, often utilizing "efficiency experts" from the business world to sharpen systems organization.

The National Baptist Conventions (NBC, Incorporated, and NBC, Unincorporated) represent the largest number of African American Baptists in the United States. These two groups maintain mission boards as well as publication and educational agencies. Each holds an annual meeting with delegates, a majority of whom are clergy, representing member churches. For many years the two conventions had no executive director who administered basic operations; they instead elected presidents, who acquired significant power in denominational authority and oversight. This is illustrated in the National Baptist Convention, Inc., and the presidency of Joseph H. Jackson (1900–1990), which lasted from 1953 to 1982. Jackson's hold on power led to a revolt in the 1960s that ended with the founding of the Progressive National Baptist Convention. In 1961 the NBC reshaped its organization and appointed its first executive director.[3]

The American Baptist Convention, USA witnessed extensive denominational reorganization during the last half of the twentieth century. The denomination traces its roots to the Triennial Convention of 1814 and through the divisions with the Southerners in 1845. In 1907 it was renamed the Northern Baptist Convention, bringing together major agencies related to missions and publications but permitting them to retain extensive autonomy. In 1950 it was again renamed, this time becoming the American Baptist Churches, as a way of linking the denomination with multiple societies—missionary, publication, historical—that also used the designation "American Baptist." The first general secretary was appointed in 1950 to enhance denominational administration. In 1972 an even more elaborate reorganization led to another name change, to American Baptist Convention in the USA. The intention of the restructuring was to allow greater representation and encourage broader "voice" in denominational affairs. As Norman Maring and Winthrop Hudson wrote, "Provisions were made to ensure that a proportionate number of men and women, clergy and laity, ethnic groups, youth, and any other minorities would be represented on the General Board, by electing representatives-at-large as needed to provide balance."[4]

Some Baptist churches and groups remain wary of denominational hierarchy "from above" with denominational systems that might undermine local church autonomy. Primitive, Old Regular, and Independent Baptists maintain much looser connections, with a predominant emphasis on the local congregation and associational or "fellowship" relationships with other churches and groups.

## The Mission Enterprise

At the beginning of the twentieth century the missionary impetus remained a major concern of Baptist groups. Mission societies, many of them founded in the nineteenth century, expanded their work throughout the world. Denominations looked for ways to garner financial support for missionary endeavors at home and abroad while encouraging a new generation of young people to consider devoting their lives to missionary service. By 1900 Baptist denominations in America maintained missionary work on every continent, aimed at converting populations, establishing churches, founding schools and hospitals, and promoting New Testament Christianity around the world. Missionary activities were so significant that concerns about doctrinal compromises by missionary personnel marked the early stages of the fundamentalist-modernist confrontations.

Mission boards in numerous Baptist denominations appointed men and women who served in home and foreign mission fields. Home mission boards funded programs aimed at Native Americans, African Americans, immigrants, migrant workers, urban tenement dwellers, and other target groups. The American Baptist Home Mission Society, founded in 1832, continued to support work with African Americans in the North and South, Native Americans in the Southwest, and immigrants in the West. In 1955 it was merged with the Woman's American Baptist Home Mission Society. A new director, Japanese American Jitsuo Morikawa, encouraged the society to extend greater ministry to college students and to the business world. Indeed, much Baptist campus ministry in colleges and universities began through the auspices of various home mission boards and societies. In a 1972–1973 denominational reorganization, the Home Mission Society was moved into the Board of National Ministries of the American Baptist Churches, USA.[5]

By the mid-twentieth century, Southern Baptists had developed the largest missionary task force to be found among Baptists in the United States. They sent out a wide variety of career missionaries whose work was funded through gifts from churches, channeled through the mission boards. Missionaries were much revered in Southern Baptist life, and young people were urged to consider the missionary calling as a life's vocation.

Missionaries founded churches, schools, and hospitals, working with Baptists "in-country" to evangelize and instruct the populace. The Foreign Mission Board of the SBC acquired property in countries throughout the world, often securing property for churches in countries, such as Italy and Spain, where it was difficult for Protestant groups to acquire land. In cooperation with indigenous Baptists, the SBC helped to establish schools, primary and secondary, as well as certain theological seminaries.

By the late twentieth century the SBC had reorganized its mission boards and tightened doctrinal requirements for missionary personnel. The Foreign Mission Board became the International Mission Board and the Home Mission Board became the North American Mission Board. A decision in 2002 required that all missionary employees of the two boards formally subscribe to the doctrines in the *Baptist Faith and Message*, the denomination's confession of faith, revised in 2000. Numerous missionaries refused to sign the statement, citing what they believed to be the traditional non-creedal nature of Baptist faith.

During the late nineteenth and early twentieth centuries, several Baptist boards entered to the Appalachian region of the southern United States, establishing churches, schools, hospitals, and training programs for "mountain people." Central Appalachia is generally considered to include portions of nine states extending from Virginia to Alabama, along with all of West Virginia. Some home mission societies received specific funds from mining companies that maintained overarching control of particular towns and regions. Congregationalist H. Paul Douglass wrote (with approval) in 1909 that "the millionaire and the missionary" would manage "the future of the mountains," by changing the individualism of the "mountaineer" into the "normally equipped American." As did missionary activity in foreign lands, home missions in Appalachia would bring Christianity and civilization, as if none had been there before.[6]

Many of these home mission efforts extended evangelical and humanitarian efforts in response to the terrible poverty and illiteracy present in an increasingly exploited region of the country. For example, Southern Baptists and other Baptist entities, state and local, began to establish "mountain schools" in the Appalachian regions of various southern states.[7] Yet some of these missionary efforts reflected an outsider's analysis of the religion already present in the region, often with dismissive or paternalistic attitudes toward the Old Baptists—Primitive, Old Regular, Free Will, and others. Indeed, scholars sometimes question the premises on which this mission work was predicated and its failure to take seriously the existence and ministry of older, more indigenous Baptist groups. For example, Deborah McCauley writes: "For home missionaries in the Appalachian region during this period, to modernize was to uplift, to uplift was to Christianize, to Christianize was to Americanize. . . . It had to do with dominion over mountain people and their land, driven by the engines of capitalism, of money, not simply the desire to help lost cousins regain their footing in the world today."[8] Mission movements often failed to take into account the ministries of churches they found when they arrived. Some of these groups were dismissed as "hyper-Calvinist," a pejorative term for a theology that was judged to be excessive and unbalanced when in fact it represented a long and venerable tradition in Baptist history.

Foreign mission agencies raised significant funds to send career missionaries abroad. They served as evangelist/pastors, educators, physicians, and agricultural advisors to native peoples. In most countries the mission agencies were able to buy extensive property for hospitals, churches, schools, and "missionary compounds," where missionaries could live in close proximity. More daring souls traveled to "new fields" to establish a Christian witness where it had not been before. By the early twentieth century, so extensive was Baptist missionary work that diverse groups sometimes divided nations or continents among themselves so as not to duplicate work and to extend the Baptist witness more broadly. For example, the American Baptist Home Mission Society and the Home Mission Board of the Southern Baptist Convention divided the island of Cuba into sections assigned to one of these denominations.

Funding for the missionary endeavors was extremely complex and became a major theme of Baptist denominational identity throughout the twentieth century. Baptist denominations urged churches and individuals to give generously to the missionary cause. Special offerings were developed for supporting the work. Missionaries "on furlough" at home were encouraged to spend a portion of their time visiting churches and informing them of the specifics of their ministries. The highlight of many denominational conferences was the "commissioning service," in which new missionaries were recognized and sent forth with prayers and blessings to proclaim the gospel to "the ends of the earth." "Prayer calendars" in many Baptist churches highlighted missionaries on their birthdays when the prayers of the faithful were focused annually on specific individuals. Missionary literature detailed the dangers and joys of missionary service, along with the sacrifices made by the missionaries and their families. Indeed, families were the backbone of the mission force; married couples were appointed together and sent out to "the fields," often accompanied by their children. (In certain Baptist denominations the male missionary was the fully appointed missionary and the wife was a "missionary associate.") Children were often home-schooled or attended English-speaking schools in-country. When those options were not available they were sent to boarding schools or back to the United States.

Women's missionary societies had been formed throughout the previous century, many among the earliest efforts to raise financial support for world evangelization. The Woman's American Baptist Foreign and Home Mission Societies raised funds for missionary work at home and abroad. Their missionaries "excelled in teaching and nursing on the mission field; they were leaders in working ecumenically, starting orphanages and boarding schools, and giving an important place to work with women and children."[9] In 1955 the two agencies merged to become the American Baptist Foreign and Home Mission Societies.

The Woman's Missionary Union, Auxiliary to the Southern Baptist Convention (WMU—1888), took up sponsorship of the Sunbeam Band, a mission education group for children, and in 1907 it developed the Young Woman's Auxiliary (later Girls' Auxiliary). Also in 1907 the union became the manager of the Woman's (Missionary) Training School, founded in Louisville, Kentucky, in 1904 to prepare single women for missionary service.[10]

## Laymen's Movements

A concern for evangelism and stewardship led to specific programs aimed at reaching men with the gospel and encouraging them to provide financial support for the Baptist missionary endeavors. The International Laymen's

Missionary Movement was an early interdenominational effort to enlist men in the service of the church's missionary calling. Baptists from several denominational groups were present in 1906 at the formation of that organization. Northern Baptists urged the organization to expand its work to both home and foreign missions, a recommendation approved in 1907.[11]

In 1908 the Northern Baptist Convention established its own "Baptist Brotherhood" as a denominational department. The "Brotherhood" was "to promote the organization of men in . . . churches, congregations and communities," toward "spiritual development, good fellowship, social betterment, civic and commercial righteousness, the reinforcement of the church, the evangelization of the world, and the brotherhood of man in Jesus Christ."[12]

The Laymen's Missionary Movement of the Southern Baptist Convention was founded in 1907 through the encouragement of Joshua Levering, a Baptist layman from Baltimore, Maryland. Its concerns were for evangelizing males, promoting missionary endeavors, and encouraging a "business-like system of giving" in Baptist churches.[13] In 1926 the organization's name was changed to the Baptist Brotherhood of the South, but it continued to emphasize missions, stewardship, and lay ministry. In 1950 it became the Brotherhood Commission of the SBC, an agency of the denomination. Its members were charged "to promote the work of their church and denomination, and enable the church through its leadership to develop, encourage, assist and guide the men in their Christian growth, influence and witness."[14] In the latter twentieth century it became the Baptist Men's Movement.

American Baptist Men, first known as the National Council of Northern Baptist Men, began in 1917 as part of a missionary fund-raising movement in the Northern Baptist Convention. It became a permanent entity in 1922, aimed at evangelization, fund-raising, and mission-action projects. African American Baptists, Free Will Baptists, and other groups developed similar organizations.

These Baptist men's organizations had several purposes: (1) to enlist the aid of Baptist males in appreciating and encouraging missionary endeavors, (2) to secure financial support from men for the local, national, and international ministries, (3) to engage men in service toward the evangelization of other men, and (4) to awaken men to their responsibilities as spiritual leaders in the family and the church.

Baptist men's groups often conducted Bible studies and prayer meetings, engaging in various service projects that enlisted men in home and foreign missionary activities. They also developed local and regional activities that included building repair, disaster relief, and short-term missionary service. In many churches Baptist men were trained in "personal witnessing" techniques for evangelizing the "lost"—those who were unconverted to Christianity. More recent activities included short-term mission trips abroad involving men and women in building projects, health clinics, and educational programs.

As international travel became more readily available, Baptist men fostered service trips to missionary programs that involved carpentry, medical care, and evangelistic campaigns at specific mission sites. Literature provided for Baptist men fostered programs of service to the local church and information regarding national and international missionary outreach. Certain groups of Baptist men were encouraged to mentor boys through Sunday School teaching, service projects, sports, and camping.

Among Southern Baptists, for example, the Baptist Brotherhood sponsored the Royal Ambassadors program, which included merit badges, camping, and service. Based on the biblical challenge to be "Ambassadors for Christ" (2 Corinthians 5:17), Royal Ambassadors challenged boys to fulfill requirements leading to ranks of Ambassador, Ambassador Extraordinary, and Ambassador Plenipotentiary. During the mid-twentieth century, Baptist men's groups often sponsored "Father-Son" breakfasts, dinners, or service projects aimed at mentoring a new generation of males in Christian faith and practice.

Men's movements continued among Baptist groups throughout the twentieth century. Many developed specific projects, such as disaster relief missions, medical treatment programs, and other short-term experiences in missionary service. At century's end, most Baptist men's organizations were declining in number except in the areas of special service and travel projects. Some Baptist men's groups have connected with various new interdenominational men's organizations, such as Promise Keepers, a movement that brings men together for praise, worship, and spiritual encouragement.

### Ethnic Baptists

The twentieth century saw increases in immigration and the growth of specific ethnic groups of Baptists, including German, Norwegian, Swedish, and Japanese Baptists. Ethnic Baptists formed numerous denominations in the late nineteenth and early twentieth centuries. These included the English and French-Speaking Baptist Conference of New England (1891); the Italian

Baptist Association (1899); the Finnish Baptist Mission Union of America (1901); the American Magyar (Hungarian) Baptist Union (1908); the Danish Baptist General Conference of America (1910); the Norwegian Baptist Conference of America (1910); the Czecho-Slovak Conference and the Polish Baptist Conference (1912); the Rumanian Baptist Association of America (1913); the Swedish Baptist General Conference of America (1914); the German Baptist Churches of North America; and the Russian Baptist Conference (1919).[15] World War I was particularly difficult for Germans in the United States and influenced the decision of many German Baptist congregations to abandon their native language in worship lest they be considered un-American.

Baptist work with Japanese immigrants began in California in 1914 by the Los Angeles Baptist City Mission Society. The second mission was instituted in 1916 when women from the First Baptist Church of San Pedro went to Terminal Island, California, to instruct women in English and crochet. By the late 1920s the Sunday school they had begun had increased from forty to four hundred members. During the 1930s two Japanese Baptist ministers, Reverend Kichitaro Yamamoto and Reverend Jitsuo Morikawa, assumed pastoral duties with the burgeoning church on Terminal Island. Morikawa, a second-generation Japanese Canadian, became one of the first Asians to gain leadership in what was then known as the Northern Baptist Convention.[16] The growing churches became part of the Japanese Baptist Union in Southern California.

As the century progressed, Baptists extended their work to the burgeoning Latino population throughout the United States, benefiting from the growth of churches in those ethnic communities. Many Baptist churches sponsored immigrant families from throughout the world, especially those fleeing war and persecution in places like Cambodia, Vietnam, Liberia, Laos, and elsewhere.

## Worship Practices in Baptist Churches

### Preaching

Throughout the twentieth century preaching was an important element of Baptist life, and in most congregations it served as the central event of Sunday worship services. It is viewed as an occasion when the congregation "gathers round the Word" of God to be presented with ideas, insights, and lessons for daily living drawn from biblical texts. Some Baptist churches utilize the "lectionary," that series of texts drawn from the Old Testament, the Psalms, the Epistles, and the Gospels, prescribed for each Sunday and offering a survey of the entire Bible on a three-year cycle. This approach to weekly texts is utilized by many Christian traditions but not mandated for Baptist usage as it is in other communions. Other Baptists, perhaps a majority, eschew use of the lectionary in favor of a more spontaneous approach to the use of Scripture in weekly worship services. Preachers are thus free to use texts as "led by the Holy Spirit" to provide spiritual, moral, and doctrinal insights for the specific local congregation. Usually, biblical texts are read before the sermon and ministers then expound on their meaning and application.

Some Baptist ministers are adamant in their insistence that "expository" preaching is the only valid approach to the biblical text. In this method the text is explained for its own inherent power. The preacher provides listeners with the textual background, context, and application as taken directly from the Scriptures. As these preachers see it, they do not need to make the text "relevant." When properly exegeted (explained) it will be relevant simply because it is the very Word of God. Many twentieth-century Baptists would agree with nineteenth-century professor John A. Broadus in his classic text on "the preparation and delivery of sermons":

> The primary idea is that the discourse is a development of the text, an explanation, illustration, application of its teachings. Our business is to teach God's Word. And although we may often discuss subjects, and aspects of subjects, which are not presented in precisely that form by any passage of Scripture, yet the fundamental conception should be habitually retained, that we are about to set forth what the text contains.[17]

Some go so far as to insist that they are not interpreting the text but allowing it to declare itself to the believing community. As Brother John Sherfey, a twentieth-century Independent Baptist pastor, declared:

> You read the Scripture out of the Bible, and then you start preaching from those verses, you know, just like I preached from this morning. And as you preach, why, God just begins to pour it on you and words'll come that you never even dreamed. Why, Lord, there's been a-many of a time I've been in the pulpit preaching and the Lord just showed me things in the Scriptures that I'd never seen before in my life—while I was preaching.[18]

Other Baptist preachers blend text, interpretation, application, and a call to commitment in churches from Sunday to Sunday. They may employ multiple methods for examining a biblical text, depending on the specific emphasis or intent of a given sermon. These preachers take varying approaches to the Sunday presentation, with topics that shape the way the "biblical story" is "retold." Baptist minister Stephen Shoemaker writes that the "Bible is not laid out like a philosophical discourse or a book of systematic theology. It is not a series of lessons or lectures. Its essential shape is story form, a grand, sweeping (if at times untidy) story." Shoemaker suggests that preaching involves "a retelling of Jewish/Christian stories as mirrors of the human condition and as signs of earth's redemption."[19]

African American Baptist preachers blend exegesis, narrative, and prophetic insights in unique ways, with vigorous preaching styles that elicit audible responses from the listening congregation. As Melva Wilson Costen writes of preaching in black churches:

> "Is there a word from the Lord?" This question, which was imbedded in the souls of the slaves, continues with African American worshipers. . . . The preached word, presented so that it is heard and experienced, allows one to know that "there *is* a way out of no way," and frees worshipers to celebrate this fact with the preacher. The word from the Lord is heard with the ears of one's total being, and it is experienced in the poetic flow of the preacher. The word elicits holistic responses that may begin in the gathered community, and will continue with worshipers as they move into the world.[20]

Well into the twentieth century Baptists discussed, and even debated, the most appropriate methods for presenting sermons. Some preachers—particularly Primitive, Old Regular, and Independent Baptists—reject any suggestion that they use manuscripts or even outlines in their homiletical presentations. They prefer instead to let the Spirit go where it will, reading and reflecting on the biblical text in preparation and then preaching "spontaneously." Other Baptist preachers use outlines, and still others use complete manuscripts. Many Baptist clergy and laity react negatively to the preacher who "reads" the sermon as too stilted or programmed for appropriate, Spirit-filled presentation.

Ministerial vestments worn in public worship represent another diverse, even divisive, element of Baptist liturgical life. In the nineteenth and early twentieth centuries, many Baptist preachers, especially in prominent pulpits, wore "frock tail coats" (tails) at worship. Twentieth-century Baptist pastors, probably a majority, wore basic business suits each Sunday, concerned that vestments—pulpit robes—might be too "high church" and set them off from the people inappropriately. Some Baptist pastors, black and white, now wear pulpit robes as a way of giving dignity to the service and avoiding a fashion show from Sunday to Sunday. In some contemporary-style services ministers may preach in sport clothes without benefit of coat and tie. One Alabama minister reported that he preferred to preach in Reeboks, a type of sports shoes that gave greater freedom of the Spirit than did Adidas or Nike!

## *The Shape of Baptist Worship*

In many Baptist churches the twentieth century brought numerous changes in the basic form of Baptist worship services. In other churches, the "order of worship" remained much as it had been a century before. Though congregations vary, a somewhat typical Sunday morning worship in many Baptist churches would involve the following elements, not unlike those found in other Protestant communions.

Invocation (an opening prayer led by a minister or lay member of the church)

Hymns (sung throughout the service by the congregation or choirs)

Prayers (almost always including some type of "pastoral prayer" offering intercession for global, regional, and personal needs)

Anthems or "special music" (offered by choirs or groups, "praise bands," orchestras, or soloists)

Offerings (money collected for the continuing work of the church and its varied ministries)

Scripture reading(s) (one or more texts read orally)

Sermon (the "proclamation of the Word" by a minister or layperson)

Call to Christian commitment (inviting people to literally or figuratively "respond" to the Christian gospel, often by publicly "coming forward" from the congregation)

Benediction or closing prayer (concluding the service and sending the people out into the world)

Some churches may use responsive readings taken from Scripture or printed in the Sunday program. More liturgically oriented Baptist congregations are apt to utilize specific confessions, responses, and collects (specific types of common prayer) blended throughout the service. More recently, some "seeker-sensitive" church services aimed at reaching the religiously nonaffiliated include the use of skits or brief dramatic enactments to highlight the theme of the service or the weekly biblical texts. In certain Baptist churches the congregation responds audibly and spontaneously throughout the entire service, punctuating particular presentations, especially the sermon, by verbal exhortations such as "amen," "hallelujah," "thank you, Jesus," or other phrases. Applause may also be a tool for congregational response and approval. This is particularly true of African America Baptist churches and congregations where a more charismatic style is normative. Some Baptist churches are less publicly demonstrative, and members may even suggest that such outbursts are excessively emotional or otherwise distracting to the service.

In most Baptist churches the pulpit is central to the worshiping congregation. Certain Baptists refer to it as the "sacred desk" from which the Word of God is proclaimed. Yet the animated style of many Baptist ministers leads them to roam the stage, pacing the platform as they preach. In certain Primitive Baptist churches and Appalachian Baptist communions, for example, the preacher may walk through the congregation, shaking hands with members or weeping throughout the sermon.

In some traditional Baptist churches the "invitation" or call to Christian discipleship remains a highlight of Sunday services, calling sinners to salvation and inviting believers to "move their membership" to the specific church. Born of frontier and urban revivalistic campaigns, "invitations" are essential to many congregations since they encourage non-Christians to "accept Christ" without delay. In highly evangelistic congregations the invitation hymn is repeated continuously until someone "walks the aisle." Indeed, the sacrament of walking the aisle remains a significant liturgical and communal element of worship in many congregations. People often speak of their conversion to Jesus Christ and their decision to receive baptism and membership in a particular church as "when I walked the aisle," or "when I came forward," or "when I shook the preacher's hand," an outward and visible sign of an inward and evangelical grace.

Worship remains a central element of Baptist life. Churches gather for worship on Sundays, for morning and often evening services. Many Baptist churches nationwide also conduct midweek services for prayer and fellowship on Wednesdays or Thursdays. In many respects the style of worship identifies, even defines, the primary directions and overall ethos of the congregation.

## Debates and Divisions: The Twentieth Century

Debates and divisions characterized, divided, and shaped Baptist church life throughout the twentieth century. Indeed, whether local, regional, or national, controversy was evident at every level. Church members argued over questions as diverse as whether the nation should go to war, what the nature of biblical revelation is, and what color the Sunday School rooms should be painted. Any of those issues could and did cause church splits. A brief survey of representative debates must suffice here.

### War and Peace

Some of the deepest divisions in Baptist life in the United States came as a result of war. Baptists North and South divided in 1845 over issues that led to the Civil War. Those two Baptist groups have never been reunited, and in many respects the roots of those divisions continue to affect Baptist denominations North and South, black and white.

While World War I created few divisions among Baptists, its aftermath led many Baptists to confront conscientious objection as a real possibility for Christian response to global conflict. On the whole, Baptist clergy and laity joined other Americans in supporting the Allied cause and denouncing the enemy, particularly Germany. Liberal and conservative alike used pro-war and anti-German rhetoric in their effort to promote democracy and freedom.

The outbreak of the war led many Baptists to join the army. In 1918 Southern Baptists issued a "Report on the World Crisis," which stated: "The issues at stake are not primarily personal or political. They are in essence religious. They are concerned with fundamental human rights and liberties. They touch the very foundations of moral law."[21] Northern Baptist editor W. I. Hargis wrote in the *Watchman-Examiner* that America and its allies were "fighting for a principle that is dearer than life. We are fighting to establish in every land the things that Jesus brought to the world and for which he laid down his life."[22]

Most Baptists refused to accept or support conscientious objection, since the war was cast as a battle against totalitarianism and for democracy. Fundamentalist A. C. Dixon placed blame for the conflict squarely on secularism and the evils unleashed in the world by Darwinian theories of human origins. He wrote: "Back of this war, and responsible for it, is Darwin's pagan teaching that the strong and the fit have the right to destroy the weak and the unfit." Darwin's influence on the "neurotic German philosopher" Friedrich

Nietzsche undergirded the aggression of the Kaiser and Germany.[23] Southern Baptist leader William Louis Poteat, president of Wake Forest College in North Carolina, confessed at the end of the war that "the German menace outraged us" and said: "We thank God that night has past [*sic*] and the day has dawned at length. We have achieved a signal victory which promises to be permanent for civilization against barbarism."[24]

Harry Emerson Fosdick (1878–1969), one of the nation's best-known liberal pastors, gave early support to the war effort. After the war, however, he was among a group of Baptists who declared themselves against all future warfare. Fosdick affirmed a pacifist position and acknowledged that although pacifists were sometimes "wrongheaded, they were 'wrongheaded in the right direction.'"[25] His concern, he wrote, was "to keep the church Christian despite the unchristian nature of war."[26]

In the years between the World Wars Baptists were not always of the same mind regarding the developing world powers. Some Baptists from the United States participated in the World Disarmament Conference in 1931 and warned that "preparedness" was not "a means of peace."[27] In 1934 Northern Baptists encouraged churches to support conscientious objectors in their ranks and to reject any war effort save for the defense of the United States[28]

Other Baptists gave affirmation to various changes brought about in the initial stages of Adolf Hitler's rule in Germany. The Fifth Baptist World Congress, held in Berlin in 1934, thrust Baptists into the early turmoil surrounding the growth of the Third Reich. More than three thousand people attended, representing more than forty Baptist groups. As a portion of its business, the congress went on record addressing "Racialism," denouncing "as a violation of the law of God, the Heavenly Father, all racial animosity and every form of unfair discrimination towards the jews, towards coloured people, or towards subject races in any part of the world."[29] At the same time, many delegates were impressed with the social and moral emphases of the Hitler regime. Boston pastor John W. Bradbury wrote: "It was a great relief to be in a country where salacious sex literature cannot be sold; where putrid motion pictures and gangster films cannot be shown. The new Germany has burned great masses of corrupting books and magazines along with its bonfires of Jewish and communistic libraries."[30] Alliance pronouncements acknowledged "that Chancellor Adolf Hitler gives to the temperance movement the prestige of his personal example since he neither uses intoxicants nor smokes."[31]

Many delegates deplored the racial attitudes of the Nazis, while others seemed less concerned. M. E. Dodd, president of the Southern Baptist Convention, wrote after his return from Germany that Jews "were not to be blamed for the intelligence and strength, so characteristic of their race, which put them forward." Yet they were using their strengths of intellect and economics "for self-aggrandizement to the injury of the German people."[32] For Dodd, governmental aggression against the Jews in Germany was regrettable but perhaps necessary. He commented: "Since the war some 200,000 Jews from Russia and other Eastern places had come to Germany. Most of these were Communist agitators against the government."[33] The Baptist World Alliance (BWA) assembly in Berlin brought out the best and the worst of Baptist responses to the social and political realities of their day. The war took its toll on the Alliance. Bombings in London forced it to move to interim and later permanent offices in Washington, DC, where it remains.

World War II and the evils of Nazism compelled Baptists and other Protestants to rethink earlier positions. The Northern Baptist Convention acknowledged the need for an armed response to the international conflict, but concluded: "We will not bless war, but we will not withhold our blessing from our sons who fight and from our country's cause."[34] Baptists generally gave their support to the war and viewed it as a fight for freedom. Nonetheless, some Baptists did serve as conscientious objectors, refusing to fight under any circumstances.

After Pearl Harbor was attacked by the empire of Japan on December 7, 1941, Japanese Americans were interned in various camps, most of them for the duration of the war. Again, the Los Angeles Baptist City Mission Society addressed the segregation of their Japanese Baptist colleagues, noting:

> We have a feeling of distinct sense of loss as these brethren in Christ depart from us. We regret the loss of this number from our local Baptist fellowship. We rejoice, however, that our work with the group was well done and that the work can never be lost. We shall maintain a prayerful interest in these Christian brethren of ours and do all that we can to help them wherever they go. The Federal Government has taken over our buildings at Terminal Island.[35]

In 1942, after President Franklin Roosevelt's Order 9066 requiring the internment of Japanese Americans, the Northern Baptist Convention issued a response through its two mission societies that protested against the "indiscriminate and enforced evacuation" of Japanese Americans and expressed "deep regret at this violation of the Christian principles of racial non-discrimination and respect for justice and fair play."[36] Years later, American Baptist leader Jitsuo Morikawa wrote:

> We give thanks to God when remember how the evacuation and intern-ment of Japanese Americans brought to the surface the true conscience of courage of the church. It was the case again where the church in nor-mal times of crisis, like the confessing church in Nazi German . . . so the church courageously responded in the time of our evacuation. When the evacuation of 120,000 from coastal towns was announced by the gov-ernment, among the first religious voices to make public protest came from Clarence Pickett of the American Friends Service Committee and John W. Thomas of the American Baptist Home Mission Societies.[37]

No war of the twentieth century divided Baptists and all Americans like the war in Vietnam, which ended with American withdrawal in 1975 and the reunification of the long-divided country. Baptist leaders supported and op-posed the war; Baptist groups offered their "official" responses on either side; and Baptist youth were divided, some serving in the military and others leaving the country to escape the draft. The family of Henlee Barnette (1911–2004), ethics professor at Southern Baptist Theological Seminary, Louisville, Kentucky, personified the divisions. One of his sons served in the military in Vietnam, while another went to Canada in protest the injustice of the draft and the war. Some Baptists were adamantly in favor of the Vietnam War, while others marched in opposition to the effort.

## The Fundamentalist-Modernist Controversy

Perhaps the most divisive issues for Baptists (and other Protestants) involved the confrontation over doctrine as evidenced in the classic fundamentalist-modernist controversy. It reverberated across multiple Baptist communions throughout the twentieth century and continues to divide many churches in the twenty-first. The controversy has numerous antecedents, including the history of an evangelical approach to religion present in colonial Puritanism and its emphasis on the centrality of Scripture, the need for conversion, and the importance of the church's mission in the world. More recently, evangel-icalism in Protestant groups included a significant reaction of conservative Christians to what was sometimes known at "modernism" or "liberalism," new developments in education, philosophy, theology, psychology, and science. By the early twentieth century conservatives were frequently labeled fundamentalists because of their desire to retain the doctrinal essentials of orthodox Christian faith.

As the theological controversies extended throughout American Protestantism, the terms *modernist* and *liberal* were often used interchangeably, especially by conservatives who attacked every effort to move the church away from tradition and orthodoxy. Others defined modernism as a more radical approach that moved beyond any revelation that could not be brought under the scrutiny of science and reason. They understood the Bible as no more or less "inspired" than any other sacred text, accepted "a strictly humanitarian view of Jesus," and called Christianity to come to terms with the realities of the modern world.[38]

Shailer Mathews (1863–1941), longtime dean of the University of Chicago Divinity School, sought to explain the "faith of the modernist." He described modernism as "a projection of the Christian movement into modern conditions. It proceeds within the religious limits set by an ongoing Christian group; it distinguishes permanent Christian convictions from their doctrinal expression; it uses these convictions in meeting the actual needs of our modern world."[39] Mathews illustrated the difficulty of drawing the lines between modernists and liberals too sharply: "Modernists are thus evangelical Christians who use modern methods to meet modern needs. Confessionalism is the evangelicalism of the dogmatic mind. Modernism is the evangelicalism of the scientific mind."[40]

Liberals were often those who retained more attachment to the uniqueness of Christianity among other religions and the significance of Jesus for both the church and the world. They are sometimes known as "Christocentric liberals" or representatives of "progressive orthodoxy." Baptist theologian William Newton Clarke (1841–1912) described this kind of liberalism in terms of its Christ-centeredness and the insistence that Christianity differed from "other religions" in that "its conception of God and of man's relation to him, and its impulse and power for the religious life, are derived from a self-revelation of God in human history, which culminated in Jesus Christ; and it is under the influence of that revelation that the Christian religious life is lived."[41]

Many of these liberals challenged traditionalism with their insistence that creeds and confessions of faith were not timeless statements of unchanging Christian orthodoxy but historically conditioned documents that could be amended and adapted with the discovery of new truth in every age. All truth was God's truth, and a faith that could not sustain itself amid new knowledge would not survive in the modern world. These liberals, especially the Baptists among them, insisted that creeds might change, but the abiding experience with Jesus was the timeless ideal that bound Christians in every age. While they generally affirmed "organic evolution," the Christocentric liberals refused to follow those of more modernist sentiments who asserted that human beings were "the product of purely naturalistic forces." Rather, they preferred a theistic evolution that held to the centrality of God's activity in creation.[42]

Using Jesus as the guide to all truth, the liberals affirmed scientific findings regarding human evolution; utilized the historical-critical method of biblical studies; appropriated new teachings found in psychology and sociology; accepted new philosophical studies, particularly "philosophical idealism;" and preached progressive social ideals based on democratic idealism.[43]

In *The Modernist Impulse in American Protestantism*, William R. Hutchinson noted that "after the Methodists, the two groups most deeply affected [by liberal influences] were the Baptists and the Disciples [of Christ]."[44] Winthrop Hudson observed that during the early 1900s, "Northern Baptists were more deeply divided, distracted, and immobilized by the Fundamentalist controversy than any other denomination."[45] E. Glenn Hinson lists a number of significant Baptists who reflect liberal outlooks regarding theology, history, and social action. He includes Walter Rauschenbusch, a founder of the Social Gospel movement; William Newton Clarke, professor of theology at Hamilton (Colgate) Seminary; and Harry Emerson Fosdick, pastor of Riverside Baptist Church, New York City. Numerous Baptist scholars and educational institutions brought liberal ideals into their curriculum, often to the chagrin of conservatives.[46]

Rauschenbusch, conservative in his evangelicalism and liberal in his social concerns, often defended what he believed to be the breadth of Baptist freedom and openness to diversity. In 1896 he defended Nathaniel Schmidt, a professor at Colgate University who had been fired for his use of higher criticism in Bible classes. He wrote:

> Whether we accept or reject particular results of critical investigation, we assert the right of competent men to investigate and communicate their results, provided they do both in the spirit of reverence and of submission to the truth. . . . Even if some of us do not belong to it ourselves, we assert the right of a liberal wing of the Baptist denomination to exist and to contribute its share to our development.[47]

In *An Outline of Christian Theology*, published in 1898, William Newton Clarke developed a theology that brought liberal approaches to the study of classic theological categories regarding the nature of God, Scripture, salvation, and faith. His concern was less with a literal reading of the Bible than with the inspiration of the same Spirit that inspired the biblical writers. Clarke believed that God's nature was essentially benevolent, grounded in mercy and forgiveness revealed in Jesus. He insisted that "all the great religions contain some truth concerning religion."[48]

Shailer Mathews taught at Colby College and the University of Chicago. From 1908 to 1933 he served as dean of the University of Chicago Divinity School. Mathews became a leading spokesperson for modernism, and its concern to bring the "truths" of modern science, philosophy, and culture to bear on traditional Christian beliefs. He suggested that doctrines and biblical interpretations are shaped by social context and change with the culture. Thus Mathews turned from Christocentric liberalism to a modernist approach to truth found inside and outside the boundaries of the Christian tradition. Hinson writes: "Believing that theologies have a practical rather than a theoretical significance, he [Mathews] turned to the natural and social sciences rather than philosophy to interpret religious doctrines."[49]

Shailer Mathews was but one of a significant number of Baptists on the faculty of the predominantly liberal divinity school at the University of Chicago. These included biblical scholars Shirley Jackson Case and John M. P. Smith, as well as theologians Gerald Barney Smith, Daniel Day Williams, and Bernard E. Meland, among others.[50]

Although perhaps not as outspoken as their Northern counterpoints, Baptists in the South were not unaffected by the liberal movement. William Louis Poteat (1856–1938) was a nationally known biologist who was one of the first professors to bring the laboratory method into college biology classes. After teaching for many years at Wake Forest College in North Carolina, he was named president of that institution and served in that office from 1905 to 1927. As both professor and president, Poteat defended the teaching of evolution, as evident in a speech to the North Carolina Baptist Convention in December 1922. In it he encouraged the Baptists to "welcome truth" since Jesus Christ was "the theme, origin, and end of all truth."[51]

In his book *The Impact of American Religious Liberalism*, Kenneth Cauthen wrote:

> The Baptist influence on twentieth-century liberalism in America, then, is of great significance. One suspects that there is an important connec-

tion between some of the theological emphases of Baptists and the development of liberalism. Baptists have always shied away from any creedal statements which would enforce strict doctrinal conformity and have stressed the freedom and competency of the individual under the leadership of the Spirit to interpret the New Testament for himself/[herself]. Moreover Baptists were among those most affected by revivalism in the nineteenth century. The stress of revivalism on conversion and Christian experience shifted attention away from concern with correctness of belief and the significance of dogma to the authority and importance of personal experience. In the light of this background it is not surprising that some of the most influential leaders of liberal thought in America came out of a Baptist, pietistic environment which had already laid the ground work for some of the most distinctive liberal emphases.[52]

Not all Baptists, of course, would agree with Cauthen's assessment. Indeed, if certain Baptists were in the vanguard of the liberal/modernist movement, others were unashamed conservatives/fundamentalists who attacked liberals even as they reasserted the timeless orthodoxy of traditional Christian dogma. Conservatives warned that these new liberal ideas would destroy the unchanging truth of the Bible, the "fundamental" doctrines of Christian orthodoxy, and the need for conversion. The theory of "organic evolution" not only undermined the veracity of the Genesis account of creation but also challenged the uniqueness of humanity as the *imago dei*, the image of God. The historical-critical method of biblical studies not only challenged the inspiration of the Bible but also placed it on the same level as any other classic text. Liberalism's more positive view of human nature was a direct threat to biblical doctrines of total depravity and human sinfulness. The minimizing of historic Christian dogmas was detrimental to the uniqueness of Christianity and the theological beliefs that were essential to Christian identity.

The conservative movement that became known as fundamentalism developed out of a variety of evangelical traditions that had long occupied the American landscape. Leaders saw themselves as part of a lineage that included revivalism, conversionism, and support for biblical authority and the creeds and confessions of historic Christianity. As George Marsden has shown, fundamentalism began with influences and ideas drawn from various religious movements, including evangelicalism, Princeton Theology, premillennialism, and the general reaction of many conservatives to the impact of new science on biblical authority and Christian doctrine.[53]

By the late nineteenth century many conservatives were convinced that the rise of liberalism was yet another "sign of the times," proving that Christ's return was imminent. Indeed, the growth of premillennialism was a major element in many, though not all, elements of the fundamentalist movement. Premillennialism is the belief, expressed in various theories, that the world is growing more evil with each passing day and can be redeemed only through the radical return of Christ before the millennial reign. Drawing on references such as Revelation 20:2–7 and linking various biblical prophecies taken from both Testaments, premillennialists suggest that Christ's bodily Second Coming is a direct intervention of the Divine, which brings deliverance for the "saints" (Christian believers) and retribution on the unjust. This return marks the beginning of a thousand-year struggle that will end in the destruction of Satan, the birth of the new Jerusalem, and the absolute reign of Christ. The church will then be "raptured" out of this world before the time of tribulation when, amid severe persecution, human beings are given one last chance to believe in Christ and escape the perils of hell.

Many Baptists, even conservatives, were slow to come to premillennial views. Some progressives remained committed to postmillennialism, the belief that the church through evangelical zeal or "Christianizing the social order" would bring in a Golden Age of spiritual renewal as a prelude to the return of Jesus Christ. Other Baptist leaders were outspoken amillennialists, who affirmed that God would bring about an end to history but denied that the Bible taught a literal millennium. Over time, however, premillennialism seemed to prevail in popular millennial speculation among large numbers of Baptists and other evangelicals.

This is not to say that premillennialists themselves agreed on the particulars of Christ's return. Some were historicists who believed that the biblical prophecies had been fulfilled and merely awaited Christ's final action. Others were futurists who suggested that many specific prophecies remained unrealized and develop a system for anticipating their fulfillment. Certain futurists developed an elaborate system known as Dispensational Premillennialism that posited a series of dispensations or "ages" when God had worked in particular ways in the world. Twentieth-century Christians, they believed, were living in the "Church Age," the penultimate era leading to the final dispensation and the return of Jesus Christ. Yet even Dispensationalists could not agree on the time for the Rapture of the church, that moment when true believers, living and dead, would be snatched heavenward to be immediately in the presence of God. Some suggested the Rapture would occur before the great time of tribulation, others thought it would occur in the middle of the tribulation, and a third group put the Rapture at the end of that terrible ordeal.

British Dispensationalist John Nelson Darby (1800–1882) and his American counterpart C. I. Scofield (1843–1921) were the chief ideologues behind the movement. Scofield's *Reference Bible* (1909), a King James Version of the Scriptures complete with notes on Dispensationalism written by Scofield, became something of a handbook for Baptist and other premillennialists. In fact, the best-selling series of novels known as the *Left Behind* series follows many of Scofield's ideas when detailing the particulars of Christ's bodily return before the millennium amid the Rapture of the faithful, was cowritten by Tim LaHaye, a well-known conservative Baptist.

Premillennialism was built on the idea that the Bible was a book that could be taken literally and studied scientifically in order to unlock its prophetic secrets. Many of its supporters insisted that intense Bible study could verify the predictions and prepare the church for the final events leading to Christ's return and the judgment of the sinful world. Efforts to promote these and other conservative doctrines led to the organization of a series of Bible conferences begun as early as the 1860s and eventually based at Niagara-on-the-Lake, Ontario, in 1883–1897. These conferences promoted the "scientific" study of the Bible, the literal nature of biblical prophecy, and the theories of Dispensational Premillennialism. They were also a direct influence on the development of fundamentalism and influenced Baptists and other Protestants well into the twentieth century.

Yet another facet of the conservative/fundamentalist movement in the United States was found in what came to be known as Princeton Theology, a particular approach to biblical interpretation and Christian orthodoxy that developed among certain Presbyterian and Reformed faculty members at Princeton Seminary in the late nineteenth and early twentieth centuries. While generally unsympathetic toward the claims of premillennialists, these scholars defended the truths of Scripture and traditional Christian doctrine against the dangers of liberalism and historical criticism. Utilizing ideals taken from Scottish Common Sense Philosophy, they asserted that the teachings of the Bible were logically defensible, "that empirical induction is the primary source of truth and that all reasonable people intuit moral absolutes."[54] They reaffirmed the dogmas of Reformed (Calvinist) theology as taught in the classic creeds and confessions of faith and promoted the "unchanging" truth and veracity of the Bible. Princeton theologians such as Archibald Alexander, Charles Hodge, Benjamin B. Warfield, and J. Gresham Machen had a profound influence on conservative-evangelicals, including many Baptists.

The movement known as fundamentalism thus developed from various conservative groups as a reassertion of classic Christian doctrines and a reaction against the liberal/modernist movement. The Baptist presence among fundamentalist leaders was evident from the beginning. Indeed, the very terms *fundamentalist* and *fundamentalism* were probably first used by Curtis Lee Laws (1868–1946), editor of the Baptist magazine *Watchman-Examiner*, in referring to those individuals who sought "to do battle royal for the Fundamentals" of the faith.[55] By 1920 Laws and some 150 other Northern Baptists had united to organize a "General conference on Fundamentals" to be held following the meeting of the Northern Baptist Convention. As they saw it, the decline of doctrinal solidarity in the denomination was contributing to the "worldliness" and "rationalism" rampant in the churches.

During the years 1910–1915 Baptist Amzi Clarence Dixon (1854–1925) helped to edit *The Fundamentals*, a multivolume set of essays that defended conservative theology and attacked "modernist" ideology from evolution to the historical-critical method of biblical interpretation. A variety of Baptist leaders wrote essays published in these volumes that were intended to provide grassroots assistance for pastors, missionaries, and other church leaders in responding to the growth of liberalism. Many Baptists were at the forefront of the fundamentalist movement of the early twentieth century, often provoking a colorful populist response to liberalism, Darwinism, and the rise of secularism.

One prominent Baptist premillennialist was Adoniram Judson Gordon (1836–1895), long-time pastor of Boston's Clarendon Street Church. Gordon asserted that this view of eschatology (last things) was insightful for understanding the "signs of the times" that anticipated the immediate return of Christ. In 1890 he was elected president of the newly formed Baptist Society for Bible Study, a seedbed of Baptist premillennial views.[56]

Leading Baptist fundamentalists were articulate in their defense of the faith. In 1918 William Bell Riley (1861–1947), Baptist educator and evangelist, began publishing *Christian Fundamentals in School and Church*, a periodical that warned of the growing influence of liberalism in Baptist educational institutions. As pastor of First Baptist Church, Minneapolis, Minnesota, he founded Northfield schools through which students were prepared for ministry, missionary work and other Christian activities. (In 1944 Riley was succeeded as president by Billy Graham, a youthful evangelist on his way up.) In 1919 Riley established the World's Christian Fundamentals Association, an organization through which William Jennings Bryan was enlisted to prosecute John Scopes in the famous "monkey trial" in Dayton, Tennessee, in 1925.[57] Riley was a longtime opponent of the theory of evolution and its place on the curriculum of state or private schools and chaired the Anti-Evolution League of Minnesota. He did not hesitate to attack the liberal members at the University of Minnesota and elsewhere as "Darwinized . . . Germanized . . . deceived and faithless professors."[58]

Riley was a major force in the effort to turn the Northern Baptist Convention away from what he saw as the denomination's growing liberalism. During the 1920s he advocated adoption of a denominational confession of faith, monitored the theology of missionaries, and opposed Darwinism. Although his efforts were essentially unsuccessful, he continued to be a prominent spokesman for fundamentalism among Baptists until his death in 1947.

Like Riley, Baptist leader J. C. Massee (1871–1965) called upon the Northern Baptist Convention to expel liberals and liberalism from Baptist schools. He chaired a conference that brought together Baptist fundamentalists shortly before the Northern Baptist Convention meeting of 1920 in an effort to "restate, reaffirm and re-emphasize the fundamentals of New Testament faith."[59] Although never a liberal, Massee later moved away from the fundamentalists, noting, "I left the fundamentalists to save my own spirit, they became so self-righteous, so critical, so unchristian, so destructive, so incapable of being fair that I had to go elsewhere for spiritual nourishment."[60] While Massee worked diligently to keep the Northern Baptist Convention from succumbing to liberalism, his distress with the militancy of certain fundamentalists illustrated the divisions within the movement itself. As he once commented to a group of friends, "There are fundamentalists and damned fundamentalists."[61]

More militant than Massee, John Roach Straton (1875–1929), pastor of Calvary Baptist Church in New York City, was a powerful supporter of the fundamentalist cause among Protestants in general and Baptists in particular. From his New York pulpit Straton challenged the developing secularism of his day, often attacked gambling, liquor, nightlife, materialism, birth control, and other vices of urban life.[62] His early-twentieth-century speculations about catastrophes that might befall the city have an eerie quality in light of the terrible destruction of the World Trade Center on September 11, 2001.

Have you ever thought of what a good husky tidal wave would do to "little old New York"? Have you ever imagined the Woolworth "skyscraper" butting headlong into the Equitable Building, through such an earthquake as that which laid San Francisco's proud beauty in the dust? Have you ever imagined the Metropolitan Tower crashing over on Madison Square Garden some time, when there were tens of thousands of people in there at some worldly, godless, celebration on the Lord's Day? Ah yes, don't worry about God's not having the means for judgment, even in this world.[63]

Straton was one of the most ardent fundamentalists of his time. His list of Baptist "infidels" included the likes of Walter Rauschenbusch, Harry Emerson Fosdick, William Newton Clarke, Shailer Mathews, and others who had "departed from the faith, and their form of infidelity is far more subtle and seductive and ruinous than the old, outspoken, sneering infidelity of the past."[64] As he saw it, liberalism was the root cause of the growing social and moral problems descending on American society.

Perhaps the most colorful, if not the most controversial, Baptist fundamentalist of the early twentieth century was J. Frank Norris (1877–1952), pastor of First Baptist Church, Fort Worth, Texas. Norris grew that church into one of the largest congregations in the nation largely through aggressive evangelism and outlandish tactics, and he was instrumental in beginning the Independent Baptist movement, a new segment of the Baptist family in America. He set his own Texas style of fundamentalist populism over against any hint of liberalism, even among Baptists who had always considered themselves thoroughly orthodox. He was a biblical literalist who brooked no moderation, asserting: "Whenever you find a preacher who takes the Bible allegorically and figuratively . . . that preacher is preaching an allegorical gospel which is no gospel. I thank God for a literal Christ; for a literal salvation. There is literal sorrow; literal death; literal hell; and, thank God, there is a literal heaven."[65]

Norris waded into community disputes, preaching sermons such as "The Ten Biggest Devils in Fort Worth, Names Given," and "Rum and Romanism." He attracted crowds by bringing a monkey into the pulpit when denouncing Darwinism and by conducting mock funerals for "demon rum" and throwing bottles into a coffin. On one occasion, when baptizing a popular rodeo cowboy, Norris permitted the man to bring his horse to watch the event.[66] In 1926 Norris shot and killed D. E. Chipps, a Fort Worth citizen who Norris thought was threatening his life. Acquitted of the charge of manslaughter, Norris continued to attack liberalism inside and outside the Baptist communion. He left the Southern Baptist Convention in the 1930s, rejecting its "hierarchical bureaucracy" that undermined the authority of the local congregation and the liberalism that he charged was rampant in such as Baylor University. This action marked the unofficial beginnings of the Independent Baptist movement, a loosely connected group of local churches that rejected denominational hierarchies and mission boards as detrimental to the autonomy of the local congregation. It also reflected a form of fundamentalist separatism, whereby conservatives distanced themselves from any hint of liberalism, refusing to participate in community or ecumenical endeavors that required the involvement of liberal clergy or churches. Such separatism meant that to know a liberal was to be a liberal. Orthodoxy required separation from any form of liberal taint.

Norris used various publications to attack liberalism in the church and the government. He founded the *Searchlight* in the 1920s and soon changed the name to the *Fundamentalist*. He also was instrumental in forming the "Premillennial, Fundamental, Missionary Fellowship," a gathering of fundamentalist Baptist pastors for fellowship, evangelism, and affirmation of orthodoxy. Conflicts within that movement over Norris's autocratic leadership style led to divisions and the formation of two new groups, the World Fundamentalist Fellowship, led by Norris, and the Baptist Bible Fellowship, made up of his opponents.[67] The latter group, based in Springfield, Missouri, produced some of the largest Protestant churches in America during the 1950s and 1960s. Jerry Falwell, one of the best-known fundamentalist Baptists of the latter twentieth century, has long maintained a relationship with the Baptist Bible Fellowship.

In 1921 a study commission investigating the presence of liberal ideology in schools related to the Northern Baptist Convention reported: "Here and there doubtless is a teacher who has departed from the Baptist faith or has lost the Saviour's spirit. . . . It is the duty of the Baptist communities . . . to displace from the schools men who impugn the authority of the Scriptures as the Word of God and who deny the deity of our Lord, but they must do it in prescribed ways."[68] Conservatives remained suspicious and were dissatisfied with the findings.

A continuing discontent with liberalism led to further calls for greater doctrinal specificity of the entire denomination. At the annual convention at Indianapolis in 1922, fundamentalists, led by W. B. Riley, urged the denomination to adopt the *New Hampshire Confession of Faith* as its doctrinal statement. Ultimately, they approved a statement put forth by Cornelius Woelfkin (1859–1928), pastor of Park Avenue Baptist Church, New York, that read: "The Northern Baptist Convention affirms that the New Testament is the all-sufficient ground of our faith and practice, and we need no other statement." The resolution passed by a vote of 1,264 to 637.[69]

The controversy continued when charges of liberalism were made against certain missionaries sent out by the Foreign Mission Societies of the

NBC. Investigations were held, and some churches withheld funding from the societies as protest against liberal missionaries. Curtis Lee Laws and other conservatives toured the mission field and responded positively to the work they found there. A 1925 investigative report praised the missionaries, their work, and their beliefs.[70]

Other fundamentalist fellowships included the Baptist Bible Union (BBU), founded in 1923 by A. C. Dixon, W. B. Riley, J. Frank Norris, and an outspoken Canadian Baptist named T. T. Shields. It promoted the cause of orthodoxy in Baptist churches and schools and rejected the teaching of evolution and the work of Social Gospel liberals. The union's "doctrinal basis" was fundamentalist, including belief in Christ's "premillennial, personal and visible" return.[71] Its demise led to the formation of the General Association of Regular Baptist Churches (GARBC), a new conservative Baptist group.

Two controversies occurred in the 1920s that galvanized Baptists on the right and the left. The first involved Harry Emerson Fosdick and his work as preaching minister for the First Presbyterian Church in New York City. In a sermon titled "Shall the Fundamentalists Win?" preached in 1921 after a return from the China mission fields, Fosdick defended liberal approaches to Scripture, doctrine, and practice. He distinguished between fundamentalists and conservatives by noting that "the best conservatives can often give lessons to the liberals in true liberality of spirit, but the Fundamentalist program is essentially illiberal and intolerant." He declared that "the new knowledge and the old faith [have] to be blended in a new combination. Now, the people in this generation who are trying to do this are the liberals, and the Fundamentalists are out on a campaign to shut against them the doors of the Christian fellowship. Shall they be allowed to succeed?"[72]

A vehement response from Presbyterian fundamentalists led to efforts to remove Fosdick from First Presbyterian Church. A special committee called upon him to resign, and although the church at first refused to accept his resignation, Fosdick ultimately departed for Riverside Church, a new congregation in a neo-Gothic building constructed in Manhattan in the 1930s with funding from John D. Rockefeller Jr.

A second controversy in the 1920s was the infamous Scopes Monkey Trial, held in Dayton, Tennessee, in the summer of 1925. With the encouragement of the American Civil Liberties Union, John Scopes, a teacher in the Tennessee public schools, agreed to violate the state's antievolution law in order to create a test case. William Jennings Bryan, Presbyterian political leader and populist, was secured to prosecute the case, and Clarence Darrow, the epitome of liberal and secular modernism, agreed to defend Scopes. Hundreds of people poured into Dayton, including a variety of Baptist evangelists led by T. T. Martin. Throughout the trial, Martin held a tent revival on the edge of town. The trial became a sideshow; Scopes was finally found guilty and fined one hundred dollars, which he never paid. Bryan, humiliated under questioning by Darrow, prepared an elaborate rebuttal that he never gave, and he died a short time later, worn out from the ordeal. Baptists themselves divided over the meaning of the effort. Also in 1925 the Southern Baptist Convention adopted Baptists' first confession of faith, delineating their conservative theological views more specifically than had been previously set forth.

During the 1950 and 1960s Independent Baptist churches were some of the largest in the country. Many of these congregations were founded by aggressive, charismatic, autocratic pastors who used a variety of evangelical and entrepreneurial methods to attract huge crowds to their services. These methods included such things as attendance contests, revival services, music groups, meals, and special events for children, youth, and families. These preachers were unashamedly orthodox in their doctrine, often attacking every vestige of liberalism in the church and state. They were active anti-communists, often linking theological liberals with communist sympathizers and "humanists." Independent Baptist pastors included Lee Robertson at Tennessee Temple Baptist Church in Chattanooga, Tennessee, Jack Hyles at First Baptist Church, Hammond, Indiana, and Jerry Falwell, founder/pastor of Thomas Road Baptist Church in Lynchburg, Virginia.

Some Independent Baptists moved into the political realm with the founding of the Moral Majority by Jerry Falwell in 1979. It attempted to involve conservative Christians in the political process in response to issues of abortion, homosexuality, prayer in public schools, pornography, and the overall collapse of American moral culture. While most of its supporters came from the ranks of the Independent Baptists and other fundamentalist-based churches, Falwell also claimed support from conservative Catholics, Mormons, and other groups. The Moral Majority was disbanded in 1989 when Falwell announced that it had achieved its goals. By century's end, some conservatives suggested that Christian conservatives should again eschew political entanglements and renew their energy for redeeming individuals for Christ.

Fundamentalism did not end in the 1920s. Baptists continued to debate and divide over its dogmas throughout the twentieth century. Divisions over doctrine in the Northern Baptist Convention led to the founding of the Conservative Baptist Mission Society in 1943 and the Conservative Baptist Convention in 1946, which later became the Conservative Baptist Association of America.

The Southern Baptist Convention did not experience significant doctrinal divisions in the 1920s. By the 1960s, however, conservatives in the denomination were complaining vigorously that liberalism was creeping into convention-related colleges and seminaries. They pointed to books and lectures given by professors at some of the six denominationally funded theological schools. In 1979 a conservative majority elected Adrian Rogers, pastor of Belleview Baptist Church in Memphis, president of the convention. Rogers then began the process of appointing trustees to denominational boards and agencies who would support the doctrine of biblical inerrancy and other "fundamentals" of the faith. This agenda was continued by a series of convention presidents determined to change the course of the denomination to more conservative directions.

These efforts were not without opposition. From 1979 to 1990 another segment of the convention known as "moderates" mounted campaigns to elect their own candidates to convention leadership. They contended that the issue was not conservative dogma but denominational control and that fundamentalists were simply involved in a takeover movement to gain control of America's largest Protestant communion. Moderates and fundamentalists confronted each other at the annual meeting of the convention held each June. So intense was the controversy that some 45,000 "messengers" from SBC churches attended the annual meeting in Dallas; it was the largest SBC meeting ever held. Conservatives won that election and all other challenges until 1990, when moderates essentially withdrew their effort to elect candidates to convention leadership.

At the beginning of the twenty-first century, Southern Baptist churches continued to experience varying divisions at every level of denominational life. While the national denomination was firmly in conservatives' control, state Baptist conventions, local associations, and individual congregations continued to move across a spectrum from strong to declining connections to the denomination. New groups such as the Cooperative Baptist Fellowship and the Alliance of Baptists have attracted many moderate-based congregations. New divinity schools and seminaries have sprung up related directly or indirectly to more moderate churches and their support. These include Baptist Theological Seminary at Richmond (Virginia); Beeson Divinity School, Samford University; McAffee School of Theology, Mercer University; Truett Theological Seminary, Baylor University; Logston School of Theology, Hardin-Simmons University; Christopher White School of Divinity School, Gardner-Webb University; Campbell University Divinity School; Wake Forest University Divinity School; and Baptist Houses at Emory, Duke, and Texas Christian Universities.

## Baptists and the Twentieth Century

At the end of the twentieth century Baptists represented the largest Protestant communion in the United States. Throughout the century, however, Baptists themselves multiplied by dividing into new denominations. Theological and ethical divisions created new churches, denominations, and schools with Baptist connections. They maintained the world's largest mission task force, sending missionaries across the world. Baptist churches, long present in rural areas of the nation, claimed increasing segments of the urban landscape. Baptists were surely among the first to develop "megachurches" and in so doing raised new questions regarding the nature of the church and the future of denominationalism itself. Early debates over the nature of biblical revelation, Darwinism, and the boundaries of orthodoxy still raged at century's end. Divisions related to women's ordination, homosexuality, and the nature of the family descended upon churches and were carried into a new century. Through it all, many Baptist groups were compelled to revisit their history and theology as a way of understanding who they are and how they relate to changing times. Indeed, in many regions of the country, Baptist identity seemed "up for grabs."

## CHAPTER FOUR

# Baptist Beliefs and Practices

Baptists believe many things. They affirm a variety of doctrines, some shared with other Protestant groups and some distinct to Baptist traditions. Their roots in English Puritanism link Baptists with such classic Reformation dogmas as *sola scriptura* (Scripture alone), *sola fide* (faith alone), and the priesthood of all believers. Like other reformers, Baptists practice only two sacraments (ordinances): baptism and the Lord's Supper. Directly or indirectly, they are influenced by Lutheran and Reformed theology, the Radical Reformation, and other Reformation movements that preceded them.

Certain beliefs, such as baptismal immersion, congregational polity, and local church autonomy, evoke a general consensus that is endemic to Baptist identity. Their concern for religious freedom and a believers' church places Baptists securely within the Free Church tradition. Yet beyond a core of distinctives, Baptists themselves often differ as to doctrinal definitions and approaches to ministry. For example, ideas relating to election and predestination, theories of biblical inspiration, and questions regarding the nature of salvation can be so divisive as to make reconciliation among Baptist groups seem impossible. Where disparities arise, one group may denounce another as "un-baptistic" or heretical and thus unworthy of the Baptist name. Debates over what constitutes a true Baptist erupt with frequency among Baptist individuals, churches, and denominations.

Baptists in the United States are heirs of a variety of doctrines set forth by the early Baptist groups, especially the seventeenth-century General and Particular Baptists, who delineated their common and distinctive beliefs in a variety of confessions of faith. These confessions provided systematic statements of doctrines around which specific churches and associates might unite. Generally longer than the ancient Christian creeds (Apostles', Athanasian, Nicene), confessions included beliefs regarding Scripture, God, faith, regeneration, baptism, church government, church officers, conscience, and relations with the state. Many Baptists in the United States and elsewhere employed those confessions as guides for their own church and denominational statements of belief.

Yet not all Baptists agree that confessions are useful. Some fear that confessions might undermine or at least challenge the authority of Scripture alone. Certain Baptists eschewed confessions all together and relied only on the Bible as their doctrinal guide. William L. Lumpkin observed that the first Baptist confessions were "sectarian, being intended to differentiate Baptists from other groups of Christians and to justify their separate existence."[1] Confessions were intended to show that Baptists were orthodox Christians with specific beliefs and practices drawn from peculiarly Baptist ways of reading and understanding the Scriptures and the history of the church.

Baptists share many of their basic doctrines with other Christian and Protestant communions. They readily affirm many of the basic tenets of classic Christian belief. Yet, as Lumpkin asserted, Baptists have "traditionally been non-creedal" and have "not erected authoritative confessions of faith as official bases of organization and tests of orthodoxy." Their commitment to the Bible as the sole authority for faith and practice made them hesitant to make elaborate use of traditional "man-made" creeds of the church. Lumpkin thus concluded that "the desire to achieve uniformity has never been strong enough to secure adoption of a fixed creed even if the authority for imposing it had existed."[2]

Nonetheless, most Baptist groups would affirm the classic doctrines delineated in such ancient documents as the Apostles', Nicene, and Athanasian creeds. In fact, the so-called Orthodox Creed (1679) acknowledged that,

> The three creeds, viz. Nicene Creed, Athanasius's creed, and the Apostles creed, [sic] as they are commonly called, ought thoroughly to be received, and believed. For we believe, they may be proved, by most undoubted authority of holy scripture, and are necessary to be understood of all Christians; and to be instructed in the knowledge of them, by the ministers of Christ, according to the analogy of faith, recorded in sacred scriptures, upon which these creeds are grounded, and catechistically opened, and expounded in all Christian families, for the edification of young and old which might be a means to prevent heresy in doctrine, and

practice, these creeds containing all things in a brief manner that are necessary to be known.[3]

For example, most would agree with the dogmas set forth in the Apostles' Creed. It states:

> I believe in God the Father Almighty, Maker of Heaven and Earth, and in Jesus Christ His only Son our Lord. Who was conceived of the Holy Spirit, born of the Virgin Mary, suffered under Pontius Pilate, was crucified, dead and buried; on the third day he rose again from the dead. He descended into Hell. He ascended into heaven and sits on the right hand of God the Father Almighty. From thence he shall come to judge the living and the dead. I believe in the Holy Spirit, the Holy Catholic Church, the communion of Saints, the forgiveness of sins, the resurrection of the body, and the life ever lasting.

These doctrines are present in various forms in most Baptist confessions of faith. Likewise, the confessions illustrate Baptist commitment to many of the basic tenets of Protestantism. They would certainly agree with Martin Luther's emphasis on *sola scriptura* (Scripture alone), *sola fide* (faith alone), and *sola gratia* (grace alone). Thus they affirm that the Bible alone is the foundational source for doctrine and practice; that justification by faith alone (not works) is the basis of salvation; and that salvation was made possible only by the grace of God offered to sinners who could not *do* anything to attain or deserve it. Baptists also rejected apostolic succession and Catholic claims that the pope was Head of the Church and Vicar of Christ on earth. With Luther and other reformers they affirmed the priesthood of all believers and the centrality of two sacraments, not the seven sacraments of the Catholic system.

Particular Baptists were especially indebted to the theology of the Genevan reformer John Calvin regarding the nature of salvation, election, and predestination. Some accepted Calvin's understanding of the Lord's Supper as conveying the spiritual presence of Christ, while others preferred the theology of Zurich's Ulrich Zwingli, who suggested that the Lord's Supper is a memorial in which Christ's presence is less in the elements of bread and wine than in the faith of the believing community. However, they parted company with the so-called magisterial reformers, by rejecting infant baptism and the union of church and state.

In this Baptists agree with the Anabaptists (Swiss Brethren, Mennonites, and others) that baptism should be administered only to those who have professed faith in the believing community, the church. Thus William L. Lumpkin suggested that "in the seventeenth century, confessions were used both to distinguish Baptists groups from one another and from other Protestants, and to show kinship with one another and other Protestant groups."[4] Even a brief survey of Baptist doctrines, especially those set forth in confessions of faith, illustrates the differences and similarities between Baptists and other Christian groups. The seventeenth-century confessions provided a foundation for later doctrinal statements by Baptists.

First, with some notable exceptions, Baptists are Trinitarians in their view of God. They affirm a belief in one God "in three persons, blessed Trinity." They insist that the God revealed in Jesus Christ is expressed in three *hypostases*: Father, Son, and Holy Ghost. The first article of the *Declaration of Faith of English People*, published by the first Baptist community in Amsterdam in 1611, confessed:

> That there are THREE which beare record in heaven the FATHER, the WORD, and the SPIRIT; and these THREE are one GOD, in all equalitie, I Jno. 5–7; Phil 2.5, 6. By whome all thinges are created and preserved, in Heaven and in Earth. Gen. I Chap.[5]

The *London* (Particular Baptist) *Confession* (1644) declared:

> In this God-head, there is the Father, the Sonne, and the Spirit; being every one of them one and the same God; and therefore not divided, but distinguished one from another by their severall properties; the Father being from himselfe, the Sonne of the Father from everlasting, the holy spirit proceeding from the Father and the Sonne.[6]

Yet Trinitarian orthodoxy did not go unchallenged among certain Baptists. For example, some eighteenth-century Baptists questioned whether the Scriptures actually taught Trinitarianism. Some were Arians in their Christology, affirming the deity of Christ but denying that Jesus was "eternal with the Father." Mirroring the theology of the fourth-century Christian Arius, these Baptists insisted that Jesus was "subordinate" to the Father, who alone was uncreated and eternal.

More recently, some Baptist women and men have challenged their tradition to reexamine the male-dominant language of Trinitarian terminology, minimizing references to the Divine gender and giving greater emphasis to descriptions of God such as Creator, Redeemer, and Sustainer. Other Baptists reject such efforts as an inappropriate attempt to undermine orthodox dogma.

Second, Baptists believe that Jesus Christ is the Son of God, the Savior of the world who became incarnate, was born of the Virgin Mary, died on the cross for the sins of humanity, and rose again on the third day. They accept the idea of final judgment and the resurrection of all faithful believers to eternal life. The London-based Baptists who composed *A Confession of Faith, of those Churches which are commonly (though falsely) called Anabaptists*, in 1644, declared that Jesus "was made man of a woman, of the Tribe of Judah, of the seed of Abraham and David, to wit, of Mary that blessed Virgin, by the holy spirit coming upon her."[7]

John Clarke's personal Baptist confession of faith made "at Boston in behalf of my Lord," in 1651 acknowledged that "Jesus of Nazareth, whom God hath raised from the dead, is made both Lord and Christ; This Jesus I say is the Christ, in English, the Anointed One, that a name above every name."[8]

Debates among twentieth-century Baptists regarding the nature of Christ (Christology), the virgin birth, and the bodily resurrection divided certain liberal and conservative Baptists. These confrontations found their way into educational institutions and divided Baptists north and south.

Third, Baptists believe that every member of the church should have a personal experience with Christ as a prerequisite for baptism, that Christ's death and resurrection provide the doorway to faith and salvation. This experience of grace facilitates a regenerate church membership, a community of believers. While affirming the need for salvation, Baptists have not necessarily agreed on who could be saved. The Particular Baptists' *London Confession* of 1644 noted:

> That Christ Jesus by his death did bring forth salvation and reconciliation onely for the elect, which were those which God the Father gave him; & that the Gospel which is to be preached to all me as the ground of faith, is, that Jesus is the Christ, the Sonne of the ever blessed God . . . [and] That Faith is the gift of god wrought in the hearts of the elect by the Spirit of God, whereby they come to see, know, and believe the truth of the Scriptures.[9]

Likewise, the Calvinistic *Somerset Confession* of 1654 stated:

> That God in his son did freely, without respect to any work done, or to be done by them as a moving cause, elect and choose some to himself

before the foundation of the world (Eph 1:3, 4; 2 Tim. 1:9), whom he in time hath, douth, and will call, justify, sanctify and glorify (Rom. 8:29, 30).[10]

The General (Arminian) Baptists understood salvation differently, as noted in their *Standard Confession* of 1660. It affirmed that "all men at one time or other, are put into such a capacity, as that (through the grace of God) they may be eternally saved."[11]

Some twentieth-century Baptists continue to divide over the way in which regeneration occurs and who can receive it. Is salvation only for the elect? Or are all persons potentially elected and receive that election on the basis of repentance and faith? Some Baptists believe that once salvation is secured it can never be lost, while others suggest that just as persons have the free will to accept Christ's salvation they also have the free will to turn from it and "fall from grace."

Fourth, faith in Christ brings believers into the church of Jesus Christ, a community that the *London Confession* of 1644 defined as

> a company of visible Saints, called & separated from the world, by the word and Spirit of god, to the visible profession of the faith of the Gospel, being baptized into that faith, and joined to the Lord, and each other, by mutuall agreement, [Covenant] in the practical injoyment of the Ordinances, commanded by Christ their head and King.[12]

The idea of "mutuall agreement" is the foundation of the covenant between God and the believers and among the believers themselves. Through the covenant, God's "presence, love, blessing, and protection" were made known to the believing individuals who were also "fitly compact and knit together, according to the effectuall working of every part, to the edification of itselfe in love."[13] Many scholars of Baptist history and theology believe that the idea of a covenant is a hallmark of Baptist identity evident from the very beginning of the movement. Through covenant, believers are drawn into community with God and with each other.

Fifth, Baptists also believe that the Scriptures of the Old (Hebrew Bible) and New Testaments constitute a special revelation from God that provides authoritative teaching on matters of faith, doctrine, ethics, and spirituality. As noted earlier, with Martin Luther and other Protestant reformers Baptists affirm *sola scriptura*, the belief that Scripture alone is the source of authority and inspiration for the church and the individual. While the traditional canon (list) of the Hebrew Scriptures (Old Testament) is the revelation of God, Baptists generally read them in light of the revelation found in the Christian Scriptures (New Testament). The truths discerned from Scripture are revealed by God to those who have "eyes to see" and "ears to hear."

In some of the first confessions of faith, biblical authority seems to be so basic that it is not given a major emphasis in the documents. Rather, each dogma is discussed in the context of specific Bible references that provide authoritative proof texts that validate the belief. The *Short Confession of Faith*, written by the Amsterdam community that became the first Baptist church in history, contained some thirty-eight articles, none of which deals specifically with biblical inspiration or authority. Its first article, however, begins with a statement on God as drawn from biblical teaching:

> We believe, *through the power and instruction of the Holy Scriptures* [italics mine], that there is one only God, who is a Spirit, eternal, incomprehensible, infinite, almighty, merciful, righteous, perfectly wise, only good, and only fountain of life and all goodness, the Creator of heaven and earth, things visible and invisible.[14]

Thus the Scriptures are viewed as the authoritative foundation for describing the nature of God.

The *Declaration of Faith of English People* (1611) did contain a statement on Scripture that acknowledged: "That the scriptures off the Old and New Testament are written for our instruction, 2. Tim. 3:16 & that wee ought to search them for they testifie off CHRIST, Jo. 5:39. And therefore to bee used with all reverence, as conteyning the Holie Word of GOD, which onelie is our direction in al thinges whatsoever "[15] The confession written as *The Faith and Practise of Thirty Congregations, Gathered According to the Primitive Pattern* (1651) also has no formal statement on Scripture but notes "That God's Word, Son, or Spirit, are one . . . God and His Word (Jesus) are one."[16] Scripture references are provided as verification of each dogma cited, yet the primary reference to the "Word of God" is Jesus and the Holy Spirit.

The *Second London Confession* (1688) is a Calvinist-oriented statement based on the earlier *Westminster Confession* written by British Puritans (Presbyterians) in the 1640s. It presents a strong statement on the authority and nature of Holy Scripture. A preamble to the document sets it in the context of Baptist support for "All the fundamental articles of the Christian religion, as also with many others whose orthodox confessions have been published to the World, on the behalf of the protestants in diverse nations and cities."[17]

Thus these Particular Baptists understood themselves as a distinct part of the Protestant movement. They also noted that "we have no itch to clog religion with new words, but to readily acquiesce in that form of sound words which hath been, *in consent with the holy scriptures* [italics mine] used by others before."[18]

The confession begins with the assertion that

the Holy Scripture is the only sufficient, certain, and infallible rule of all saving Knowledge, Faith, and Obedience; . . . Therefore it pleased the Lord at sundry times, and in divers manners, to reveal himself, and to declare that His will unto his Church; and afterward for the better preserving, and propagating of the Truth, and for the more sure Establishment and comfort of the Church against the corruption of the flesh, and the malice of Satan and of the World, to commit the same wholly unto writing.[19]

In its thirty-seventh article, the *Orthodox Creed* (1657) concludes:

The authority of the holy scripture dependeth not upon the authority of any man, but only upon the authority of God, who hath delivered and revealed his mind therein unto us, and containeth all things necessary for salvation; so that whatsoever is not read therein, nor may be proved thereby, is not to be required of any man, that it should be believed as an article of the Christian faith, or be thought required to salvation.[20]

While these statements describe Baptist commitment to the authority of Scripture, Baptist individuals and subgroups have not always agreed on the nature of that inspiration. Some Baptists are biblical inerrantists who understand such words as *infallible* to mean that the Testaments are without error in any topic they address—faith, morals, doctrine, science, sociology, and psychology. Other Baptists affirm the importance of biblical authority and inspiration but do not assert an inerrantist position. Still others promote a modern historical-critical analysis of biblical content and background. Many affirm biblical authority in the context of their own religious experience and personal piety. The question of biblical authority became one of the most divisive issues in Baptist life in the United States throughout the twentieth century.[21]

Sixth, Baptists generally agree that a "personal experience" with Jesus Christ, an encounter with divine grace, is necessary for all who would claim membership in the church. At best, all members of the church are required to testify to a salvific encounter by which they have been called to conversion in Christ. Candidates for baptism must have professed faith and been affirmed, even voted on, by the local congregation. The church, therefore, is a believers' church, composed only of those who have made the proper profession of faith.

The *Somerset Confession* (1656) provides one of the most concise statements of the meaning of this "justification" made possible through the life, death, and resurrection of Jesus Christ. It declares:

> That justification is God's accounting and declaring that man justified from the guilt and condemnation of all his sin, who hath received Jesus Christ and doth believe in him (in truth and power) according to the record given of him by God in scripture. . . . That justification from the guilt and condemnation of sin is only obtained through faith in that man Jesus Christ, crucified at Jerusalem, and by God raised from the dead.[22]

As Baptists understand it, no person can claim to be a Christian apart from justification by faith.

Amid their concern for a "regenerate church membership" Baptists confronted another dilemma concerning the proper candidate for salvation, centering on the question of election, predestination, and free will. Calvinistic Baptists affirmed that salvation was possible only for the elect, those whom God had chosen before the foundation of the world. The *Second London Confession* (1688) stated:

> Those of mankind that are predestinated to life, God, before the foundation of the world was laid according to his eternal and immutable purpose, and the secret Councel and good pleasure of his will, hath chosen in Christ unto everlasting glory . . . neither are any other redeemed by Christ, or effectually called, justified, adopted, sanctified, and saved, but the elect only.[23]

and

> Those whom God hath predestined unto Life, he is pleased, in his appointed, and accepted time, effectually to call by his word, and Spirit, out of that state of sin, and death, in which they are by nature, to grace and Salvation by Jesus Christ.[24]

The gospel might be preached to the entire world, but only the elect would be able to hear and respond.

General or Arminian Baptists disagreed. For them the entire human race was *potentially* elected. Those who came to faith were *actually* elected to salvation. The early group of Baptists in Amsterdam (1612) wrote:

> That GOD before the Foundation of the World hath Predestinated that all that believe in him shall-be saved, Eph. 1.4, 12; Mark 16.16. and all that believe not shall be damned . . . and this is the Election and reprobacion spoken of in the Scripture, concerning salvacion, and condemnacion, and not that GOD hath Predestinated men to be wicked, and so to be damned, but all men being wicked shall be damned, for GOD would have all men saved and come to the knowledge of the truth.[25]

Salvation was open to all who would exercise free will in choosing to believe in Christ. The *Standard Confession* (1660) noted "that all men at one time or other, are put into such a capacity, as that (through the grace of God) they may be eternally saved."[26]

These assertions regarding the nature of election and free will had implications for infants and adults. Since the Baptists did not baptize infants, they were compelled to address the eternal state of infants and children. General Baptists insisted that all infants were in a state of grace and would therefore be saved. The *Standard Confession* noted:

> That all Children dying in Infancy, having not actually transgressed against the Law of God in their own persons, are only subject to the first death, which comes upon them by the sin of the first *Adam*, from whence they shall be all raised by the second *Adam*.[27]

Particular Baptists were bound to the doctrine of total depravity, a condition present in infants as well as adults. Thus, the *Second London Confession* asserted:

> Elect Infants dying in infancy, are regenerated and saved by Christ through the Spirit; who worketh when and where, and how he pleaseth: so also are all other elect persons, who are uncapable of being outwardly called by the Ministry of the Word.[28]

These Calvinistic Baptists believed that while only elect infants would be saved, all the elect would receive the gift of grace, even if they were unable to hear the preaching of the gospel ("Ministry of the Word"). For Particular Baptists, salvation was not possible to the non-elect, be they infants or adults. General Baptists disagreed, opening the door to the salvation of all infants, since they were moral innocents in the sight of God. The high infant mortality rate present in seventeenth- and eighteenth-century communities made the question of the eternal destiny of infants a very important matter.

The concern for salvation and conversion was inseparable from the practice of believer's baptism, administered to all persons who professed their faith and sought membership in a Baptist church. Thus Baptists insisted that baptism be administered to believers only. As noted earlier, the first Baptist communities in Amsterdam and London (1608 and following) administered baptism by affusion, pouring water on the head three times in the name of the Father, the Son, and the Holy Spirit. It was not until 1641 that they instituted the practice of baptism by immersion, known to seventeenth-century Baptists as "dipping."

Baptism, therefore, is the door to the church, administered to those who can testify to a work of grace in their hearts. The *Declaration of Faith of English People* (1611) in Amsterdam noted: "That everie Church is to receive in all their members by Baptisme upon the confession off their faith and sinnes wrought by the preaching off the Gospel, according to the primitive [New Testament] Instruction."[29] The document described "Baptisme or washing with Water" as "the outward manifestacion off dieing unto sinn, and walking in newness off life." It also noted: "And therefore in no wise apperteyneth to infants."[30]

Early Baptists in America echoed this idea. John Clarke wrote:

> I Testifie that Baptism, or dipping in Water, is one of the Commandments of this Lord Jesus Christ, and that a visible believer, or Disciple of Christ Jesus (that is, one that manifesteth repentance towards God, and Faith in Jesus Christ) is the only person that is to be Baptized, or dipped with that visible Baptism, or dipping of Jesus Christ in Water.[31]

Obadiah Holmes (1607?–1682), another colonial Baptist, was even more direct in his description of baptism. His own confession of faith declared:

> I believe that the true baptism of the Gospel is a visible believer with his own consent being baptized in common water by dipping or, as it were, drowned to hold forth death, burial, resurrection, by a messenger of Jesus into the name of the Father, Son and Holy Spirit.[32]

These early confessions set the pattern for the continuing Baptist theology of the church and the suggestion

> That the church off CHRIST is a company off faithful people I Cor. 1.2, Eph.I.I separated from the world by the word & Spirit off GOD. 2 Cor. 6, 17. being knit unto the LORD, & one unto another, by Baptisme. I Cor. 12.13. Upon their owne confession of the faith. Act. 8.37. and sinnes. Mat. 3.6.[33]

Clearly, church membership was based on a confession of faith followed by baptism. While they may differ on many things, Baptists continue to affirm that idea as central to their beliefs.

The *London Confession* (1644) utilized by the Particular Baptists echoed the earlier General Baptist understanding of faith and baptism while asserting that the rite should be administered only by immersion. It stated: "That Baptisme is an Ordinance of the new onely upon persons professing faith, or that are Disciples, or taught, who upon profession of faith, ought to be baptized." The adjacent article noted that "The way and manner of the dispensing of this Ordinance the Scripture holds out to be dipping or plunging the whole body under water: it being a sign."[34] Immersion/dipping signified the soul's being washed in Christ's blood; identification with Christ's death, burial, and resurrection; and was a pledge of the resurrection of the individual believer.[35] The *Second London Confession* (1688) set forth the theology of baptism succinctly. It stated:

> Those who do actually profess repentance towards God, faith in, and obedience, to our Lord Jesus, are the only proper subjects of this ordinance. The outward element to be used in this ordinance is water, wherein the party is to be baptized, in the name of the Father, and of the Son, and of the Holy spirit. Immersion, or dipping of the person in water, is necessary to the due administration of this ordinance.[36]

Baptists, therefore, are "deep water" Christians, immersing the entire body of the new believer in outdoor creeks or rivers, or in special baptismal pools built into the worship space of a specific congregation. Some early Baptists even administered the laying on of hands to the newly baptized as a sign of the coming of the Holy Spirit upon the newly professed Christian.[37]

Baptists understood baptismal immersion to be the entrance to faith and the church. Some of the early Baptists referred to it as a "sacrament," an outward and visible sign of an inward and spiritual grace. Even when they used the word *sacrament* to describe the rite, they were often careful to distinguish its meaning from the baptismal theology of Roman Catholics or even some other Protestants. Thus they came to use the word *ordinance* to refer to both baptism and the Lord's Supper.

Concerning the Lord's Supper, the *Propositions and Conclusions* written by the General Baptists in Amsterdam in 1612 suggested that the Supper should be received only by "baptized persons" and was a "spiritual supper, which Christ maketh of His flesh and blood: which is crucified and shed for the remission of sins (as the bread is broken and the wine poured forth), and which is eaten and drunken (as is the bread and wine bodily) only by those which are flesh."[38] Yet the authors of the same document were careful to say what the ordinances of baptism and the Supper were NOT. It stated: "That the outward baptism and supper do not confer, and convey grace and regeneration to the participants or communicants: but . . . they serve only to support and stir up the repentance and faith of the communicants till Christ come."[39] The confession also noted: "That the *sacraments* [italics mine] have the same use that the word hath; that they are a visible word, and that they teach to the eye of them that understand as the word teacheth the ears of them that have ears to hear . . . and therefore as the word pertaineth not to infants, no more do the sacraments."[40]

The *Declaration of Faith of English People* (1611) says simply that the Lord's Supper "is the outward manifestacion off the spiritual Communion between CHRIST and the faithful mutually I. Cor. 10.16,17. to declare his death until he come. I Cor. 11.26."[41] The *Second London Confession* (1688) declared that the Supper was instituted by Christ "for the perpetual remembrance, and shewing forth the sacrifice in his death, confirmation of the faith of believers in all the benefits thereof, their spiritual nourishment, and growth in him." It was not, however, "offered up to his Father, nor any real sacrifice made at all, for remission of sin of the quick[living] or dead; but only a memorial of that one offering up of himself, by himself, upon the crosse, once for all; and a spiritual oblation of all."[42] The document also denied the Catholic understanding of the Supper as accomplishing transubstantiation, the belief through the proper words of institution uttered by the priest at the altar, the elements of bread and wine are transformed into the very body and blood of Jesus Christ.[43] This confession, grounded in Reformed theology, followed John Calvin's interpretation of the Lord's Supper as a spiritual experience of Christ's presence, noting that believers "spiritually receive, and feed upon Christ crucified & all the benefits of his death: the

Body and Blood of *Christ,* being then not corporally, or carnally, but spiritually present to the faith of Believers."[44]

Other Baptists moved away from the idea of Christ's spiritual presence in the Supper, preferring instead to emphasize the memorial nature of the rite. The *Faith and Practise of Thirty Congregations* (1651) noted "that Jesus Christ took Bread, and the juice of the Vine, and brake, and gave to his Disciples, to eat and drink with thanksgiving; which practice is left upon record as a memorial of his suffering, to continue in the Church until he come again."[45]

In their approach to church government (polity) Baptists are Congregationalists. That is, they believe that the authority of Christ is mediated through the community of believers, the church. The *London Confession* (1644) described the church as "a company of visible Saints, called & separated from the world, by the word and Spirit of God, the visible profession of the faith of the Gospel, being baptized into that faith, and joined to the Lord, and each other, by mutuall agreement."[46] The church, therefore, was bound together by a covenant with God and among the members one with another.

As Baptists see it, each congregation is autonomous, and may make its own decisions as to its ministers, ministries, and programs. This idea of congregational autonomy is evident in the earliest Baptist churches. The Amsterdam group wrote in the *Declaration of Faith of English People* (1611):

> That though in respect of CHRIST, the Church be one, Ephes. 4.4. yet it consisteth of divers particular congregations, even so many as there shall be in the World, every of which congregation, though they be but two or three, have CHRIST given them, with all the means of their salvation.[47]

Congregations took seriously their calling to admit people to the covenant. In many Baptist congregations from the seventeenth to the twentieth centuries, new converts were required to profess their faith before the entire congregation or at least before representative clergy and laity. If the congregation had doubts or questions about the veracity of the profession, they could choose to reject or defer the candidate's admission to baptism and church membership. In a sense, members were evaluated and voted into membership formally or informally. And, if individuals could be voted into membership, they could also be voted out. Most Baptist churches have abolished the vote on accepting persons for membership. Some retain the practice, at least in the form of welcome and recognition of new members.

Throughout their history, many Baptist churches have taken their disciplinary responsibilities seriously. The *Second London Confession* (1688) stated: "As all Believers are bound to joyn themselves to particular *Churches*, when and where they have opportunity so to do; So all that are admitted unto the priviledges of a *Church*, are also under the Censures and government thereof, according to the Rule of *Christ*."[48] Members of the church were thus subject to discipline when they crossed the boundaries of orthodoxy or ethics. Members were encouraged to repent and be reconciled to the community of faith. If that did not happen, then they were excommunicated and put out of the congregation. The *Propositions and Conclusions* (1612), written by the General Baptists in Amsterdam, was quite specific when it came to the issue of excommunication. It declared that

> none are to be separated from the outward communion of the Church but such as forsake repentance, which deny the power of Godliness (2 Tim. iii. 5), and namely that sufficient admonition go before, according to the rule (Matt. Xviii. 15–18), and that none are to be rejected for ignorance or errors, or infirmities as long as they retain repentance and faith in Christ.[49]

The confession also set forth harsh response to those who resisted repentance. It stated

> that persons separated from the communion of the church, are to be accounted as heathens and publicans (Matt. xviii.), and that they are so far to be shunned, as they may pollute: not withstanding being ready to instruct them, and to relieve them in their wants: seeking by all lawful means to win them: considering that excommunication is only for the destruction of the flesh, that the spirit may be saved in the day of the Lord.[50]

Discipline was generally believed to be the domain of each congregation. The *London Confession* (1644) stated that "Christ has likewise given power to his whole Church to receive in and cast out, by way of Excommunication, any member; and this power is given to every particular Congregation, and not one particular person, either member or Officer, but the whole."[51] Excommunication was not the work of popes, bishops, or clergy but that of the entire congregation of faithful believers.

The *Second London Confession* acknowledged that all believers who were "admitted unto the privileges of a *Church* are also under the Censures and government thereof, according to the Rule of *Christ*."[52] The *Faith and Practise of Thirty Congregations* warned "That if any one of the fellowship neglect the watching over his own heart, and so break out into an evil life and conversation. . . . then ought not such a one to break bread with obedient walkers."[53]

Baptist congregations gave extensive attention to church discipline well into the twentieth century. Discipline continues in many Baptist communions and is especially evident among certain Appalachian groups, including the Primitive and Old Regular Baptists. In these congregations discipline may take the form of "churching," whereby recalcitrant individuals are literally put out of the church in hopes that this drastic action will compel them to turn from their sins, repent, and seek restoration. Other Baptists mourn the absence of discipline in many congregations and attribute that loss to moral laxity, the size of congregations that makes discipline unmanageable, or the problems of deciding what public and private actions deserve the church's attention.

## Officers of Baptist Churches

Baptists have generally understood that the New Testament church had two specific offices for carrying out the work of the ministry. These included pastors (sometimes called elders) and deacons. The *Declaration of Faith of English People* (1611) asserted: "the Officers off every Church or congregation are either Elders, who by their office do especially feed the flock concerning their soules, Act. 20.28, Pet. 5.2, 3. or deacons Men, and Women who by their office releave the necessities off the poore and impotent brethren concerning their bodies, Acts 6.1–4."[54] This succinct description indicates that the pastor was to give attention to the spiritual needs of the congregation while deacons were responsible for responding to the immediate physical needs of the members of the church.

The *London Confession* (1644) reflected the influence of Reformed theology in delineating the four offices characteristic of Presbyterianism. It noted that "every Church has power given them from Christ for their better well-being, to choose to themselves meet persons into the office of Pastors,

Teachers, Elders, Deacons, being qualified according to the Word."[55] Later, these offices were apparently combined formally or informally with duties of pastor-teacher and deacon-elder.

Some Baptist churches past and present permit only duly ordained ministers to administer baptism and the Lord's Supper, while others acknowledge that any believer may so function as given permission by the individual congregation. Again, the London Confession noted that the ordinance of baptism was to be dispensed by a "preaching Disciple," "it being no where tyed to a particular Church, Officer, or person extraordinarily sent, the Commission injoyning the administration, being given to them under no other consideration, but as considered Disciples."[56]

The individuals who are recognized as ministers or deacons were (and are) generally ordained by the local church in a service that involves prayers, reading of the Scripture, a sermon or "charge" to the candidate, and the laying on of hands. This symbol usually was carried out by the ordained ministers and deacons present. In some cases it might involve the entire congregation of believers, who were invited to participate. The Standard Confession described "Elders or Pastors" who were to "oversee, and feed his Church." They were to be ordained and commissioned to "feed the flock with meat in due season, and in much love to rule over them, with all care, seeking after such as go astray." Deacons were to provide "free and voluntary help" as "Overseers of the poor."[57] The Second London Confession (1688) identifies Pastors (Elders) and Deacons as the two officers of the church, each elected by the church and set aside with prayer and "the Imposition of hands." Pastors were to give themselves to the "Ministry of the Word, and Prayer." They were to "preach the Gospel" and "live of the Gospel" as well. Preaching was not confined only to the pastors, however, but extended to "others also gifted and fitted by the Holy Spirit."[58] The confession also asserted that baptism and the Supper were to be "administered by those only, who are qualified and thereunto called according to the commission of Christ," a statement that apparently meant duly ordained pastor/elders.[59]

The Orthodox Creed described three offices in Baptist life, including "Bishops or Messengers; or Elders, or Pastors; and Deacons, or Overseers of the poor."[60] The office of Messenger, although short-lived among early Baptists, was apparently a traveling evangelist who moved from place to place mediating in church disputes and preaching broadly. They were responsible to associations of churches that chose them and set them aside.[61]

From the beginning of their movement, Baptists have sought to be citizens of two worlds, affirming their loyalty to their specific governments and "magistrates," while acknowledging a higher citizenship in the kingdom of God. This higher calling often required them to act as dissenters for the sake of conscience and Christian conviction. While the early Baptists do not speak often about the priesthood of all believers, so-called, they emphasize the role of the individual conscience in many of their confessions of faith. Indeed, the concern for conscience seems a hallmark of Baptist identity from the beginning of the movement. Yet the earliest Baptists seem to suggest that conscience begins with God, not with the individual. The *Propositions and Conclusions* ( 1612) recognized that the magistrate's office was permitted by God "for the good of mankind" that, among other things, "justice and civility" might "be preserved." Yet it also warned that

> the magistrate is not by virtue of his office to meddle with religion, or matters of conscience, to force or compel men to this or that form of religion, or doctrine: but to leave Christian religion free, to every man's conscience . . . for Christ only is the king, and lawgiver of the church and conscience (James iv.12).[62]

In other words, God alone is judge of conscience, and thus all human beings are responsible to God alone for the religious and spiritual choices they make. As the Baptists who wrote the *Propositions and Conclusions* saw it, a personal experience of grace brought religious knowledge that transcended all "outward" resources. They concluded

> That the new creature which is begotten of God, needeth not the outward scriptures, creatures, or ordinances of the Church, to support or help them (2 Cor. Xiii. 10,12; I joh. ii. 27; I Cor. I. 15, 16; Rev. xxi. 23), seeing he hath three witnesses in himself, the Father, the Word, and the Holy Ghost: which are better than all scriptures, or creatures whatsoever.[63]

Other Baptist confessions emphasize the need of all Christians to be obedient to the divinely ordained powers and government, and several assert that Baptists themselves strive to be good citizens. The *Standard Confession* (1660) was written in the midst of persecution from the Stuart monarchy and the Anglican establishment. It affirmed the need for all citizens to be subject to the "higher Powers," yet unashamedly declared: "But in case the Civil Powers do, or shall at any time impose things about matters of Religion, which we through conscience to God cannot actually obey, then we with

*Peter* also do say, that we ought (in such cases) to obey God rather than men; Acts. 5.29."[64]

The later *Orthodox Creed* (1679) gives particular attention to liberty of conscience, insisting that "The Lord Jesus Christ . . . is only Lord of Conscience; having a peculiar right so to be. . . . And therefore he would not have the consciences of men in bondage to, or imposed upon, by any usurpation, tyranny or command whatsoever, contrary to his revealed will in his word."[65] Again, these Baptists emphasized that God (in Christ) alone was the judge and lord of conscience, an idea that shaped the responses Baptists might make to the demands of church or state. It continued:

> And therefore the obedience to any command, or decree, that is not re-vealed in, or consonant to his word . . . is a betraying of the true liberty of conscience. And the requiring of an implicit faith, and an absolute blind obedience, destroys liberty of conscience, and reason also, it being repugnant to both, and that no pretended good end whatsoever, by any man, can make that action, obedience, or practice, lawful and good, that is not grounded in or upon the authority of holy scripture, or right reason agreeable thereunto.[66]

The concern for conscience led Baptists to stand at the forefront of the effort to secure complete religious liberty, not simply for sectarian Christian groups, and other heretics outside the established church, but also for atheists and non-believers who were responsible to God, not to the state, for their religious choices.

## Baptist Beliefs: The American Experience

Baptists in the United States are heirs of these beliefs, often expressed in confessions of faith reflecting varying degrees of diversity, paradox, and even contradiction. Many of the early colonial churches did not use formal confessions, perhaps because members sought to place primary emphasis on Scripture as the only appropriate source of "faith and order." Confessions were also problematic because many of these early Baptist churches included members with both Arminian and Calvinist sentiments.[67] As Baptists moved south and west, the General (Arminian) position became less influential among eighteenth-century Baptists, and Calvinism in various forms shaped the theology of newly organized churches. These churches often organized around three documents: a confession of faith, guiding belief; a church covenant, directing churchly relationships; and "rules of decorum," governing church business.

The first Baptist confession of faith used in the American colonies was originally compiled by Benjamin Keach and his son Elias for use in the Tallow Chandler's Hall Church, London. The document was probably the *Second London Confession* (1688) with the addition of two articles, one that permitted the singing of hymns, not simply the Psalms, and the other that permitted the laying on of hands to the newly baptized. Known in the colonies as "Keach's Confession," it was used in 1712 to resolve a response to a doctrinal dispute in the Baptist church at Middletown, New Jersey.[68]

Keach's Confession paralleled the first official confession approved by a Baptist association in America. Known as the *Philadelphia Confession*, it was accepted by the Philadelphia (Baptist) Association in 1742. Like Keach's document, it duplicated the *Second London Confession* (1688) with the addition of articles on hymn singing and the laying on of hands. The former article made room for the singing of "psalms, hymns, and spiritual songs" in "the whole church" and among "private Christians." The laying on of hands was a continuation of practices promoted by the so-called Six Principle Baptists, and the article stated: "We believe that (Heb 5 12 and 6 1 2 Acts 8 17 18 and 19 6) laying on of hands (with prayer) upon baptized believers, as such, is an ordinance of Christ, and ought to be submitted unto by all such persons that are admitted to partake of the Lord's Supper."[69]

This confession was republished frequently and used widely by churches and associations. Later associations such as the Charleston Association in South Carolina dropped the section on the laying on of hands, and other Baptist groups soon followed suit. The *Philadelphia Confession* expressed the basic beliefs of Calvinist or Reformed Baptist traditions in the United States.

Eighteenth-century Baptists in America also utilized Benjamin Griffith's work, *A Summary of Church Discipline*, (1743), which became something of a manual for use in Baptist churches. It was attached to the *Philadelphia Confession* as a further guide for churches. Griffith's *Essay on the Authority and Power of an Association* (1749) articulated a definition of Baptist associations that shaped those early Baptist cooperative endeavors. It stated "that several such independent churches, where Providence gives them their situation convenient, may, and ought, for their mutual strength, counsel, and other valuable advantages, by their voluntary and free consent, to enter into an agreement and confederation.[70] Other Calvinists such as the Primitive and Old Regular Baptists developed confessions that extended Calvinist assertions regarding election, predestination, and Divine sovereignty.

By the nineteenth century a more modified Calvinism had developed among many Baptist communions in the United States, influenced by the revival movements that spread across the new nation. This revival fervor affected he rise of the so-called modern mission movement, by which Baptists and other Protestant bodies sent missionaries to the far reaches of the globe. These religious developments, along with the rise of a strong democratic idealism, sent Baptists and others looking for a theology that opened the door to greater emphasis on free will, human participation in the salvific process, and the possibility that election might extend to all who chose faith in Christ. The *New Hampshire Confession of Faith*, appearing in 1833, was one confessional response to this effort to modify traditional Calvinism. In a sense, the confession, first commissioned by the Baptist Convention of New Hampshire, uses the language of Calvinism, but in such a way as to open the door to a much broader understanding of the nature of salvation, free will, and predestination.

The confession begins with a statement on the Scriptures that would become both an affirmation of faith and an object of lively debate for a century and a half. It noted:

> We believe [that] the Holy Bible was written by men divinely inspired, and is a perfect treasure of heavenly instruction; that it has God for its author, salvation for its end, and truth, without any mixture of error, for its matter; that it reveals the principles by which God will judge us; and therefore is, and shall remain to the end of the world, the true centre of Christian union, and the supreme standard by which all human conduct, creeds, and opinions should be tried.[71]

In many ways, the *New Hampshire Confession* represents a revision of Baptist doctrines in a more modified Calvinist direction, with less-specific references to election, predestination, or salvation. It opens the door to the possibility of election for all who choose Christ through repentance and faith. The statement on election notes:

> That Election is the gracious purpose of God, according to which he regenerates, sanctifies, and saves sinners; that being perfectly consistent with the free agency of man, it comprehends all the means in con-

nection with the end; that is a most glorious display of God's sovereign goodness.[72]

Thus, by the mid-nineteenth century and through the twentieth, Baptists—at least some of them—were using the language of Calvinism but defining it in ways that allowed them to speak of both election and free will. Thus they could retain a certain degree of traditional orthodoxy while opening the door to the possibility of missionary outreach and a divine mandate to take the gospel to the world as if all who heard it had the capability of choosing grace. It was an effort to "have it both ways," retaining election but extending it to all who chose to believe.

Changes in or controversies over Baptist belief are evident throughout the twentieth century. The General Association of Regular Baptist Churches (GARBC) was founded in 1932 as a response to liberalism in the Northern Baptist Convention (later the American Baptist Churches, USA). A revision of its conservative confession, approved in 1972, acknowledges that the purpose of the denomination is not only to promote evangelization and missionary endeavors, but also to confront "worldliness, modernism and apostasy."[73] The denomination's articles of faith insist that Scripture is "verbally and plenarily inspired" and "infallible and inerrant in all matters of which it speaks."[74] The document requires churches and individuals in the GARBC to affirm "a literal, historical account of the direct, immediate creative acts of God without any evolutionary process," and the assertion that "all men are descended from the historical Adam and Eve, first parents of the entire human race."[75] The GARBC document stresses the premillennial return of Christ, including the "Tribulation" and the "Rapture."[76]

Other conservative Baptists have not hesitated to articulate the "fundamentals" of faith, a list that included the classic "five points": biblical inerrancy, Christ's virgin birth, the substitutionary atonement theory of Christ's death on the cross, Christ's bodily resurrection, and Christ's bodily Second Coming. These doctrinal affirmations are seen as the theological nonnegotiables for the church and the individual.

Perhaps no other Baptist denomination has been more in the public eye regarding its belief system than the Southern Baptist Convention. Since at least 1979 the denomination has struggled between moderate and conservative individuals and churches over the nature of belief. The denomination's confession of faith, known as the *Baptist Faith and Message*, first approved in 1925, was taken primarily from the *New Hampshire Confession of Faith*, with additional articles dealing with religious freedom, Christian education, and cooperative relationships among Baptists.[77] Although the SBC was founded in 1845, it did not have an official confession of faith until 1925. Approved at the height of the fundamentalist/modernist controversy in America, the confession was not of major interest to most Southern Baptists, who generally reflected a strong theological conservatism. It was revised substantially in 1963 in a response to controversies that developed around biblical authority and "academic freedom" issues at Baptist-related schools. A third revision of the confession was approved in 2000 to give increasing specificity to conservative issues.

Revisions illustrate the way in which Southern Baptists sought to respond to controversies the descended on them at various stages of their history. For example, the 1925 confession said of "Education:"

> Christianity is the religion of enlightenment and intelligence. In Jesus Christ are hidden all the treasures of wisdom and knowledge. All sound learning is therefore a part of our Christian heritage. The new birth opens all human faculties and creates a thirst for knowledge. An adequate system of schools is necessary to a complete spiritual program for Christ's people. The cause of education in the Kingdom of Christ is co-ordinate with the causes of missions and general benevolence, and should receive along with these the liberal support of the churches.[78]

In the revised document of 1963 the statement on "Education" reads:

> The cause of education in the kingdom of Christ is co-ordinate with the causes of missions and general benevolence and should receive along with these the liberal support of the churches. An adequate system of Christian schools is necessary to a complete spiritual program for Christ's people. In Christian education there should be a proper balance between academic freedom and academic responsibility. Freedom in any orderly relationship of human life is always limited and never absolute. The freedom of a teacher in a Christian school, college, or seminary is limited by the pre-eminence of Jesus Christ, by the authoritative nature of the Scriptures, and by the distinct purpose for which the school exist.[79]

In the first document, Jesus Christ is the source of all "wisdom and knowledge." In the revision, professorial freedom is "limited" by "the pre-eminence of Jesus Christ." The second document sets boundaries on the nature of intellectual investigation in ways that the first does not. The revised confession of 2000 combines both of those articles.[80]

## Baptist Beliefs: A Study in Paradox

This brief survey of Baptist beliefs demonstrates that Baptists share many doctrines with other Protestant denominations. Their emphasis on a believers' church and immersion baptism are important elements of their unique identity, yet even those doctrines are not exclusive to Baptists. Perhaps the uniqueness is found in the way in which Baptists hold these doctrines in tension or paradox, moving across a spectrum that explains both the distinctiveness and the diversity of Baptist theology. These include the following:

1. Biblical authority and liberty of conscience. Baptists readily assert their commitment to the authority and veracity of Scripture as the source of doctrine, ethics, spirituality, and guidance for the individual and the community of faith. At the same time, they acknowledge the role of individual conscience in shaping the individual's response to faith, convictions, and actions.

2. Regeneration (conversion) known through dramatic conversion and gradual nurture. Baptists are committed to the idea of a believers' church, in which all the members can testify to an experience of God's grace. All who claim membership in Christ's church are to be regenerated, made new by faith in Christ. This concern for conversion led many Baptists to testify and encourage a dramatic experience of grace, sometimes immediate and life changing. In America revivals were an important means of drawing persons to faith in which individuals struggled with sin, repentance, and salvation. These conversions seemed dramatic events that transformed the life of the individual. Yet Baptists also nurtured children to faith in more gradual and less immediate means. They wrote catechisms that provided basic doctrinal and moral teaching to children. Later Baptists created Sunday schools and other children's programs for nurturing youth to faith. Thus some Baptists speak of their regeneration as a drastic moment or series of experiences leading to a radical conversion. Others were nurtured to faith, often acknowledging that they "never knew a time" when they did not believe in Jesus. Whatever the form, regeneration (conversion) is a hallmark of Baptist identity.

3. Local autonomy and associational cooperation. Baptists place great emphasis on the autonomy of each local congregation. The authority of Christ is mediated through the believing community bound together by a covenant with God and with one another. The local congregation is the chief source of

Baptist authority and organization. Most Baptist congregations are autonomous but not necessarily independent. They develop associations or unions with other churches for fellowship, encouragement, and cooperative ministries. This "connectionalism" may be regional, national, or international.

4. Sacraments/ordinances: Baptism and the Lord's Supper (foot-washing). Baptists observe two events that link them with the earliest Christians: baptism and the Lord's Supper. Baptism is administered not to infants but to those who can claim an experience of grace. Thus baptism follows "profession of faith." The mode or method of baptism is immersion, the dipping of the whole body in water as a sign of new life, cleansing, and burial and resurrection with Christ. Some Baptists, particularly in the Appalachian region of the United States, practice the washing of feet as described in John 13. Members wash each other's feet as a symbol of servanthood and humility. This is usually done in conjunction with the Lord's Supper.

5. Priesthood of the laity and the calling out of ministers. Baptists believe that conversion is the great equalizer. All believers are called to minister and serve through the power of the Holy Spirit. With Martin Luther and other Protestants, Baptists assert that there is no mediator but Christ himself, so individuals need no other high priest. Each new believer is a minister, called to carry out Christ's gospel in the world. Yet Baptists also recognize and "set aside" people for specific ministerial functions—those who carry out the "ministry of the word." Ministers are "called out" and ordained within specific communities of faith (churches). They then serve the church in specific ministerial ways. Some Baptists put great emphasis on the role of the laity, while others give greater attention to ministerial leadership and authority. Often those tensions collide when it comes to administering local churches.

6. Loyalty to the state and radical religious liberty. Baptists' historic commitment to religious liberty has often set them at odds with the state on a variety of matters. Throughout American history Baptist individuals and groups have opposed various government activities, from the appointment of an ambassador to the Vatican, to aid to parochial schools, to government incursion into the religious realm. At the same time Baptists have consistently asserted their loyalty to the state, with many posting the American flag in their worship settings, encouraging patriotism, and serving in the military. By the late twentieth century, Baptists were divided over issues of prayer in public schools, "faith-based funding" for religious communities, and government vouchers for use in parochial (some Baptist) schools. These disputes threaten to divide Baptists even more extensively in the new millennium.

## Beliefs Affect Practices

These and other distinguishing marks of Baptist identity extend across a wide range of doctrine and practice in Baptist churches throughout the United States. They reflect a denomination that occupies both ends of the Protestant theological spectrum from Calvinist to Arminian positions on grace, free will, and predestination, a remarkable dichotomy for any religious tradition. Such distinctions mean that multiple Baptist communions hold both common and contradictory doctrines. While a majority of Baptists no doubt reveal an overall conservative response to classic Christian orthodoxy, there exists a strong and often vocal liberal segment within the tradition as well. Issues of theology, conversion, social consciousness, and individual conscience fuel internal debates over baptism, church membership, government, Scripture, denominational control, ministerial authority, and an array of social issues including abortion, gender, race, and economics. Thus, in spite of—or at least alongside—their distinctive dogmas, Baptists encounter many of the same controversies as the society at large.

## CHAPTER FIVE

# Baptist Groups

## Denominations, Subdenominations, and Churches

More than sixty distinct groups in the United States claim the name Baptist in some form or another. These varied Baptist communions span the country and reflect a surprising diversity of theological positions. Some have roots in the earliest days of the colonial experience, while others are of more recent origin. Some began with other names and as part of coalitions that no longer exist. Many contemporary Baptist groups grew out of schisms that befell their parent bodies. Their numbers give evidence of the old saying "Baptists multiply by dividing."

Certain Baptists have embraced denominational and organizational structures willingly, while others have run from them like the plague. Baptist denominations often originated as cooperative endeavors of churches and associations uniting in order to accomplish common tasks that they could not carry out alone. Some were founded around specific doctrines that distinguished them from other Christian and Baptist subgroups. Still others grew out of schisms born of controversies within churches and denominations.

Some Baptist denominations are linked with churches spread across the nation, while others occupy particular regions—Appalachia, the South, the Midwest, urban or rural. Some are localized in regional subdenominations. While all Baptist groups share certain common beliefs, each individual communion reflects unique characteristics, emphases, and approaches to specific dogmas.

Baptist denominationalism began with the development of early associations such as the Philadelphia Association formed by five churches in 1707. Other associations were formed linking local churches in fellowship and cooperative ministry. State conventions brought together churches and associations in a specified region of the country. The first national denomination originated in 1814 with the formation of the General Missionary Convention of the Baptist Denomination in the United States for Foreign Missions. It soon came to be known as the Triennial Convention because it met every three years. This missionary society was founded to support Adoniram and Ann Hasseltine Judson, Congregational missionaries who accepted Baptist beliefs on their way to serve in India in 1812. On arrival they received immersion, moved to Burma and petitioned Baptists in America for support. The Foreign Mission Society was formed as a result. The Home Mission Society began in 1832. Each of these societies was autonomous and received funds from individuals, churches, and associations in the North and the South. These and other societies united many Baptist churches in the United States in collective missionary action.

Soon the Triennial Convention developed links to three freestanding societies: the American Baptist Missionary Union (later called the American Baptist Foreign Mission Society), the American Baptist Home Missionary Society, and the American Baptist Publication Society. These groups illustrate the "society" approach that characterized certain Baptist denominations throughout much of their history. By organizing societies that addressed specific benevolences of service or ministry, Baptist churches could potentially work together without threatening the autonomy of the local congregation. This "benevolence-based" approach made each society an entity unto itself, with little or no connection to other societies or denominations.

The Triennial Convention divided in 1845 over the question of appointments for slaveholding missionaries and the founding of the Southern Baptist Convention. In some sense, the Triennial Convention was less a full-blown denomination than an organizational clearinghouse for various societies developed by the churches. After the split, the Northern churches retained this benevolence-based connectionalism, which allowed individuals and churches to pick and choose where they wished their funds and energies to be given. It also contributed to substantial waste of time and money in duplication of governing bodies, separate fund-raising strategies aimed at a similar constituency, competition for support, and a limited sense of the entire spectrum of ministry in the church. Likewise, state Baptist conventions and missionary societies in the North seem to have retained significant autonomy, often developing their own programs exclusive of those of the supposed denominational activities. The following is a brief survey of many, though not all, the Baptist groups in the United States.

## American Baptist Churches in the USA

The denomination now known as the American Baptist Churches in the USA (ABCUSA) dates its origins to the founding of the General Missionary Convention of the Baptist Denomination in the United States for Foreign Missions (Triennial Convention) in 1814. After the split with Southern Baptists, the convention continued to function through its various societies for benevolent activities. These societies were active during the Civil War, sending missionaries to "foreign fields" and participating in a variety of missionary efforts among Native Americans and freed slaves. During the postwar years, the American Baptist Home Missionary Society (ABHMS) helped to underwrite the founding of numerous African American colleges in the South, including Shaw University (North Carolina), Spellman Seminary (Georgia), Bishop College (Texas), and other institutions. In 1882, for example, the Northern society spent more than $84,000 to fund programs in the South, while the SBC Home Mission Board spent less than $29,000.[1]

Disagreements between Baptists in the North and the South heightened after the Civil War. Southerners insisted that Northern Baptists were intruding into the South and Southwest in territories where the SBC was prominent. Northerners insisted that they were simply carrying out missionary work long associated with the Triennial Convention. Disputes about territory endured until the end of the nineteenth century and led to a joint conference between representatives of the SBC and the American Baptist Home Mission Society held at Fortress Monroe, Virginia, in September 1894. The result was a three-point agreement that permitted the ABHMS to continue work with African American Baptist schools in the South but enabled Southern Baptists to raise funds to support the schools as well. It also allowed for cooperation between the two Baptist groups in further work with African Americans. In addition, the document specified that neither of the denominations would begin new ministry in regions were the other was already at work. Yet, as Robert A. Baker observed, "Despite the fine words and good spirit of the Fortress Monroe Conference . . . the agreement was not effective. Indeed, it was often ignored by white and black Baptist associations and churches."[2] Controversies over regional boundaries combined with theological and cultural differences to prevent reunion of Baptists North and South. Unlike their Presbyterian and Methodist counterparts, Baptists never reunited after the divisions caused by slavery and the Civil War.

Baptist women in the North were among the first to found women's missionary societies to raise funds for and encourage interest in missionary endeavors. The first of these was the Boston Female Society for Missionary Purposes, established in 1800 by Baptist Mary Webb (1779–1861). Webb, a person with significant physical disabilities, inspired Baptist and Congregational women to join in forming and funding the society and was secretary-treasurer of the organization for half a century. In 1877 the Woman's American Baptist Home Mission Society began under the sponsorship of Baptist women in New England. A year later the society extended its membership nationally and began to send out missionaries, many of whom were women, to raise funds, and to offer mission-education programs for congregations.[3]

A Baptist women's foreign missionary society was founded in the eastern and western United States in 1871. The union of these two groups in 1913 produced the Woman's American Baptist Foreign Mission Society as a national effort to raise funds and send missionaries abroad. The society sent out women who founded schools, orphanages, and programs for women and children in countries throughout the world. In 1955 it became part of the American Baptist Foreign Mission Society.[4]

In 1907 representatives of churches, associations, and state conventions located largely in the North and the West joined members of the American Baptist Publication, Home and Foreign Societies to form a new entity called the Northern Baptist Convention (NBC). New York governor Charles Evans Hughes was chosen as the first president. The societies retained their individual autonomy and were known as "cooperating organizations" with the new convention. State Baptist conventions and local mission societies were designated as "affiliating organizations." This new denomination represented something of "a compromise between the old independence and the desired cooperation." Essentially, it meant that the societies continued to maintain their legal and ecclesial independence but agreed to meet together biennially and allow designated delegates from member churches to serve as "voting members."[5] This arrangement was aimed at protecting local church autonomy while strengthening a new denominational connectionalism in specific ways. One of the organizational documents suggested that the convention's work was "purely advisory," while another insisted that the Northern Baptist Convention was established "to promote denominational unity and efficiency in efforts for the evangelization of the world."[6]

No sooner was it officially organized than the new convention began to make overtures toward other denominations in the nation and the world. The NBC was among the charter members of the Federal Council of Churches of Christ founded in 1911, the forerunner of the present National Council of Churches of Christ. That same year it became a member of the Faith and

Order movement, one of the early stages of what would become the World Council of Churches. Also in 1911, a union with the Free Will Baptist General Conference was secured.[7]

The first steps toward a collective budgetary program were initiated in 1920 with the General Board of Promotion, a movement that led eventually to the World Mission Budget. In 1934 the Executive Committee became the General Council, charged with "all the powers vested in the Northern Baptist Convention and which the Convention had not expressly reserved to itself."[8] In 1950 the denominational name was changed to the American Baptist Convention, and the first General Secretary (chief administrative officer) was elected. Five years later the two women's mission agencies united their administration with that of the home and foreign mission societies, thus utilizing the same officers, managers, and administration. These mission agencies, along with the American Baptist Historical Society, the Ministers and Missionaries Benefit Board, and the American Baptist Board of Education and Publication, continued to be "cooperating organizations" with the convention. The denomination has connections to numerous theological schools, including Andover Newton Theological School (Newton, Massachusetts), Eastern Baptist Seminary (St. David's, Pennsylvania), Northern Baptist Seminary (Chicago), Central Baptist Seminary (Kansas City, Kansas), Colgate Rochester Seminary (Rochester, New York), and American Baptist Seminary of the West (Berkeley, California).

In 1972 the name was again changed to the American Baptist Churches in the USA, and a significant revision took place in the way the denomination was organized. Greater effort was made to extend representation on boards and agencies in a more centralized connectionalism by which societies were numbered among the convention's program boards whose representatives participated in the annual denominational meeting. New "covenants of relationships" were composed in order to establish the connections between some sixty regional and national bodies. Significant effort was made to extend denominational leadership toward greater inclusion of women and people of color (Asians, African Americans, Latinos, Native Americans, and others). For example, the American Baptist Churches of the South (ABCOTS) is a regional gathering of churches (many of which are African American–based churches), in the southern region of the country. Those initiatives have borne fruit, and the leadership of the ABCUSA reflects that diversity.[9]

Controversies regarding doctrine and practice affected American Baptist life throughout the twentieth century and are discussed in greater detail in succeeding chapters. Divisions between fundamentalists and liberals were evident in the Northern Baptist Convention by the 1920s, creating calls for greater creedal specificity and scrutiny of the views of professors teaching in Baptist-related schools and on the mission fields. Fundamentalists were generally dissatisfied by the denominational response to their concerns.

During the 1960s significant reorganization occurred in the ABC, with the formation of several commissions to study denominational structures. A Commission for the Study of Administrative Areas and Relationships Project (SAAR) was formed in 1962 and developed recommendations regarding geographic regions and relationships between local churches and the national denomination. In 1968 the Study Commission on Denominational Structure (SCODS) was organized, and its proposed reorganization was implemented in 1972. Four areas of mission were set forth for American Baptists:

> 1. To bear witness to the gospel of Jesus Christ in the world and to lead persons to Christ.
> 2. To seek the mind of Christ on moral, spiritual, political, economic, social, denominational and ecumenical matters, and to express to the rest of society, on behalf of American Baptists, their convictions as to the mind of Christ on these matters.
> 3. To guide, unify and assist American Baptists in their witness in the world, in preparing members for the work of ministry, and in serving both those within and outside the fellowship of Christ.
> 4. To promote closer relations among American Baptist churches and groups within the whole body of Christ and to promote understanding with other religious bodies.[10]

During the last twenty-five years of the twentieth century, the ABCUSA confronted numerous controversies and denominational dilemmas. Controversies over doctrine during the period of the 1920s to the 1950s led to the exodus of various individuals and churches and the formation of new Baptist denominations such as the Conservative Baptist Convention. These divisions related to differences regarding such issues as the authority of Scripture, the atonement of Christ, salvation, and the nature of the church. Later debates included divisions over the role of women in the church, abortion, the ordination of homosexuals and the celebration of homosexual unions, contemporary worship styles, the uniqueness of the Christian religion, and the nature of the church's world mission.

At the beginning of the twenty-first century, American Baptists are a relatively small denomination (1.5 million) with a national presence evident in churches spread from coast to coast. Their strength is particularly evident in the Northeast, the Midwest, and the West. In the South the denomination is linked to the American Baptist Churches of the South, a group of predominantly African American Baptist congregations. In 2003 the ABCUSA claimed some 1.2 million members. The denomination maintains affiliation with, but not ownership of, a variety of institutions, including 15 universities and colleges, 6 theological seminaries, and approximately 122 hospitals and community-related agencies. The denomination helps to fund a variety of missionaries who carry out evangelistic, agricultural, and medical ministries in the United States and abroad. Their publishing house, Judson Press, provides books and other literature for churches and the general public.

### Seventh Day Baptists

Seventh Day Baptists are one of history's oldest Baptist communions, originating in England during the mid-seventeenth century. They affirm basic Baptist dogmas—regenerate church membership, baptismal immersion, congregational autonomy, and religious liberty—while insisting that biblical teaching requires worship on Saturday, the divinely ordained Sabbath. Sabbatarianism was present among numerous English Puritans of the 1600s, with those who accepted Baptist views and participated in General or Particular Baptist congregations. The earliest Sabbatarian Baptist church was probably the Mill Yard congregation in London, established around 1650.

The movement was brought to America by Stephan Mumford, who migrated from England to Newport, Rhode Island, in 1664, participating in the First Baptist Church there. The Sabbatarians remained in the church for a brief period until divisions occurred and they departed to found the first Seventh Day Baptist communion in the colonies in 1671. The two churches continued fraternal relations, even sharing the same pastor at one point more than twenty years later. Another church was formed at Piscataway, New Jersey, in 1705, and a third communion of German Seventh Day Baptists organized a communitarian settlement at Ephrata, Pennsylvania, in 1728.[11]

Seventh Day Baptists formed their first General Conference in 1802. The new constitution declared that "no church in our union can receive into their fellowship a person, except they observe the seventh day for a Sabbath: neither such as have not been baptized by immersion."[12] A periodical was begun in 1821. In 1844 it became *The Sabbath Recorder*, a denominational resource that continues to be published.

Missionary efforts were carried out through various localized missionary societies until 1828, when a denominational agency, the American Seventh Day Baptist Missionary Society, was founded. Much of its early work was focused on missionary activity in the United States, including an effort to convert Protestants to "Sabbath-keeping." In 1838 another society, the American Seventh-day Baptist Society for the Promotion of Christianity among the Jews, was founded. It was the first of several institutional efforts to convert "Sabbath-keeping" Jews into "Sabbath-keeping" Christians. During the nineteenth century various attempts to evangelize Jews in the United States and Palestine were undertaken, but they met with little or no success. Those endeavors were terminated by 1890.[13]

Missionaries were also sent to China, where they remained until the Communist insurgency of 1950. Other missions have developed in response to various Sabbath-oriented groups in places such as Jamaica, Guyana, Malawi, India, Burma, and the Philippines. A World Federation of Seventh Day Baptist Conferences was established in 1965. It claimed seventeen members in 1993.[14]

The denomination maintains connections with three undergraduate institutions located in Alfred, New York; Milton, Wisconsin; and Salem, West Virginia. Alfred University also maintains a theological school, begun in 1871. It was a founding member of both the Federal (National) and World Councils of Churches, but withdrew during the 1970s when the organization moved in directions that the Baptists felt were threatening to local church autonomy. Seventh Day Baptists retain membership in the Baptist World Alliance, the North American Baptist Fellowship, and the Baptist Joint Committee on Public Affairs.[15]

During the nineteenth century, Seventh Day Baptist women were appointed to the mission field and ordained to pastoral ministry. Perie Burdick (later known as Experience Randolph) was ordained in 1885 and was the first woman to engage in pastoral ministry in the denomination. Women were first included as official delegates to the General Convention in 1866. A Women's Board of the General Conference was founded in 1884 through the influence of Mary C. Bailey. It continues to raise support for missionary and other church programs.[16]

## The Southern Baptist Convention

The Southern Baptist Convention (SBC) is the largest Baptist denomination in the nation and the world. It dominates large segments of the American

South and maintains a presence throughout much of the country. During the latter twentieth century, the convention's size, evangelistic efforts, and activities in the public arena sometimes made it appear to be the denomination that defined Baptists' identity in the United States.

As noted earlier, the Southern Baptist Convention began in 1845 as a direct result of controversies over slavery that divided Baptists North and South. As abolitionist influence increased among Baptists in the North, the tensions with Southerners also increased. Finally, Georgia Baptists proposed a "test case" by presenting the name of Southerner James Reeve as a candidate for appointment by the Home Mission Society. The Executive Board of the Society rejected Reeve's candidacy on the grounds that it was a direct violation of earlier resolutions that forbade the introduction of slavery into denominational procedures. Alabama Baptists responded by insisting that the society declare that slaveholders would be considered equally with non-slaveholders for missionary appointments. The governing board of the convention declared that no new missionaries would be appointed if they retained ownership of slaves and concluded: "One thing is certain; we can never be a party to any arrangement which would imply approbation of slavery."[17]

Southerners insisted that their rights had been violated when the General (Triennial) Convention changed the rules, adding requirements that were not a part of the original agreement. In response, a group of Baptists gathered at First Baptist Church, Augusta, Georgia, in May 1845 to form the Southern Baptist Convention. William Bullein Johnson (1782–1862), one of the early leaders, proposed the creation of "one Convention, embodying the whole Denomination, together with separate and distinct Boards, for each object of benevolent enterprise, located at different places, and all amenable to the Convention."[18] Johnson's plan was based not on the loose-knit society method of the Triennial Convention but on a system in which individual agencies and boards were linked to the central convention. Johnson was elected president of the convention, and his vision for the denomination was evident in the constitution approved on May 10, 1845. Its preamble stated that the SBC was founded as "carrying into effect the benevolent intentions of our constituents, by organizing a plan for eliciting, combining and directing the energies of the whole denomination in one sacred effort, for the propagation of the Gospel."[19] Implied in this was the belief that by refusing to appoint slaveholders, the Northerners had undermined the calling of Southerners who felt the mandate to take the gospel to the world.

The earliest denominational agencies included only home and foreign mission boards, both of which began appointment of missionaries rather quickly. The Foreign Mission Board appointed its first missionaries to China in September 1845. Two new missionaries, Samuel C. Clopton and George Pearcy, were sent out, and the board assumed support of J. Lewis Shuck, a Southerner already in China under appointment by the Triennial Convention. The Domestic (Home) Mission Board was slow in securing support and securing missionaries to work with Native Americans and to work in the West.[20] A "Bible Board," charged with circulating the Scriptures, was founded in 1851.

In 1859 the Southern Baptist Theological Seminary was established on the campus of Furman College in Greenville, South Carolina. The first faculty included James P. Boyce (1827–1888), John R. Broadus (1827–1895), Basil Manly Jr. (1825–1892), and William Williams (1821–1877). The trustees approved an *Abstract of Principles*, a statement of faith to be signed by professors, who were required to teach "in accordance with, and not contrary to" the document. The founders asserted that the school would train those who had limited or extensive academic backgrounds.

In the early years the convention developed connections with local churches, regional associations, and state Baptist conventions, each of which could send "messengers" to the biennial, later annual, meetings. Later on, messengers were permitted only from churches that gave a basic amount of money to the denomination.

Although most early Southern Baptists were not slaveholders, they generally gave their support to the Confederacy. Many ministers served as chaplains in the Confederate Army, and the convention issued frequent resolutions in support of the Cause throughout the war years (1861–1865). Stories of dramatic conversions and deathbed confessions filled the pulpits of the period. One famous volume, titled *Christ in the Camp: Religion in Lee's Army*, documented a variety of revivals and spiritual awakenings that were said to have occurred among the troops.[21]

In the aftermath of the defeat at Appomattox, the SBC, like its region, was devastated, with churches and school destroyed, constituency despondent, and funds depleted. The Southern Baptist Theological Seminary reopened with one blind veteran as the "student body" and moved to Louisville, Kentucky, in 1877 to escape the war-ravaged region. Numerous Southern Baptist leaders struggled with the theological implications of their defeat, especially given the claims that slavery was supported by biblical mandates. Some even wondered if a failure to evangelize slaves properly had led to Divine judgment against the Southerners. As Charles Reagan Wilson has shown, many Southern Baptists were among the devotees of the "Lost Cause," that effort to mythologize the religious meaning of the war in Southern society. In a sense, Southern Baptists came to perpetuate one of the great myths of Southern identity: The people who lost the war retained the vision. The defeated people would vindicate their original ideals so that even in defeat they would be more moral, more evangelical, and more orthodox than their Northern counterparts ever would be. Growth was slow in coming, but the denomination's leaders worked diligently to conquer their region for Christ.[22]

The division with the North continued in spite of early efforts at reunion. In 1845 Southern Baptists claimed some 351,951 members, 130,000 of whom were African American. Emancipation and the end of the war witnessed a mass exodus of black members, who formed new churches and denominations. Yet by 1890 there were 1, 235,908, of which a large majority were white.[23]

New denominational or related agencies were established in the latter nineteenth century. The Bible Board was replaced with the Sunday School Board, established in 1863 and charged with publishing literature for use in churches. It fell on difficult times, shut down, and was not reorganized until 1891. The Woman's Missionary Union was founded in 1888 to raise funds for missionary endeavors at home and abroad. Fears that women's activities might contradict biblical admonitions for female silence and male authority in the church influenced the decision to make the organization and "auxiliary" not officially connected to the SBC, a relationship it continues to retain.

Like other Baptists, Southerners were and remain an independent lot, concerned that denominational prerogatives not overshadow the autonomy of local congregations. Baptist organization linked churches to a variety of broader relationships, each itself autonomous yet connected in various ways. Associations are gatherings of churches in a given town, county, or region. State conventions bring together participating churches in a particular state in the United States. The national denomination (SBC) involves local churches that unite for specific purposes involving missions, publications, theological education, and other endeavors.

Convincing local churches to join in these efforts was no easy matter. It took years of encouragement and programmatic identity. Indeed, by the twentieth century the SBC had developed an increasingly intense identity grounded in Southern culture and Southern Baptist denominational programs. Missionary appointments increased, a denominationally based corporate funding program known as the Cooperative Program began in 1925, organizations for men, women, and children were expanded, and additional seminaries were founded.

In 1925 the convention approved its first official confession of faith, the *Baptist Faith and Message*, delineating doctrines regarding Scripture, salvation, the church, baptism, the Lord's Supper, and other issues. By the 1950s Southern Baptists had six theological seminaries spread from North Carolina to California: Southern Baptist Seminary (Louisville, Kentucky), Southwestern Baptist Theological Seminary (Fort Worth, Texas), New Orleans Baptist Seminary, Midwestern Baptist Seminary (Kansas City, Missouri), Southeastern Baptist Seminary (Wake Forest, North Carolina), and Golden Gate Baptist Seminary (Mill Valley, California). The Depression and the embezzlement of funds by a denominational employee created financial crises that took years to overcome. By the mid-twentieth century, however, the denomination had developed an extensive constituency, greater financial solvency, and extended its influence beyond the South with new state conventions in other regions of the country. Evangelism was a major tool used by the denomination and its member churches to reach the population with the claims of Christianity, bring people to faith, and expand membership in the SBC.

Beginning around 1980, the SBC became involved in a denomination-wide controversy between conservatives and moderates regarding doctrine (particularly the doctrine of biblical inerrancy), denominational control, and assorted other theological and ethical issues. Conservatives succeeded in electing a series of convention presidents who appointed people of like belief to convention boards and agencies, thereby effecting a "course correction" that turned the denominational agenda in more theologically and ethically rightward directions.

While the core of the convention remained intact, certain individuals, churches, state Baptist conventions, and Baptist-related schools have distanced themselves (to varying degrees) from traditional connections to the SBC system. In 2003 denominational leaders announced a crisis of funding evident in a significant decrease in contributions to the national denomination through the convention's Cooperative Program.

### Appalachian-Based Baptists

The central Appalachian region of the American South is home to a variety of small, sectarian Baptist communions, many of which have similar characteristics and occupy space and identity as what has sometimes been called "Appalachian Mountain religious groups." These churches often view themselves as retaining and perpetuating the "old-timey" faith that characterized not only the beliefs of the earliest settlers in that particular region but also the faith of the earliest Christians, passed on from the New Testament era. Their denominational relationships are often left to local churches and regional associations, with limited national organization. They developed numerous rituals and styles of church life that characterize much of Baptist life in the region.

## Primitive Baptists

While the Primitive Baptist movement began as a direct result of divisions over the denominational and missionary organizations, most Primitive Baptists themselves would insist that they are directly linked to the earliest Christian communities (hence "primitive") in faith and practices. They assert that their doctrines and church order are identical to those of the first generation of Christian churches. Historically, these congregations and associations maintain limited denominational structures, sometimes rejecting "manmade" denominations as antithetical to New Testament teachings. Theirs is a radical congregationalism centered in the belief that every church should "govern itself according to the laws of Christ as found in the new Testament, and no minister, association, or convention has any authority over the [individual] churches."[24]

The Primitive Baptist movement began as a direct reaction among some Baptists to two important developments among nineteenth-century Baptists: denominationalism and missions. The first took shape as early as 1827 when the Kehukee Association in North Carolina objected to the increased emphasis among some Baptists on participation in missionary, publication, and other national or regional societies. These Baptists declared that such organizations had no basis in Scripture and were a threat to the autonomy and authority of local congregations. While they were usually willing to join together in associations of churches on a local or regional level, they did not want those "fellowships" to dictate policies to individual congregations. They refused to align themselves with denominations for fear that such a hierarchy would claim control of their churches and their consciences. One document concluded: "We . . . declare a non-fellowship with all such human institutions" and "all societies and traveling beggars for their support, believing them to be the emissaries and agents of antichrist, and opposed to the true kingdom of Jesus Christ."[25]

Primitive Baptists also support a particular kind of Calvinism that places strong emphasis on election and predestination of individuals on the basis of the activity of an overarching Providence. They believe that all people are totally depraved and therefore deserve damnation by a just and righteous God. However, a merciful God has chosen to save some by unconditionally electing certain individuals for salvation "before the foundation of the world." All those born into the world are therefore in the elect or the non-elect. These Baptists contend that God alone is the author of salvation and therefore any effort by human beings to make salvation happen or compel others to conversion is simply a form of "works righteousness" that implies that sinners can affect their own salvation. They eschew participation in missionary societies both because such societies have no precedent in the New Testament and because they represent a futile human attempt to interfere with the sovereign work of God. Again, since God alone is the source of salvation, missionary efforts are another form of works righteousness. Thus some Primitive Baptists reject the need for mission societies and in some cases the very idea of missionary activity altogether. They oppose Bible societies, Sunday schools, theological seminaries, revivals, and other means of presenting the gospel apart from divine intervention.

As noted earlier, Daniel Parker (1781–1844), a frontier Baptist preacher and debater, was one of the early opponents of revivals and other "human means" to promote salvation. Parker's understanding of election and divine sovereignty led him to promote a doctrine of "two seed in the spirit predestinarianism," which suggested that every individual born into the world had either the seed of salvation or the seed of damnation as set forth by God's sovereign plan. While Primitive Baptists have not been explicit regarding the doctrine of the two seeds, they agree with Parker regarding the eternal destiny of the elect and the non-elect from the time of conception. Parker's beliefs took root in a highly Calvinistic group known as the Two-Seed-in-the-Spirit Predestinarian Baptists. This small Baptist group continues with only two small churches, one near Jacksboro, Texas, and another in Putnam County, Indiana.[26]

Likewise, the "Black Rock Address," composed by Calvinist Baptists, stated the case for the opposition by certain Baptist groups to mission boards, revivals, Sunday schools, and revival meetings, rejecting Sunday schools, mission boards, theological seminaries, and other "man-made" agencies that had no precedent in the New Testament.

Generally, Primitive Baptists affirm the following doctrines:

1. All persons are totally depraved because of the "fall" of Adam and Eve. Thus they deserve punishment from a just and righteous God.

2. God, in mercy, unconditionally elected some persons for salvation before the foundation of the world. This was done by God's own choice, not on the basis of anything that the elect could accomplish in themselves.

3. The death and resurrection of Jesus Christ provides the means of redemption for the ELECT. It is thus a "limited atonement."

4. All who are in the elect will be saved—experience the grace of God and the forgiveness of sins—in God's time and through God's redemptive activity, before they die. Any attempt to create salvation through use of "altar calls," "sinner's prayers," or other evangelistic formulas is merely blasphemous human means of trying to participate in the salvation process. The conversion process may involve years of struggle, waiting, and listening for the movement of God on the heart of the individual. Instant conversions are possible but seldom occur among Primitive Baptists. New converts are asked to relate their conversion story to the members of the church or the elders, who then decide together whether it seems a valid experience that will lead to baptism and church membership.[27]

5. One Primitive Baptist document notes: "We believe that sinners are called, converted, regenerated and sanctified by the Holy Spirit, and that all who are thus regenerated and born again by the Spirit of God shall never fall away."[28]

6. Many Primitive Baptist churches do not promote revival meetings, Sunday schools, missionary activity, or denominational organizations.

7. Most Primitive Baptist ministers are "bi-vocational," that is, they support themselves through secular employment and serve churches with little or no remuneration. Indeed, many Primitive Baptist churches and ministers reject the idea of a "hireling" or paid ministry.

8. Primitive Baptists do not believe that women can serve as pastors or even as official lay leaders of congregations. While informal leadership inside the "woman's sphere" of activity is substantial, formal offices of leadership are not open to women.

9. Primitive Baptists generally form local associations of churches for fellowship and mutual encouragement. They reject the idea that the association should have authority over local congregations. Some congregations eschew all churchly connections beyond the local community of faith.

10. A substantial number of Primitive Baptist congregations support only the use of the King James Version (KJV) of the Bible (1611) as the authorized text for the church and the individual. In fact, they evaluate the or-

thodoxy of a church or individual in terms of its use of the KJV as the only valid text.

11. Primitive Baptists generally practice three sacraments. Baptism by immersion is usually administered outdoors in creeks or rivers and is a sign of the new believer's faith in Christ and cleansing from sin. It is a profound and often highly emotional event. The Lord's Supper, observed with bread and wine (usually unfermented grape juice) is administered by deacons periodically in each church (monthly, quarterly, or annually). The washing of feet, usually administered in conjunction with the Lord's Supper, is a sign of the servanthood of all believers. It is carried out "in decency and in order," with members of the same sex washing each other's feet in observance of the practice detailed in the Gospel of John, chapter 13.

12. While Primitive Baptist churches are spread throughout the United States, they are particularly strong in the South and Southwest, especially in the central Appalachian region of the South.

13. Primitive Baptist churches continue to observe a practice of church discipline known as "churching" or "exclusion," whereby recalcitrant members or those who have been determined to be continuing in known sins such as drunkenness, adultery, lying, cheating, criminal behavior, or other practices that bring judgment on the individual and disrepute on the church are excommunicated from the congregation. The intent of the action is to bring judgment on the individual and encourage repentance through the practice of what might be called "tough love."

Primitive Baptists are a diverse lot, with numerous subgroups that span a wide theological spectrum from staunchly predestinarian to affirmatively Universalist. These groups include the following:

1. Single Predestinarians affirm that God has elected some persons for salvation, but avoid pressing this idea to include damnation of the non-elect.

2. Double Predestinarians believe that God chose some people for salvation and others for damnation.

3. Evangelical Predestinarians permit churches to use Sunday schools, preaching services, and other "means" to reach the elect with the gospel message.

4. Primitive Baptist Universalists (a small sect not recognized by other Primitives) insist that life on this earth purges all people, ultimately toward the redemption of the whole world in Christ.[29] These "no-hellers" as they are sometimes (incorrectly) identified, believe that while Adam's death brought sin to all people, Christ's death provides universal salvation. As one Primitive Baptist Universalist observed: "After this fleeting transitory exis-

tence in the present evil world, . . . ALL mankind will possess Eternal Life, the Life of God, and His Son Jesus Christ. (Though it has not been revealed to me whether they all will occupy the same [eternal] station.) But we are assured ALL will be heirs with Christ, and be satisfied and God glorified."[30]

Primitive Baptists maintain a national denomination, but their primary strength is in local congregations sometimes working together in regional associations of churches. Many churches are small, sometimes holding Sunday services once a month. Rural congregations are often "stem family churches," composed of the members of a few families that have intermarried. Anglo-Saxon Primitive Baptists number fewer than 100,000, while the National Primitive Baptist Convention of the USA (primarily African American) claims more than a million members and has a much more elaborate denominational organization, which includes benevolent societies and Sunday schools.

## Old Regular Baptists

Appalachian studies scholar Howard Dorgan is among those who view the Old Regular Baptists as a distinct subdenomination of the Baptist family. He writes that the "Old Regular view themselves as a special people, not in the sense of having been 'particularly elected' as the Primitives believe, but in the sense of being 'redeemed' and 'zealous of good works,' of 'denying ungodliness and worldly lusts,' as having been 'called . . . out of darkness,' and as living 'soberly, righteously, and godly.' "[31]

The origin of the Old Regular Baptists can be traced to the founding of the New Salem (Baptist) Association in eastern Kentucky in 1825. The beliefs and practices of the Old Regulars, many of which parallel those of the Primitive Baptists, are directly related to the practices of the churches in that nineteenth-century association. The Union Association, founded in 1859, exists today as a nongeographic association incorporating more than sixty churches from Ypsilanti, Michigan, to Green Cove Springs, Florida, and including numerous congregations in Kentucky and Virginia.[32] The New Salem Association used the name Regular Baptist until 1892, when the name Old Regular Baptist first appears. It probably reflects the traditional approach of the churches, as well as an increasing attempt to distinguish them from the Primitive Baptist communions.[33]

Like their Primitive Baptist counterparts, these churches are strongly Calvinist in doctrine, administer baptism by immersion in outdoor creeks and rivers, celebrate the Lord's Supper in conjunction with the washing of feet, refuse to permit women to preach or preside at church meetings, and promote the use of the King James Version of the Bible. They reject mission societies and boards, Sunday schools, revivals, and any outward, "human" effort to compel people to be saved.

Yet where the Primitives affirm a belief "in the doctrine of eternal and particular election," the Old Regulars assert a belief in "the doctrine of election by grace, for by grace are you saved through faith."[34] Old Regulars also contend that none of their dogmas "shall be considered as to hold with particular election and reprobation so as to make God partial, directly or indirectly, nor to injure any of the children of men." This represents an effort to soften the harsh predestination whereby God chooses and damns particular individuals at will.[35] It is somewhere in between the strict predestinarian views of the Primitives and the general atonement views of the Arminian or General Baptists. Baptism, however, is seldom administered in Old Regular churches to those who are under thirty years of age.

Howard Dorgan's extensive study of the sermon style of the Appalachian Baptist churches convinced him that the Old Regular Baptists tended to demonstrate a more emotional form than their Primitive Baptist counterparts. Most preaching among the Old Regulars is spontaneous (without notes) and exuberant, moving rapidly from joyous shouts to tearful appeals and back again. They also utilize a particular vocal cadence, evident in many mountain churches, that involves particular styles of breathing and timbre in delivery of sermons. Amid a variety of distinctive styles, Old Regulars use "an elongated upward-sliding wail that rises on a phrase like 'Oh, God,' peaks in power and emotion, and then cascades downward through a series of briefer and weaker miniwails, each lower in volume and pitch than the previous, until the speaker settles on a base line for several rhythmical moments before starting the pattern all over."[36]

Old Regular churches also exercise discipline by expelling or "churching" unrepentant members. They require baptism of all who profess faith in Christ and believe that all those who are truly converted cannot lose their salvation but will persevere to the end. Writing in 1999, sociologist Clifford Grammich reported some 19,257 Old Regular Baptists "in 326 churches of 94 counties spread as far apart as Arizona, Florida, Maryland, and Washington state."[37]

## United Baptists

The United Baptists are another of the Appalachian Mountains subdenominations, with membership primarily in Kentucky, Virginia, West Virginia, and the Carolinas. They are heirs of two theological traditions, Calvinist and Arminian. They trace their origins to efforts to unite groups of Regular and Separate Baptists in the late eighteenth and early nineteenth centuries. Regular Baptists were Calvinists who affirmed the need for conversion but were less responsive to the revival movements sweeping American Protestant communities during the period. Their worship was orderly and tended to mirror that of the Presbyterians and others in the Reformed tradition. Separate Baptists were pro-revivalists whose worship was spontaneous and emotional.

In 1801, for example, Separate Baptists from the South Kentucky Association and Regulars from the Salem and Elkhorn Association united and essentially blended their divergent theologies. Today they tend to use the language of Calvinism—election, salvation, regeneration—but define it with more Arminian definitions that take seriously free will and salvation for all who come on repentance and faith. United Baptists number some 60,000 members in approximately 500 or more churches. Some churches observe open communion, others closed communion. They practice immersion baptism and celebrate the Lord's Supper, usually preceded by foot-washing.[38]

## *Union Baptists*

Union Baptists, another of the Appalachian Baptist subgroups, began as a result of a schism with the Primitive Baptists over support for the Union position in the Civil War. The first Union Baptist association was founded in Ashe County, North Carolina, in 1867 by a group of Union supporters who came out of the Senter Primitive Baptist Association.[39]

Union Baptists continue to exist in four Appalachian associations: the Mountain Union Association, the Union Baptist Association, the Primitive (Union) Baptist Association, and the Friendship (Union) Association. The churches related to these associations are located primarily in Grayson County, Virginia, and Ashe and Alleghany Counties in North Carolina. Dorgan reports that the Primitive and Friendship associations may not be as clear about their Union Baptist identity as the other two.[40]

Union Baptists, while a small group, continue to promote doctrines that place emphasis on "election by grace" and give place to human free will. They conduct Sunday schools and revival meetings, sometimes even permitting radio broadcasts of their services. They maintain fellowship with other Baptist groups in the region, and their churches have considerable diversity in worship styles and doctrinal emphases. Unlike the Primitives, the Union

Baptists are not averse to inviting preachers from other Baptist subgroups to "proclaim the Word" in their churches. While associations may affirm specific doctrinal positions, they often include a disclaimer that the "Association has no right to Lord it over God's heritage, or infringe over the internal right of any Church."[41] Dorgan notes that the Union Baptists are so small in number that it is not so much that they are "antimissionary as they are nonmissionary." Most of their churches number no more than twenty-five to one hundred fifty people, and they are not connectional enough to be able to secure funds for missionary endeavors.[42]

Certain Union Baptist churches continue the practice of "lining out" hymns, an old, traditional method of Protestant hymnody whereby the leader sings a line of a Psalm or hymn and the congregation then repeats it. In a sense, Union Baptists, like other Baptist subgroups in Appalachia, retain many practices that were common in frontier or colonial churches in America. While their numbers are small and generally getting smaller, they are important case studies in the power of early Baptist life and liturgy in farm and mountain regions.[43]

## Arminian Baptists

The first Baptist community in Amsterdam was Arminian in its approach to theology, believing in the general atonement of Christ, the freedom of the individual will, and the cooperation between grace and free will in the process of salvation, and also insisting that believers could reject the faith and "fall from grace" along the way. These ideas were carried forth by the General and Free Will Baptists in America.

### Free Will Baptists

Free Will Baptists originated in the United States in 1727 with Paul Palmer (d. 1750?) and a group of General Baptists in North Carolina. This church was soon led by Joseph Parker (d. 1791?), who helped found churches throughout the region. A confession of faith, published in 1812, referred to the new denomination as Free Will or Free "Willer" Baptists because of their idea that "Christ died for all," not simply the elect.[44] These Baptists affirmed Christ's general atonement, the importance of human free will in cooperation with God's saving grace, and the possibility that those who choose salvation at one point in life could also choose to reject it at some later

time (falling from grace). Thus, salvation required not only a strong emphasis on justification (entering to faith), but also on sanctification (going on in
grace).

Other Baptists groups also developed with a concern for Arminian ideas.
These included United Baptists in western North Carolina, Free Will Baptists in New England, and Separate Baptists in Kentucky. Southerners formed
a Triennial Conference that lasted from 1896 to 1910, then was reorganized
in 1920. New England Free Will Baptists united with American Baptists in
1911, and in 1917 various churches located in Texas, Missouri, Nebraska,
Kansas, and Oklahoma formed the General Co-operative Association of
Free Will Baptists. In 1935 the latter body united with the Southerners to
found the Free Will Baptists in America, the largest free will Baptist denomination. It claims approximately 230, 000 members.[45] Free Will Baptists are
thoroughgoing Arminians who practice three ordinances: baptism, Lord's
Supper, and foot-washing.

### General Association of General Baptists

The General Association of General Baptists represents a reaffirmation of
Arminian Baptist theology in the Midwest during the nineteenth century.
Benoni Stinson (1789–1869) helped begin that movement as a response to the
prevailing Calvinism of Indiana and Kentucky Baptist churches and his
own belief that "Christ tasted death" for every human being. He preached
these views as pastor of the Liberty Baptist Church in Howell, Indiana,
and used that congregation to form a General Baptist association. The movement spread throughout the larger region, and the General Association of
General Baptists was founded in 1870 with a home mission board begun in
1871 and a foreign mission board founded in 1903. Oakland City College was
founded in Indiana in 1891. The General Baptists have an extensive missionary ministry and claim a membership of nearly 75,000 in approximately 820
churches.[46]

While many Baptist communions—Southern Baptists, Independent Baptists, American Baptists—do not claim Arminianism as an explicit theology,
many of their churches reflect an almost implicit Arminian approach with respect to issues of general atonement, free will, and the possibility that all who
call upon Christ by repentance and faith can be saved. Their effort to promote
perseverance of the saints and repudiate falling from grace has often led them
to call themselves "modified Calvinists," but in fact they might better be designated "modified Arminians."

## Ethnic Baptist Groups

Numerous Baptist denominations trace their beginnings to immigrant or ethnic-based churches, some of which developed distinct identities after they arrived in the United States. These include the following denominations.

### *Baptist General Conference*

The Baptist General Conference began officially in 1852 in Rock Island, Illinois, founded by two Swedish immigrants, Anders Wiberg and Gustaf Palmquist. Wiberg and Palmquist had been strongly influenced by Swedish Pietism, a movement within the Lutheran church that emphasized devotional use of the Bible, personal conversion, simple worship services, and the preaching of "heart religion" by regenerate pastors.[47] This evangelical zeal had a direct impact on the growth of the movement among newly arrived immigrants, and by 1871 there were some fifteen hundred members of Swedish Baptist churches in seven states. In 1879 a national denomination, known as the Swedish Baptist General Conference, was established, and by 1902 it claimed 324 churches with a total membership of approximately 22,000. Swedish Baptists organized in Winnipeg, Canada, in 1894.[48]

During the early years of the movement some financial support was provided by the American Baptist Home Mission Society and the American Baptist Publication Society, agencies connected to Northern Baptists. Swedish Baptists participated in the missionary activity of the American Baptist Foreign Mission Society until 1944, when a separate missionary society was formed. Today the mission board provides support for work in countries such as India, Japan, the Philippines, Ethiopia, Mexico, Argentina, and Brazil.[49]

In 1871 John Alexis Edgren, a Chicago Baptist pastor, established a periodical called *Zions Wacht* (Zion's Watch). It later became the *Standard*, a denominational newspaper that continues to publish denominational news. Also in 1871, Edgren founded a theological and missionary training school in Chicago. It moved to St. Paul, Minnesota, in 1914 and became Bethel College and Seminary, both still supported by the Baptist General Conference. The college has a student body of approximately 2,000 while the seminary has some 500 students.[50] Church services were conducted in the Swedish language well into the twentieth century, but by the 1950s most congregations had made the transition to English. After 1945 the word *Swedish* was no longer used to describe the denomination, and it became the Baptist General

Conference. In 1980 the conference claimed 779 churches, with a membership of 133,698. The denomination maintained connections with the Baptist World Alliance, the Baptist Joint Committee on Public Affairs, and the National Association of Evangelicals. By the late twentieth century, many younger pastors and leaders were less connected to the denomination's Swedish heritage, and new non-Anglo-Saxon churches and membership increased dramatically. For example, there were 60 non-Anglo churches in the conference in 1980 and 139 in 1992. Albert W. Wardin writes that "during the 1991–1992 church year, of the sixty new churches added to the BGC, forty-two were non-Anglo churches."[51] Many current congregations continue to identify themselves with their Baptist heritage but with a strong appreciation for and involvement in the broader conservative-evangelical community in the United States. In the mid-1990s the Baptist General Conference claimed 132, 994 members in 786 churches.[52]

## North American Baptist Conference
### (General Conference of German Baptist Churches in North America)

The North American Baptist Conference represents a large segment of German-heritage churches in the United States and Canada. Konrad Anton Fleischmann (1812–1867) was perhaps the earliest organizer and leader of the German Baptist communities in the United States. Born in Germany and converted to Baptist views in Switzerland in 1831, Fleischmann arrived in the United States in 1839. He was soon appointed by the American Baptist Home Mission Society to work with German immigrants.[53] The first German Baptist congregations were present in the United States by 1840.

The earliest gathering of German Baptist pastors and laity took place in Philadelphia in 1851, with a second such meeting the next year in Rochester, New York. Rochester Theological Seminary, founded in 1850, had a major influence in shaping the German Baptist identity in America. August Rauschenbusch and his son Walter were both professors there and made significant contributions to the institutional and ideological thought of the movement. August Rauschenbusch was instrumental in founding the North American Baptist Seminary as part of the German Department of the Rochester school. It existed as a freestanding German seminary on the Rochester campus until 1947 when it moved to Sioux Falls, South Dakota, where it continues to this day.

Walter Rauschenbusch (1861–1918), professor of church history at Rochester Seminary, is sometimes known as the "father of the Social Gospel" in

America. As a pastor in Hell's Kitchen, New York, and then as a seminary professor, he wrote extensively on the social implications of Christianity for dealing with poverty, industrialization, and the corporate exploitation of workers.

Immigration to the United States and western Canada brought Germans and German Russians, many of whom became Baptists. Anti-German sentiments during World War I hastened the decision to relinquish German language for English in worship and at other public events. The denomination also began supporting its own ministries during those years. The second world conflict with Germany influenced the decision to give up the reference to German in the denomination's name, and it became the North American Baptist Conference in 1944.[54]

The denomination's mission board funds work in the Republic of Cameroon, West Africa. The Cameroon Baptist Convention now has more churches and members than the North American Baptist Conference. Additional mission work is conducted in the Philippines, Japan, Mexico, and Brazil. The denomination continues to maintain connections with churches in both Canada and the United States and claims 42, 689 members in 267 churches.[55]

## Hispanic Baptists

Baptist mission work in Spanish-speaking countries began in the nineteenth century with missionaries sent to Cuba, Puerto Rico, and Central and South America. Mexican Baptist churches were founded in Laredo and San Antonio, Texas, by the 1880s. Bible schools for training indigenous Spanish-speaking pastors were established in the early twentieth century, and the Mexican Baptist Bible Institute (now the Hispanic Baptist Theological Seminary) began in San Antonio in 1947. The Hispanic Baptist Convention of Texas originated in 1910. During the late twentieth and early twenty-first centuries, churches and ministries were founded throughout the nation in response to the growing Latino/Hispanic population. American Baptists USA, Southern, and Independent Baptists count significant numbers of Spanish-speaking congregations among their numbers.[56]

## Independent Baptists

Many observers may suggest that all Baptists are "independent," given their concern for individual conscience and congregational autonomy. Nonetheless, the label "independent" applied to some groups of Baptists means that they generally eschew denominational organizations, mission boards, or other official connections that they believe undermine the local church. Any cooperative efforts they may undertake are referred to as "fellowships" of churches or pastors. Independent Baptists often affirm the church's missionary imperative and the need to evangelize the world but prefer to fund and send out missionaries through individual congregations rather than through missionary societies or agencies. Independent Baptist churches or groups tend to be fundamentalist in their theological orientation, placing particular emphasis on the classic "five points": (1) biblical inerrancy, (2) the virgin birth of Jesus, (3) Christ's substitutionary atonement, (4) Christ's bodily resurrection from the dead, and (5) Christ's literal Second Coming to judge the world and mark the end of time.

Doctrinal orthodoxy is indeed a major emphasis of Independent Baptists. Their leaders often identify themselves as "Bible-believing Christians," in contrast to those other groups and persons they believe to be unbiblical, unorthodox, and outside the boundaries of true Christian faith. So concerned are many of these Baptists to avoid the taint of liberalism that they consider themselves to be "Separatist Fundamentalists," who refuse to associate with any groups that they consider to be theological liberals. They insist that true Christians must "obey the Biblical injunction to separate from apostasy, theological compromise and worldliness."[57] For these Baptists "to know a liberal is to be a liberal"; thus they reject any participation in community or ecumenical alliances or activities that might include those whose views and practices are heretical. Even after the "conservative resurgence" in the Southern Baptist Convention, many Independent Baptists continue to criticize the SBC for its compromises in methods and dogmas. For example, certain Independents attack the SBC for its association with the Baptist World Alliance (too ecumenical), Promise Keepers (an ecumenical evangelical men's movement), and the "Growth/Church Marketing Movement" that appears to be "secularizing today's church."[58]

Independent Baptist fellowships include the Baptist Bible Fellowship, the World Fundamentalist Fellowship, and the Southwide Baptist Fellowship. These groups are not denominations or subdenominations, but instead represent gatherings of churches and preachers for mutual affirmation, communication, and evangelism.

While various forms of orthodox separatism were evident among early Baptists, the Independent Baptist movement may be traced historically to the fundamentalism and antidenominationalism that developed around "the Texas tornado," J. Frank Norris, longtime pastor of First Baptist Church, Fort Worth. Norris broke away from the Southern Baptist Convention in the

1920s and 1930s, rejecting what he called the "denominational machine" that sought to impose requirements on its member churches. He was an outspoken separatist fundamentalist who denounced any hint of compromise with liberalism. Churches, educational institutions, the "liquor trade," Catholics, and Communists were frequent targets of his aggressive rhetoric. He was also an entrepreneur in using a variety of attention-getting tactics to bring people to his church. On certain occasions he buried liquor bottles outside the church, and he attacked Darwinism by bringing a monkey to church.[59] Other pastors and churches, many inside the Southern Baptist Convention, identified with his movement and were sometimes referred to as "Norrisites."

In 1939 Norris founded the Fundamental Baptist Bible Institute (now Arlington Baptist College) to educate preachers for fundamentalist Baptist churches. However, his autocratic leadership created tensions with many of his colleagues, and in 1950 some broke away and founded the Bible Baptist Fellowship, based in Springfield, Missouri. That group, which exists today, helps collect funds from churches to support individual missionaries. (It is not a bona fide mission board.) It also has connections to a periodical titled *The Baptist Bible Tribune*. Also in 1950 the Baptist Bible College was organized with G. Beauchamp Vick (1901–1975), a former Norris associate, as president. Jerry Falwell, pastor of Thomas Road Baptist Church in Lynchburg, Virginia, is perhaps the most nationally known minister associated with that movement. Like other fundamentalist Baptist fellowships, the group is connected to the school, the newspaper, a mission fund collection agency, and a pastors' association.[60]

The Southwide Baptist Fellowship is a similar association of fundamentalist Baptist preachers organized by Lee Roberson (1909–) during his four decades of ministry at Highland Park Baptist Church in Chattanooga, Tennessee. Like Norris, Roberson was a fierce opponent of any group or individual he thought to be liberal. In 1956 he led certain Southern Baptist clergy and laity in founding the Southern Baptist Fellowship, a movement that later became known as the Southwide Baptist Fellowship. In 1960 he also began Baptist International Missions, Inc., a clearinghouse for local church funding and appointment of missionaries. It now claims more than five hundred missionaries in more than sixty countries.[61] The Southwide Baptist Fellowship was a favorite of the controversial editor John R. Rice (d. 1980) of Murfreesboro, Tennessee. Rice's journal, the *Sword of the Lord*, was an aggressive vehicle for advancing the fundamentalist cause, linking fundamentalist churches, and attacking liberalism wherever it might be found.[62]

## General Association of Regular Baptist Churches (GARBC)

Born of disagreements between fundamentalists and liberals in the Northern Baptist Convention, the General Association of Regular Baptist Churches was founded in Chicago in 1932 by representatives of twenty-two churches formerly associated with the Baptist Bible Union (BBU). The BBU was organized in the 1920s by a group of pastors who were disturbed by the failure of the Northern Baptists to take a more conservative approach to dogma. The GARBC soon agreed to participate in two independent Baptist mission endeavors, Baptist Mid-Missions (1920) and the Association of Baptists for World Evangelism (1927). Support for additional missionary organizations was added later.[63]

Robert T. Ketcham (1889–1978) shaped the GARBC from its beginning, serving as vice president, president, and editor of its newspaper, *Baptist Bulletin*, and devising the group's organizational structures. The denomination is characterized by an emphasis on evangelism and missions, its fundamentalist doctrinal orientation, and its strong concern for biblical "separatism," refusing to take part in any endeavor linked to liberalism. Its leaders refuse to participate in the World Council of Churches or the National Association of Evangelicals and reject all connection with Billy Graham crusades.

The GARBC claims some 1,500 churches with a membership of around 150,000. Its churches are located in the North, the West, Florida, and portions of Canada.[64]

## Conservative Baptist Association of America

The Conservative Baptist Association of America, a loose confederation of churches located primarily in the West and Northwest, began as a direct result of doctrinal and missionary controversies in the Northern Baptist Convention (American Baptist Churches, USA). The controversy developed over questions of biblical inspiration, Christology, and salvation related to the so-called fundamentalist/modernist debates of the 1920s and beyond. In 1920 a group of pastors and laity formally expressed their concerns regarding the liberalism that they believed to be growing in Northern Baptist life, especially in church schools and among church-appointed missionaries. They called for a special investigation of missionaries to determine their theological positions and made a series of efforts to establish more-specific doctrinal norms as a basis for missionary appointment. The investigation turned up no major trends toward liberalism, and the attempts to tighten doctrinal guidelines proved unsuccessful. This led to the departure of numerous conservative congregations from the NBC. Finally, in 1943, another failure to secure more-stringent doctrinal requirements for missionaries led to the founding of the Conservative Baptist Foreign Mission Society (CBFMS), the first stage of what would ultimately become a new denomination. The newly formed mission society continued to be supported by churches and individuals who were still part of the Northern Baptist Convention but who felt they could no longer support that denomination's mission society. In 1946 the NBC took action that forbade member churches to support another mission agency (the CBFMS), thereby forcing the departure of the conservative churches. Representatives of those churches met in Atlantic City, New Jersey, in 1947 and formed the Conservative Baptist Association of America, taking a significant number of congregations out of the NBC.[65]

Strongly evangelistic, many of these conservative churches cooperated with the National Association of Evangelicals and various nondenominational evangelical groups. Other, more fundamentalist churches, resisted cooperation with the broader evangelical community, again fearing a compromise with various unorthodox doctrines and actions. Within seven years of the founding of the new denomination, some two hundred congregations that had identified with this ultraconservative approach departed for other fundamentalist alliances.

The denomination has connections with the Conservative Baptist International Mission to the Americas, an undergraduate school; the Southwestern Bible College in Phoenix, Arizona; and three theological institutions: Denver Seminary in Colorado; Western Seminary in Portland, Oregon; and Eastern Conservative Baptist Seminary. During the 1970s home and foreign mission agencies moved with the denominational staff to facilities in Wheaton, Illinois, and increased cooperation. Efforts to bring these autonomous bodies into greater structural connection remain unsuccessful. By the last decade of the twentieth century the group reported some 200,000 members in 1,197 congregations.[66]

## Landmark Baptist Groups

As noted earlier, Landmarkism is a movement that began in the nineteenth century as an attempt to trace Baptist ecclesiology (theory of the church) directly back to Jesus and the earliest Christian communities. Landmark churches promote the idea that Baptists represent the true church, that only members of a specific congregation can receive communion in that congregation, that infant baptism is a false baptism, and that immersion outside a Baptist communion is also false (alien immersion). They reject mission boards as nonbiblical and hesitate to develop elaborate denominational connections beyond the local church. Several Baptist groups combine fundamentalist doctrine with Landmark ecclesiology. These include the American Baptist Association (ABA), the Baptist Missionary Association (BMA), and certain separatist Landmark churches and associations.

## American Baptist Association

The American Baptist Association developed in Texas and Arkansas in the early twentieth century out of divisions between Landmark Baptists within the Southern Baptist Convention who felt that denominational "hegemony" undermined the autonomy of the local congregation. Between 1900 and 1903, Landmark Baptists founded three state-based associations: the Baptist Missionary Association of Texas, the State Association of Missionary Baptist Churches of Arkansas, and the Baptist General Assembly of Oklahoma.[67] A general association of these churches was established in 1905 in Texarkana, Arkansas. They issued a document calling on the SBC to abandon mission boards and financial requirements for membership while offering equality of representation to each member congregation. The document noted:

> We love peace, but we love principle better. First pure and then peaceable. Besides, we do not think we are guilty of causing the division which has been troubling our Zion. . . . We want the money and the associational basis of representation eliminated from the Constitution [of the SBC] and a purely church basis substituted instead. We believe in the churches to whom the Lord gave the commission, and that a church which is willing to co-operate should be entitled to a seat in this Convention by messenger, whether it be large or small, rich or poor, without any specified sum of money being fixed as the basis of co-operation.[68]

When the SBC rejected their demands, the Landmarkists broke away and founded the General Association of Baptists, later known as the Missionary Baptist General Association. The Baptist Missionary Association of Texas continued operation as a separate entity. These groups came together in 1924 to found the American Baptist Association (ABA), and this time the Texas BMA participated.[69]

Ben Bogard (1868–1951) was one of the most outspoken leaders of ABA churches in Arkansas. He frequently challenged SBC denominational procedures and theological positions. In 1934 he was instrumental in founding the Missionary Baptist Seminary, based in his congregation, the Antioch Missionary Baptist Church, Little Rock. He also instituted publication of Sunday school materials, a practice that the ABA continues. It later established three other Bible school/seminaries.

The ABA has upwards of 250,000 members, with some 40 percent in Arkansas, and headquarters in Texarkana, Texas. It continues to espouse Landmark ideals with a strong emphasis on fundamentalist dogma and local church autonomy. In 2003 it developed a new relationship with the Conservative Baptists of Texas, an SBC-affiliated group that broke away from the Baptist General Convention of Texas.

## Baptist Missionary Association of America

Conflicts over representation at associational meetings led to a schism in the American Baptist Association and the organization of the Baptist Missionary Association of America in Little Rock in 1950. These churches rejected the ABA practice of admitting "messengers" to associational meetings who were not members of the churches they were supposed to represent. They continued to promote conservative doctrines and set themselves over against the denominational system of the Southern Baptist Convention. The Baptist Missionary Association of America organized schools through specific associations, not local churches. While much of its membership is located in Texas, it also has constituencies in Mississippi, Arkansas, and other parts of the country. Its churches provide direct funding to missionaries at home and abroad. The association maintains a seminary in Jacksonville, Texas.[70]

## African American Baptist Denominations

African American Baptist denominations make up at least 25 percent of the Baptists in the United States. They also represent the largest religious communions in the country with predominantly African American constituents.

Several of today's denominations were formed out of earlier organizations that began in the aftermath of slavery.

The early antebellum Baptist churches in the South were integrated largely because slaves were not permitted to have their own congregations. Blacks were included in the membership and frequently listed on the membership roles.

While the earliest African Baptist church was probably the Silver Bluff Church founded on the Georgia/South Carolina border in the mid-1700s, it was not until emancipation that Baptist denominations really took shape. There is some indication that about 10 freestanding African American Baptist congregations existed by 1800. At the end of the Civil War there were perhaps more than 200 African American Baptist churches, around 75 in the North and 130 in the South. Others remained in integrated churches that generally broke apart after the war.[71] This exodus occurred in the 1870s and 1880s as growing numbers of African Americans recognized that they were second-class members of traditional Baptist churches. Individual congregations were formed and denominations grew out of various coalitions of churches in the North and the South. Many of the current African American Baptist groups are part of what some refer to as the National Baptist "family," in which some churches have multiple connections with a variety of denominational subgroups.

The first African American Baptist associations developed in Ohio and included Providence (1834) and Union (1836) and the Wood River Association, Illinois, in 1839. The first national denominational organization was founded in 1840 as the American Baptist Missionary Convention and included only three churches. The Western Colored Baptist Convention was founded in 1853 by various churches located in Illinois and Missouri. After a hiatus during the Civil War, it reorganized in 1864 to become the Northwestern and Southern Baptist Convention and included churches in a broader region of the Great Lakes and the Mississippi Valley.[72]

Denominational coalitions also formed through associations and state conventions. African American Baptist state organizations were established in Kentucky in 1865, North Carolina and Arkansas in 1867, Virginia and Alabama in 1868, Mississippi in 1869, Georgia in 1870, Louisiana and Tennessee in 1872, Florida and Texas in 1874, South Carolina in 1876, and West Virginia in 1878.[73] These conventions were composed of representatives from individual churches throughout the specific state. They met annually for worship, fellowship, and discussions related to common missions and benevolent activities.

## National Baptist Convention, USA, Inc.

The National Baptist Convention was founded in 1895 by representatives of three African American groups: the Baptist Foreign Mission Convention (1880), the National Baptist Education Convention (1882), and the American National Baptist Convention (1886). Debates over the implementation of the church's missionary imperative led to the first of several divisions in the convention when the Lott Carey Foreign Missionary Convention was formed in 1897. Elias C. Morris, a freed slave and pastor from Arkansas, was elected the first president. He retained the office for twenty-eight years, and he was only the first of a series of convention presidents who served lengthy terms. The new denomination organized mission, education, and young people's boards that paralleled the work of its founding organizations. Membership was extended to messengers from churches, associations, or state conventions. By 1906 the convention claimed a connection to churches numbering 2,261,607 members and had become the primary denomination for "a large percentage" of African American Christians.[74]

A publishing house was founded in 1896, and by 1898 it became an independent corporation, the National Baptist Publishing Board. Led by the entrepreneurial R. H. Boyd (1843–1922), the publishing board became a $2 million operation within the first decade. Located in Nashville, Tennessee, it soon acquired the most modern printing press in the South and even began to manufacture furniture for churches and schools.[75]

Divisions in the life of the convention developed rapidly. In 1897 questions arose regarding the importance of missions and participation with (white) American Baptist boards of publication and missions. While the majority of National Baptists sought a distinctly African American–based denomination, others favored stronger cooperation with whites in the missionary endeavor, and in two gatherings in 1897–1898, the Lott Carey Foreign Missionary Convention was formed; this organization continues to provide extensive support for African American missionary efforts worldwide. Various attempts have been made to bring the National and the Lott Carey Conventions into closer connection. Based in Washington, DC, the National Convention supports missions in Zimbabwe, Liberia, South Africa, Haiti, and India. The Carey Convention continues to receive funds from churches affiliated with the National Baptist Convention.[76]

In 1915 divisions over control of the National Baptist Publishing House and the approval of a denominational charter led to another schism and the creation of the National Baptist Convention of America. R. H. Boyd, secretary of the publishing house, asserted that the organization was legally independent of the convention. This claim and subsequent recommendations for recognition of the independence of the publishing house created a significant controversy in the NBC. In 1915 the "Boyd group" organized a new denomination, the National Baptist Convention, Unincorporated, in Chicago, Illinois. They insisted that since the publishing house was independent, it could align itself with the denomination of its choice—the newly formed denomination. This denomination is also known as the National Baptist Convention of America.[77]

E. C. Morris died in 1924 and was succeeded as president of the NBC by L. K. Williams, who served until 1940. During these years a layman's organization was founded, and a new building in Nashville was completed. David V. Jemison followed Williams as NBC president, serving from 1940 to 1953. Under his leadership the convention purchased the National Baptist Bath House in Hot Springs, Arkansas, which provided a place for African Americans to vacation in the highly segregated society of the South.

Joseph H. Jackson, president of the convention from 1953 until 1982, held great power over the denomination for nearly thirty years, overseeing a restructuring effort and extending connections to churches. His opposition to certain methods of civil disobedience utilized by Martin Luther King Jr. and other civil rights leaders was a hallmark of his tenure. Jackson was succeeded by T. J. Jamison, who served as president from 1982 to 1994 and was followed by Florida pastor Henry Lyons. Lyons was forced to resign because of legal and financial controversies and was succeeded by the president, William J. Shaw, in 1999. In response to the scandals of the Lyons tenure, Shaw promoted policies known as VISA—Vision, Integrity, Structure, and Accountability—in convention life.[78]

## Progressive National Baptist Convention

During Joseph Jackson's term as president of the NBC, Inc., a major controversy developed about denominational control and residual issues related to methods for securing civil rights. In 1956 certain members of the NBC sought to set tenure regulations for the convention president. L. V. Booth, Gardner Taylor, and Martin Luther King Jr. were among the ministers seeking to limit terms of convention officers. Their conflicts with Jackson and his supporters created differences over procedures and policies that led to the involvement of the federal courts in issues regarding voting processes at the

1961 convention. Jackson ultimately won the vote, and it appeared that the matter was closed. L. V. Booth (d. 2002), longtime Baptist pastor in Ohio, led a movement to begin a new denomination, and in 1961 the Progressive National Baptist Convention was born. Contending that they had been "expelled" from the NBC, numerous ministers insisted that they were distinct from the earlier "[Gardner] Taylor group." Rather, L. V. Booth summoned pastors to begin "an entirely new movement under new leadership. Persons who are concerned with redeeming the Baptist initiative and restoring a Democratic Thrust are invited."[79] The Progressive National Baptist Convention was born of those efforts.

The convention maintains associated relationship with the American Baptist Churches in the USA, with numerous churches "dually aligned" with both denominations. The denomination's mission endeavors are related to the Baptist Global Mission Bureau, and it has affiliation with the Urban League, the Southern Christian Leadership Conference, and the NAACP.[80]

## Newer Baptist Groups

During the latter twentieth century, several new groups of Baptists were organized, generally in response to developments within the Southern Baptist Convention. These "alliances" or "fellowships" were formed by moderates in the Southern Baptist Convention who finally decided that their efforts to thwart a "conservative take-over" of denominational boards and agencies were futile and that their energies might be better utilized in creating new ministries with like-minded and like-hearted individuals and churches. They seemed less willing to take the label of *denominations*, since many of their member churches also retained a de facto "dual alignment" with the old SBC and their own new organization, because denominations seemed in transition, and because they were hesitant to organize too elaborate a structure too quickly.

### Alliance of Baptists

The Alliance of Baptists is a relatively new Baptist organization, founded in 1986 under the name of the Southern Baptist Alliance. It was instituted largely in reaction to the increasingly rightward direction of the Southern Baptist Convention and the inability of moderates in the denomination to stop what they considered to be a takeover of trustee boards in convention agencies and seminaries. Founded on December 2, 1986, by a group of twenty-three individuals, the alliance drafted a purpose statement declaring that it was "an alliance of individuals and churches dedicated to the preservation of historic Baptist principles, freedoms and traditions and the continuance of our ministry and mission within the Southern Baptist Convention." In 1991 the phrase "within the Southern Baptist Convention" was abandoned. In 1992, in an effort to distinguish itself as a new gathering of Baptists, the organization changed its name to the Alliance of Baptists. Alan Neely, former SBC missionary and seminary professor, was named interim director, and in 1989 Baptist historian and ethicist Stan Hastey became the full-time executive director, with offices in Washington, DC.[81]

The Alliance is a loose confederation of churches participating together for fellowship and shared ministries in the United States and throughout the world. It was instrumental in founding a new seminary, Baptist Theological Seminary, in Richmond, Virginia, in 1988, and has developed connections with Baptist groups in Cuba, Zimbabwe, and Eastern Europe.

By 1992 the Alliance listed 2,331 "individual members" and 133 subscribing churches with a total membership of 73,496.[82] In the beginning at least, many of these churches retained some financial or traditional connection to the Southern Baptist Convention, with members often given the option of designating their funds to Alliance or SBC causes. By the early twenty-first century fewer Alliance churches were officially related to the SBC. The group meets annually and sponsors the Global Mission Offering, which is used for a variety of programs and grants to churches and schools. It also developed mechanisms to facilitate the licensure of hospital and military chaplains. Its ties are largely to congregations in the South, Southwest, and Midwest. In the early twenty-first century the Alliance had developed significant, if informal, connections to the United Church of Christ (UCC) and the Progressive National Baptists. Its more positive response as an "open and affirming" group toward women in ministry and homosexuals has often brought criticism from other Baptist groups.

### Cooperative Baptist Fellowship

The Cooperative Baptist Fellowship is another Baptist group that arose from the conflict in the Southern Baptist Convention. Conversations regarding the formation of the organization began at a Consultation attended by some 3,000 persons in Atlanta, Georgia, in 1990 after moderate Southern Baptists again lost in eleven years of attempts to elect a convention president who was

not aligned with conservative attempts to "take over" or "reclaim" control of
the SBC. Discussions at that meeting centered on distinguishing between the
Baptist visions evident among conservatives and moderates in the SBC.
These included biblical authority, theological education, mission, and
women in ministry.[83]

The Cooperative Baptist Fellowship (CBF) was officially begun a year
later at another Atlanta convocation. Its statement of purpose declared: "Our
purpose is to lead people to a saving knowledge of Jesus Christ and to carry
out the Great Commission [Matthew 28:19–20] through inclusive global mission in which all Baptists can participate." That statement was later revised to
read: "The Cooperative Baptist Fellowship is to enable the people of God to
carry out the Great Commission under the Lordship of Jesus Christ, in a fellowship where every Christian exercises God's gifts and calling."[84] The Coordinating Council of clergy and laity was chosen to guide the new organization, and Cecil Sherman, a longtime Southern Baptist pastor, was chosen
as the first director. He was succeeded by Daniel Vestal, another prominent
pastor and an unsuccessful SBC presidential candidate in 1990. In fact, Vestal
was the last moderate candidate to challenge conservatives for the presidency
of the SBC.

Based in Atlanta, Georgia, the CBF is another confederation or society
of Baptists with membership available to Baptist-related schools, individuals,
and churches. In one sense, it reflects many of the attributes of a denomination—funding missionaries and schools, validating chaplaincy candidates,
and promoting particular types of "moderate" Baptist identity. In another
sense, it is a loose-knit fellowship or society with many member churches
that retain connections to the SBC as well. Its annual meetings serve as something of a clearinghouse for a variety of parallel Baptist organizations related
to publication of literature, ethics, women in ministry, missions, theological
education, and peacemaking (to name only a few). Nonetheless, a growing
number of churches across the South and elsewhere in the nation have
stepped away from old SBC connections and now consider themselves CBF-
related churches. In 2003 the decision of the Baptist World Alliance to admit
the CBF to its membership prompted an immediate negative response from
representatives of the SBC and the decision of that Baptist organization to
begin a process of reducing funding to the international Baptist organization.

### State Baptist Convention Realignments

Amid the controversy in the SBC, various state Baptist conventions in the
SBC have realigned themselves in more conservative or more moderate di-

rections. The state conventions of Virginia and Texas made significant adjustments in their organizations during the 1990s that pointed them more toward the moderate position in denominational politics. This led to two new state conventions organized by conservatives, the Conservative Baptists of Virginia and the Southern Baptists of Texas. The SBC continues to recognize and receive funds from both groups. Other state conventions have remained formally intact but with a variety of funding and organizational models that tend to favor one side or the other or that allow for participation from both groups.

## Baptist Organizations: Permanent Transition

By the early twenty-first century it was clear that many if not all Baptist denominations and subgroups were experiencing a time of permanent transition in their corporate and institutional life. Old denominational alignments were fraying, disconnecting, or being renegotiated. Fewer and fewer Baptists thought of their primary religious identity in terms of a denominational identity. Localism and congregational autonomy, long present in Baptist life, became increasingly assertive in the new century. National denominations found funding and other forms of support increasingly difficult to secure. Considerable denominational "switching" was evident among Baptist church members, who often deserted the tradition for a wide variety of religious communions ranging from high church Anglicanism to Charismatic-Pentecostalism. Some Baptist churches were minimizing the Baptist name or dropping it all together. At the same time, new Baptist groups such as the Alliance of Baptists and the Cooperative Baptist Fellowship also appeared on the scene as a result of schism in older denominations, i.e., the SBC. The future promises to bring many changes to Baptist organizational life amid a growing challenge regarding the extension of Baptist identity to a new generation that is less interested in sectarian forms of Christian expression.

## CHAPTER SIX

# Bible, Ordinances, and Polity

## Debates and Divisions Among Baptists

"Where there are two Baptists, there are at least three opinions," so the saying goes, and that is often true. Baptist churches and denominations sometimes seem to be involved in perpetual controversies locally, regionally, nationally, and interpersonally. In fact, one could make the case that the entire Baptist system of theology and polity creates an ethos in which controversy is not simply possible, it is highly probable. Controversies over the Bible, baptism, communion, church membership, discipline, women in ministry and women's roles in the church, war, mission action, and ministerial authority, relations with other Christian and non-Christian groups, evangelism, and a wide variety of ethical issues abound in Baptist life. Some of the most enduring debates are related to the deepest sources of Baptist identity, among them attitudes toward the use and authority of the Bible, the meaning and interpretations of baptism and the Lord's Supper, and various ways of understanding the nature of the church, particularly local congregations.

This chapter surveys certain representative controversies as a way of identifying divisive issues and illustrating diverse Baptist responses that are evident from group to group and church to church.

### Baptists and the Bible: Debates Over Biblical Authority

There is no doubt that Baptists take very seriously their claim to be "people of the Book" and are committed to the authority of Holy Scripture for their understanding of the nature of faith, doctrine, and morals. Baptists teach, preach, and love the Bible as the primary source of authority for the individual and the church. They insist that to the best of their ability they understand their beliefs and practices to mirror those of the New Testament church and the norms it represents for Christian people. Baptists have often asserted that the Bible alone is their sole rule of faith beyond "man-made" creeds, confessions, or other ecclesiastical directives. Some even set their kind of biblical authority over against that of other Christians, and even against that of other Baptists. Jerry Falwell, Baptist pastor and television preacher, is among those who refer to themselves as "Bible-believing Christians," to be distinguished, it would seem, from those who claim to be Christians but do not believe the Bible.

Baptists have long been distinguished among Protestants for their basic knowledge of the Bible's content and their commitment to biblical exposition in the preaching and teaching ministries of the church. Their confessions of faith delineate doctrines—salvation, immersion, polity, church officers, and religious liberty—that include selected biblical references for validation. In most Baptist congregations, Sunday schools and other study groups provide extensive opportunity for the laity to investigate the history and contents of the Bible. Young people are taught Bible stories from an early age and in many Baptist communions are encouraged to memorize lengthy passages of Scripture.

Yet in spite of their commitment to the Bible, Baptists differ over how to interpret biblical content and the nature of biblical authority itself. Indeed, the Bible is at the center of every debate, division, and schism in Baptist life. Amid this concern for biblical authority are divisions over the meaning of the text and the proper method for interpreting it (hermeneutics). Baptists readily divide with other Christians and among themselves regarding the ways in which the Bible may be understood and applied. In other words, Baptists may be "people of the Book" (the Bible), but they do not always agree on what "the Book" actually says and how it is to be interpreted.

Disagreements over the correct or orthodox biblical doctrines were there almost from the beginning. General (Arminian) Baptists used the same Bible as Particular (Calvinist) Baptists, but the two groups held contradictory beliefs regarding the nature of salvation, election, free will, predestination, and other theological nonnegotiables. Seventh Day Baptists appeared in seventeenth-century England and America, convinced that Saturday was the biblically mandated day of worship. They insisted that numerous teachings from the "first covenant" (Old Testament) were still in effect and were not to be ignored.

Six Principle Baptists read Hebrews 6:1–2 as proof that they should observe the laying on of hands in two ways, once for all the newly baptized and again for those who were set aside for special ministries in the church (ministers/elders and deacons). Each of these groups believed that its dogmas came directly from the Scriptures. They all may legitimately claim the name Baptist, but they read the Bible in distinctly different ways.

## The Bible and Baptist Confessions of Faith

The first confessions of faith written by the earliest Baptists (in Amsterdam) did not contain a specific statement on Scriptures. The *Propositions and Conclusions* written by the (General) Baptists in 1612 declared:

> That the scriptures of the Old and New Testament are written for our instruction, 2 Tim. 3:16 & that we ought to search them for they testifie of CHRIST, Jn. 5:39. And therefore to be used with all reverence, as containing the Holy word of GOD, which only is our direction in all things whatsoever.[1]

The *Second London Confession*, a Particular Baptist document published in 1688, gave extensive attention to the doctrine of Scripture. It noted:

> The Holy Scripture is the only sufficient, certain, and infallible rule of all saving Knowledge, Faith, and Obedience; Although the light of Nature, and the works of Creation and Providence do so far manifest the goodness, wisdom and power of God, as to leave men unexcusable; yet are they not sufficient to give that knowledge of god and His will, which is necessary to Salvation."[2]

This statement was reproduced in the *Philadelphia Confession of Faith*, an early Calvinist confession approved for use by the Philadelphia Baptist Association in 1742.

The *New Hampshire Confession of Faith*, 1833, offered a "modified Calvinist" approach to Baptist theology. Its section on Holy Scripture notes:

> We believe [that] the Holy Bible was written by men divinely inspired, and is a perfect treasure of heavenly instruction; that it has God for its author, salvation for its end, and truth, without any mixture of error, for its matter; that it reveals the principles by which God will judge us; and

therefore is, and shall remain to the end of the world, the true centre of Christian union, and the supreme standard by which all human conduct, creeds, and opinions should be tried.[3]

Clearly, Baptists have not hesitated to affirm the Bible as a divinely inspired guide for the individual and the church in matters of faith, salvation, and doctrine. In short, Baptists agree over the centrality of the Bible as the "word of God for the people of God," yet by the late nineteenth century they were beginning to debate the nature and meaning of biblical inspiration itself. Some even chose to write their theories of biblical inspiration directly into their confessions of faith. The *Articles of Faith* of the Baptist Bible Union of America, founded in 1921 as an early fundamentalist group, is very specific about the authority and inspiration of Scripture, with particular attention to the doctrine of biblical inerrancy. It notes:

> By "THE HOLY BIBLE" we mean that collection of sixty-six books, from Genesis to Revelation, which, as originally written, does not contain and convey the word of god, but IS the very Word of God.
>  By "INSPIRATION" we mean that the books of the Bible were written by holy men of old, as they were moved by the Holy Spirit, in such a definite way that their writings were supernaturally inspired and free from error, as no other writings have ever been or ever will be inspired.[4]

In 1970, the First Baptist Church of Dallas, Texas, amended its version of the *Baptist Faith and Message*, the confession of faith of the Southern Baptist Convention, to include a theory of inspiration asserting "that the Scripture is inerrant and infallible in its original manuscript which is taken to be verbally inspired."[5]

These confessional statements illustrate the centrality of the Bible in Baptist life amid different ways of articulating the nature of biblical authority. During the latter twentieth century, debates arose, less over the authority of the Bible than over the definition of biblical inspiration.

## *Biblical Criticism and Biblical Inerrancy: Debating Inspiration*

Throughout the twentieth century, Baptists in the United States divided over modern theories of biblical interpretation and inerrancy. Historical-critical methods of Bible study encouraged analysis of texts by using the tools of modern scholarship, bringing Scripture under the same scrutiny as any other ancient document. William Brackney delineated the "classic concerns" evident in this method of hermeneutical investigation, noting:

> For instance, in light of physical science, could the events described as miracles in the Bible actually have violated the laws of nature? The literal, bodily resurrection of Jesus Christ was an all-important miracle, most Baptists thought. Second, did the biblical figures have the ability to foretell specifically the events of the future, or was "prophecy" written after the events?[6]

Brackney suggests that during the early twentieth century Baptist scholars generally fell into two groups regarding the modern use of the Bible. The first he calls the "orthodox" movement, composed of such scholars as Alvah Hovey at Newton Seminary and E. Y. Mullins of the Southern Baptist Theological Seminary. They tended to spiritualize or take a more devotional approach to difficult passages in the biblical text and "assumed a literary and theological unity" of the Testaments, Old and New.[7] They affirmed the absolute veracity of the text but often sought to avoid debates about the Bible's inerrancy.

A second group gave greater acceptance to modernist approaches to the text. These included Walter Rauschenbusch and Shailer Mathews, founders of the Social Gospel movement, as well as theologians William Newton Clarke and William Adams Brown. They denied the unity of Scripture, a literal reading of the Genesis accounts of creation, and, in many cases, the literal belief in Christ's virgin birth.[8] Harry Emerson Fosdick, one of the most prominent liberal Baptists of the twentieth century, denied that the virgin birth was "an historic fact" and acknowledged that there were many "lovers of the Bible" who never thought of the Bible in terms of its plenary (full) verbal inerrancy. Rather, he concluded, "that static and mechanical theory of inspiration seems to them a positive peril to the spiritual life."[9]

Fosdick's views and ministry were anathema to a third group of Baptists, who accepted the plenary verbal theory of biblical inspiration, evident in the complete inerrancy of the text. They believed that the entire history of the Baptist denomination was centered in the absolute veracity of Scripture as expressed in the doctrine of biblical inerrancy. They insisted that the Bible was infallible and inerrant in every topic it discussed, not only doctrine, faith, and morals, but also science, biology, history, and other matters addressed in the text. Baptist leaders who favored biblical inerrancy in the early twentieth century included William Bell Riley, J. C. Massey, A. C. Dixon, and J. Frank

Norris. By the 1920s those men were representative of a large number of pastors and laity, north and south, who were increasingly concerned about the liberal drift in Baptist leadership and in Baptist-related schools of higher education. Speaking at a conference of conservative Baptists held in Buffalo, New York, in 1920, A. C. Dixon declared: "One of the greatest needs of the Christian Church today is a university with the Bible at its center as the standard of all truth, religious, moral, historic, and scientific, and the Lord Jesus Christ preeminent in the realm of knowledge as in all other realms."[10]

Inerrantists believe that the Bible is verbally inspired in every area it addresses, not only on such obviously "religious" issues as faith, ethics, and doctrine but also, when addressed, biology, geography, history, astronomy, and all other areas of life and thought. The theory of inerrancy means that the text, some suggest only in its original manuscripts, is completely without error. Those whose methods of interpretation point out errors or inconsistencies are guilty of the worst of heresies, undermining the authoritative text of Scripture as inspired by the Holy Spirit. For some Baptist churches and denominations, biblical inerrancy is the nonnegotiable norm for interpreting the authority and inspiration of the Bible. Others affirm the authority of the Bible but resist theories of inspiration as normative for all who would claim the Baptist name. Still others are thoroughgoing liberals who value the Bible and affirm its significance for the church but decry inerrancy and infallibility as rational categories that undermine serious biblical scholarship. Throughout the twentieth century, and into the twenty-first, Baptist denominations and other factions have divided over issues related to biblical inspiration. A few specific examples must suffice.

### The Northern Baptist Convention

As noted earlier, the Northern Baptist Convention (NBC) was officially formed in 1907 as an outgrowth of numerous Baptist societies that continued their individual activities after the schism with Southern Baptists in 1845. The convention and its related societies funded missions, publications, and other church resources and maintained direct and indirect connections with a variety of Baptist colleges and seminaries. As a growing number of individuals became concerned about the rising influence of liberal approaches to the Bible and other doctrines, inerrantists in the NBC called for a renewed emphasis on the "fundamentals" of the faith. In 1922 they embarked on an effort to make the *New Hampshire Confession of Faith* the official doctrinal statement of the denomination. Instead, the convention simply reaffirmed the New Testament as the "all-sufficient ground of our faith and practice." That statement, William Brackney notes, "was broad enough to include almost all churches in the Convention but not too broad for many fundamentalists." It continues to be the only statement on Scripture approved by the group, now known as the American Baptist Churches, USA.[11] During the 1920s, some fundamentalist-minded Baptists left the NBC over that decision, and a larger group departed in the 1950s with the formation of the Conservative Baptist Convention, a new denomination born of issues related to the authority of Scripture and the meaning of Baptists' worldwide mission.

## The Southern Baptist Convention

The Southern Baptist Convention generally escaped serious schism during the controversies of the 1920s, largely because its churches and leaders were more uniformly conservative and because fundamentalists in the South tended to challenge the denominational system as illustrative of unbiblical and un-Baptist ways of organizing the churches. They did, however, approve their first confession of faith, the *Baptist Faith and Message*, in 1925, primarily in response to the controversies rocking American religious life. As noted, that confession has been revised several times, most notably in 1963 and 2000, each time related to questions of biblical authority. The statement on the Holy Scriptures in each of the editions illustrates changes in denominational concerns for the authenticity of the biblical text.

The 1925 article is taken largely from the *New Hampshire Confession*:

We believe that the Holy Bible was written by men divinely inspired, and is a perfect treasure of heavenly instruction; that it has God for its author, salvation for its end, and truth, without any mixture of error, for its matter; that it reveals the principles by which God will judge us; and therefore is, and will remain to the end of the world, the true center of Christian union, and the supreme standard by which all human conduct, creeds and religious opinions should be tried.[12]

The 1963 revision states:

The Holy Bible was written by men divinely inspired and is the record of God's revelation of Himself to man. It is a perfect treasure of divine instruction. It has God for its author, salvation for its end, and truth, without any mixture of error, for its matter. It reveals the principles by which God judges us; and therefore is, and will remain to the end of the world, the true center of Christian union, and the supreme standard by which all human conduct, creeds, and religious opinions should be tried. The criterion by which the Bible is to be interpreted is Jesus Christ.[13]

The 2000 revision essentially repeats the earlier statement but changes the reference to Christ at the end in ways that affirm him as central to God's revelation.[14]

These modifications are illustrative of a decades-long struggle over biblical inspiration that tore apart the Southern Baptist Convention (SBC). Debates over the Bible, modernity, and science were evident in the SBC as early as the 1920s, when schools like North Carolina's Wake Forest College began teaching evolution. It was manifest in the 1960s when Ralph Elliott, professor of Old Testament at Midwestern Baptist Theological Seminary in Kansas City, Missouri, published a book titled *The Message of Genesis*, using historical-critical methods in interpreting the Genesis texts. Elliott suggested that many of the stories in Genesis should be understood as "parables" rather than as literal explanations of the world, that certain traditions developed that were not to be understood as "historical," and that claims of longevity attributed to certain biblical characters were probably not to be taken literally.[15] Elliott responded by reasserting his commitment to biblical authority and Baptist freedoms. He wrote:

> This I know. I love the Bible with my very life and bow before it as inspired, authoritative, and all sufficient guide for life and faith. But I still have to interpret. I would hope that the Holy Spirit would continue to breathe over its pages within the depths of my life that when I am caught in error I may see and admit and better still, that its illumination might guide my heart and head in ways of truth

He concluded with the insistence that his commitment to Scripture was "central," but his "methodology is as varied as are Baptists."[16]

Many Southern Baptist leaders were not convinced. Since Elliott was a professor at a seminary owned and operated by the SBC, conservatives called for an investigation and urged his removal. The school administration initially permitted Elliott to retain his position, but he was subsequently removed in 1962, not for what he had written but for his refusal to cease publication of the monograph. The "Elliott Controversy" was at least one influence on the decision of the convention to revise its confession of faith in 1963. It illustrates the struggle between conservative-fundamentalists and liberal-moderates in one segment of the Baptist family. Earlier, the convention passed a resolution affirming the "Bible as the authoritative, authentic, infallible Word of God."[17]

Not long afterward, "messengers" to the SBC voted to cease publication of the first volume of the Broadman Commentary series because the British author, Henton Davies, also used the historical-critical method in his survey of Genesis and set forth the multiple-document theory that the first book of the Torah represented not one story written by Moses but diverse stories from various periods of Hebrew history. The volume was withdrawn, and a new commentary was written by another author.

Biblical inerrancy was central to the effort of conservatives to gain control of the convention from "moderates," whom they claimed had dominated SBC life long enough and in the process had facilitated creeping liberalism in the institutions if not in the churches. In 1979 the conservatives began a successful process whereby they elected a series of convention presidents committed to appointing only inerrantists to the trustee boards of denominational agencies. Moderates fielded their own candidates but were consistently unsuccessful. Within a decade the changes had begun, and by the 1990s faculties and administrators in the six seminaries owned by the denomination had been replaced with those who accepted a thoroughgoing inerrantist approach to biblical studies. By 2000, the mission agencies had been reorganized and the confession of faith revised in more conservative directions.

Throughout the controversy, conservatives insisted that the central issue was the "total trustworthiness" (inerrancy) of the Bible. In 1987, conservative Baptist leader David Dockery wrote that inerrancy meant that

> when all the facts are known, the Bible (in its autographs) properly interpreted in light of which culture and communication means had developed by the time of its composition will be shown to be completely true (and therefore not false) in all that it affirms, to the degree of precision intended by the author, in all matters relating to God and his creation (including matters of history, geography, science, and other disciplines addressed in Scripture).[18]

Yet even the inerrantists could not agree on which specific theory of inspiration was appropriate to the doctrine of biblical inspiration. Dockery traces at least six different types of inerrancy claimed by varying Baptist individuals and groups:

1. *Naïve inerrancy* assumes that God actually dictated the Bible to the writers.

2. *Absolute inerrancy* affirms that the Bible is accurate and true in all matters and that the writers intended to give a considerable amount of exact data in such matters.

3. *Balanced inerrancy* affirms that the Bible is completely true in all the Bible affirms, to the degree of precision intended by the writer.

4. *Limited inerrancy* maintains that the Bible is inerrant in matters of salvation and ethics or faith and practice.

5. *Functional inerrancy* contends that the Bible inerrantly accomplishes its purpose. This does not equate inerrancy with factuality.

6. *Errant but authoritative* is a view built on an encounter view of inspiration. It sees the Bible not as revelation but as a pointer to a personal encounter with God. Questions of faith and falseness are of little concern.[19]

In a work titled *Baptists and the Bible*, Tom Nettles and Rush Bush surveyed a variety of British and American Baptist leaders regarding the nature and authority of Scripture. They believed that Baptists were essentially inerrantist in their historic views of biblical authority and concluded:

> "Infallible" is a time-honored expression used by Baptists to describe the result of inspiration. . . . They used "infallible" as a word that made a theoretical claim about the nature of Scripture as an inspired volume—it is inherently truthful in facts and ideas and is, therefore, incapable of misleading the careful interpreter in what it affirms or denies.[20]

They generally interpreted Baptist use of words such as "inspiration," "infallibility," and "authoritative" to refer to inerrancy. Not all Baptists agree with that position.

During the 1970s and 1980s conservatives in the SBC raised an alarm against what they believed to be threats to biblical authority throughout convention life, especially in seminaries and colleges. They believed that the use or misuse of the historical-critical method of biblical studies was sowing doubts about the veracity of the text itself among a new generation of Baptist ministers and laity. They published books and articles insisting that certain professors and pastors were undermining biblical inerrancy and setting the convention on a "slippery slope" toward liberalism and denial of the veracity of Scripture. Prominent conservative leader Paige Patterson wrote:

> Until a factual or theological error is actually substantiated beyond every reasonable doubt, it remains for Southern Baptists and other evan-

gelical scholars to use the historical-critical method only insofar as it helps us capture meaning and never to the extent that it risks breeding doubt in a malleable public. Whenever the critics beckon us to embark upon an odyssey to locate a canon within the canon, we must stoutly resist, knowing that such a pilgrimage is as futile and as destructive as was the search for the Holy Grail.[21]

Walter Harrelson, American Baptist leader and dean of Vanderbilt Divinity School, responded:

And those who are content simply to affirm the literal and historical and factual truth of the entire Bible, without regard to time and circumstance or the purpose of the Bible's authors and transmitters of tradition, run the risk of doing the very last thing that they wish to do: making the Bible irrelevant to the needs and concerns of contemporary men, women, and children, or imposing upon them a mistaken notion of what the Bible makes central in faith and in life.[22]

He concluded: "At this time in our Baptist history, faithful historical-critical approaches to the Scripture can help us to move beyond the impasse that we confront. It [sic] can do so by showing evangelicals and nonevangelicals alike the critical necessity of passing on intact the truth and power of the Bible." Patterson and Harrelson illustrate that two deeply committed Baptists could radically disagree over methods for interpreting the Bible and using it in the churches.

During the 1980s and 1990s, debates raged in the Southern Baptist Convention between inerrantists and non-inerrantists over the nature of biblical inspiration, the veracity of the biblical text, and the implications of biblical authority for all areas of church life. Inerrantists charged that liberals in seminaries, colleges, and churches were undermining biblical authority in ways that were detrimental to evangelical outreach, church growth, and the truth of Christian faith. Non-inerrantists warned that debates over theories of biblical inspiration were destructive to the unity of the convention and its overarching tasks of evangelism and missions. Once conservatives gained control of the national denomination, the volatile rhetoric cooled a bit. Professors and missionaries who were unable to conform to the inerrantist view of Scripture and other conservative demands departed the convention, as did dissident moderates, who began to form new organizations.

The popular use of the Bible illustrates another facet of inerrancy issues beyond the more academic and esoteric debates between scholars. Throughout the public debate a kind of popular inerrancy prevailed and continues to prevail among many Baptists, both clergy and laity. It is the belief that the text of the Bible is so infallible that any effort to challenge even the theory of inerrancy and propose other ways of understanding the authority of the Bible is to deny the truthfulness of the text altogether. In other words, any equivocation on the doctrine of inerrancy would place one on the slippery slope toward a completely liberal or antagonistic approach to the veracity of all Scripture. Inerrancy or nothing has often been the popular response to the debate. Moderates and liberals who sought to nuance the discussion were dismissed as denying the text entirely or in the first stages of what would lead to such a denial.

By the 1990s inerrancy had become the normative public hermeneutic for the Southern Baptist Convention, and those who did not accept it were forced to go elsewhere or at least give up efforts to offer alternative views. An inerrantist interpretation of the articles in the convention's confession of faith was required of all denominational employees, including seminary professors and missionaries. SBC leaders were convinced that the reassertion of biblical inerrancy was a "course correction" that turned the convention from the path of liberalism back toward the traditional orthodoxy inherent in Baptist theology.

### Independent Baptists

Independent Baptists eschewed denominations and grounded their conservative theology in biblical inerrancy that bordered on literalism. Early leaders of the movement such as J. Frank Norris, pastor of First Baptist Church in Fort Worth, Texas, and Lee Robertson, of Tennessee Temple Baptist Church in Chattanooga, believed that their calling was to rescue Baptists from the "slippery slope" of liberalism. Norris wrote:

> Whenever you find a preacher who takes the Bible allegorically and figuratively . . . that preacher is preaching an allegorical gospel which is no gospel. I thank God for a literal Christ; for a literal salvation. There is literal sorrow; literal death; literal hell; and, thank God, there is a literal heaven.[23]

They asserted that many of the Baptist denominations had turned away from the Bible in their development of denominational bureaucracy, mission boards, ecumenical dialogues with unbiblical denominations and in their support for colleges and seminaries that accepted liberal ideas born of Darwinism, historical-critical methods of biblical studies, and other modernist-oriented issues.

As biblical separatists, Independent Baptists are among the most outspoken defenders of inerrancy, with emphases bordering on literalism. Some link such literalism with the King James Version of the Bible (1611). Indeed, a surprising number of fundamentalist Baptist churches promote the KJV as the only truly inspired English translation. The *Statement of Faith* of the Baptist Bible Fellowship, based in Springfield, Missouri, notes:

> We are Bible Believing Baptists. A Bible Believing Baptist is one who believes in a supernatural Bible preserved for us in the King James Version, which tells of a supernatural Christ, Who had a supernatural birth, Who spoke supernatural words, Who performed supernatural miracles, Who lived a supernatural life, Who died a supernatural death, Who rose in supernatural power, Who ascended in supernatural splendor, Who intercedes as a supernatural priest and Who will one day return in supernatural glory to establish a supernatural kingdom on the earth.[24]

The Baptist Bible Fellowship links biblical inerrancy with the foundation of Christian doctrine in its formal *Statement of Faith*. It declares:

> 1. By "The Holy Bible" we mean that collection of sixty-six books, from Genesis to Revelation, which, as originally written does not only contain and convey the Word of God, but IS the very Word of God.
> 2. By "inspiration" we mean that the books of the Bible were written by holy men of old, as they were moved by the Holy Spirit, in such a definite way that their writings were supernaturally and verbally inspired and free from error, as no other writings have ever been or ever will be inspired.[25]

Thus these Baptists insist that the original manuscripts of the Old and New Testaments were completely without error and that they are the direct word of God. Their belief in the supernatural nature of the text and its verbal inspiration suggests that the biblical materials are indeed the direct words of God.

## Baptists and the Bible

All of this discussion indicates that Baptists talk incessantly about the Bible, affirming its authority while teaching and preaching from its hallowed pages.

Increasingly, however, Baptist leaders across the theological spectrum are forced to recognize that a growing number of people in their churches lack basic knowledge of Bible content and information. Even many faithful members are aware of certain prominent books and passages but are limited in their ability to deal with or identify with the text itself. In a real sense, divisions over the Bible inside Baptist communities are less related to theories about the text than to the hermeneutics or method of interpreting the text itself. There is little doubt that all Baptist traditions face this challenge in the twenty-first century.

## Baptism: Unifying and Dividing

Baptism by immersion is at the center of Baptist identity. All Baptist congregations in the United States and around the world practice the baptism of Christian believers, carried out by dipping the entire body in water. It represents identification with Jesus' baptism as described in the gospels. It is also a sign of death and resurrection, in which the believer is "buried with Christ in baptism, raised to walk in newness of life." Immersion is also a symbol of cleansing from sin and an "outward and visible sign" of the inward transformation of divine grace. William Brackney noted that baptism by immersion remains the "essence" of Baptist distinctiveness. At the same time, perhaps no other issue has been as consistently divisive as baptism in Baptist theology and practice. Baptists unite and divide over the meaning of baptism and its role in Christian communities.

The earliest Baptist communions in Amsterdam and London did not practice immersion. They seemed less concerned with the mode of baptism than with establishing churches composed of believers, each of whom confessed personal faith in Jesus. Baptism was administered only after the proper profession had been made and affirmed by the community of faith. Since infants could not make such a profession, and because no evidence of infant baptism could be found in the New Testament, Baptists rejected the practice. Those Baptists who had received baptism as infants generally denied the validity of that earlier event and received what they believed to be the appropriate (New Testament) baptism.

The earliest mode of baptism was not immersion, but trine affusion, pouring water on the head three times in the name of the Father, the Son, and the Holy Spirit. This "drenching" of the new believers was normative among both General and Particular Baptist congregations until sometime around 1641, when immersion became normative, probably through the influence of the Collegiant Mennonites in Amsterdam. They had instituted immersion baptism earlier in their history, and British Particular Baptists apparently visited them and brought the practice back to London, instituting it in the early 1640s. Baptists pointed to the New Testament, interpreting the Greek word for *baptize* to mean immersion, and sought to mirror the baptism of Jesus by John the Baptizer in the River Jordan. Immersion remains the normative baptismal mode for Baptist congregations.

Early immersions in England and the America were conducted outdoors in rivers and streams, a scandalous activity in seventeenth-century England, where infant baptism was the norm. In 1646 Daniel Featley, a prominent Anglican critic, wrote with disdain of the baptismal practices of the new sect present in England:

> They preach, and print, and practice their Hereticall impieties openly; they hold their Conventicles weekly in our chiefe Cities, and Suburbs thereof, and there prophesie by turnes; and . . . they build one another in the faith of their sect, to the ruine of their soules; they flock in great multitudes to their Jordans, and both Sexes enter into the River, and are dipt after their manner with a kinde of spell containing the heads of their erroneous tenets, and their engaging themselves in their schismaticall Covenants, and (if I may so speak) combination of separation. And as they defile our Rivers with their impure washings, and our Pulpits with their false prophecies and phanaticall enthusiasms, so the Presses sweat and groan under the load of their blasphemies.[26]

While the New Testament speaks of the church as having "One Lord, one faith, one baptism," Baptists debated the meaning of the act as practiced in other denominations and within their own fellowships. Questions arose over the role of baptism in determining church membership, the place of the non-immersed in church life, and the relationship with other Christian denominations in which infant baptism was normative.

Early in Baptist history, divisions soon arose over "open" or "closed" membership and "open" and "closed" communion. Some congregations accepted both the immersed and the non-immersed into membership. For example, the congregation in Bedford, England, served by John Bunyan, the author of *Pilgrims Progress* and *Grace Abounding to the Chief of Sinners*, permitted members who had received infant baptism, believers' baptism, or no baptism at all. Other congregations were stricter, offering membership only to those who had been baptized (by immersion) following a profession of faith.

In the United States, denominational interchange and ecumenical dialogue raised numerous dilemmas regarding membership regulations in Baptist churches. When non-Baptists chose to join Baptist churches, questions arose as to whether to accept those who had not received baptismal immersion but had been professing Christians for years. Baptists thus had to decide if they would require immersion of all members or allow options for individuals who had received baptism by other modes in other denominations.

Likewise, congregations divided over admission to communion, with some permitting all professing Christians to receive the Lord's Supper, whatever mode of baptism they had received. Other churches practiced closed communion, allowing only immersed believers to be admitted to the table. These practices continued to dominate baptismal debates among Baptists into the twenty-first century.

## Baptism and Baptist Landmarkism

Perhaps no movement of Baptists shaped baptismal debates in the United States like the phenomenon known as Old Landmarkism. This effort, begun in the South in the 1850s, linked Baptist identity to a succession of churches from the New Testament era, largely on the basis of baptismal and congregational purity. It began over a question of Baptist relationships with other denominations, primarily the issue of whether "pedo-Baptist" ministers (those who baptized infants) were eligible to preach in the Baptist church and was raised by J. R. Graves, pastor of the First Baptist Church in Nashville, Tennessee, in 1859. In response to Graves's request, J. M. Pendleton, pastor of the First Baptist Church in Bowling Green, Kentucky, published a volume titled *An Old Landmark Reset*, in which he explored the definition of a true New Testament church and set Baptists over against all other Christian communions. Pendleton concluded that non-Baptist ministers should not be permitted to address Baptist congregations, since they were not members of the "true church" and lacked the proper form of baptism. Their infant baptism had no precedent in the New Testament, and therefore they were unbaptized. Their churches—Methodist, Presbyterian, Lutheran, and other Protestant groups—were not churches at all, but "societies" where Christianity could be practiced in a remedial way, outside genuine ecclesial community. Using Proverbs 22:28, "Remove not the ancient landmarks which thy fathers hath set," Pendleton concluded that all other denominations were not true churches since they lacked the "landmarks" of ecclesiastical veracity. Landmarkism, therefore, was a search for the true church, with the resulting conclusion that Baptists alone had maintained genuine New Testament faith in a succession of churches that stretched from Jesus and John the Baptist to their Baptist counterparts in Nashville, Bowling Green, and elsewhere.

J. R. Graves soon published a text titled *Old Landmarkism: What Is It?* in which he distinguished seven "marks" of the true church, each maintained solely by Baptists:

1. There is no [universal] church, but a body of immersed believers, who have been immersed by one who has himself been immersed, after conversion and a hope of salvation.

2. There are authorized no ministers, but immersed preachers, acting under the authority of a regular church—and who have been ordained by a presbytery of immersed believers.

3. There is no peculiar sanctity to a house of worship, no special sacredness to a pulpit, nor is one spot or locality . . . more consecrated than another; except as the associations connected with its occupancy, or the purpose to which it is devoted, render it sacred.

4. Since nothing is more evident than the fact, that we teach more effectively by example than by precept—therefore, so long as we appropriate our pulpit for official preaching of the gospel by those whom we consider duly baptized and ordained to the ministerial office, it is equally evident that is it improper for us to invite those teachers to occupy them, when we know they are neither baptized nor ordained, and especially since they claim it to be, and construe the act on our part into a recognition of their claims, and thus confirm their followers in error.

5. That a body of immersed believers is the highest ecclesiastical authority in the world, and the only tribunal for the trial of cases of discipline . . . and no association or convention can impose a moral obligation upon the constituent parts composing them.

6. That no association or convention has the right to demand support for any project or scheme which they have originated, but may only recommend, advise, and urge the performance of duty in subservience to the great Christian voluntary principle.

7. That Baptists never dissented from anything but sin—and are not protestants, but have been, in all ages, the Repudiators of Popery.[27]

Landmarkism appeared at a time when denominational competition was extremely high, with multiple groups attempting to prove that their beliefs and practices were closest to the original Christian communities. Since Baptists had no prominent historical founders comparable to Martin Luther, John Calvin, John Knox, or John Wesley, their claims to originality rested with a succession of dissenting churches across Christian history, outside and over against Roman Catholicism. These dissenters, dubbed "Baptist in everything but name," included Montanists (second century), Paulicians (third century), Donatists (fourth century), Albigensians/Cathari (thirteenth century), Waldensians (fourteenth century), and Anabaptists (sixteenth century). Of course, these groups were anything but Baptist, with few Baptist characteristics. For example, the medieval sect known as the Cathari or the Albigensians, eschewed baptism and the Lord's Supper and denied the flesh so vehemently that some even attempted to starve themselves to death.

Landmarkism was in large part a response to the Restorationist movement identified with such nineteenth-century individuals as Barton Warren Stone and Alexander Campbell. Though they differed on many doctrines and practices, both Stone and Campbell believed that denominationalism had obscured the teachings of the New Testament church. They sought a church composed of "Christians only" and believed that they were restoring the church as it was in the first century. Restorationists rejected all practices that could not be documented in the New Testament, including reverend titles, denominational systems, mission boards, and other "hierarchies." They practiced immersion baptism and administered communion every Sunday. Campbell and others insisted that faith was a simple confession that Jesus is the messiah and that baptism was an essential experience administered "for the remission of sins." Many Baptist congregations were divided over Restorationism, with some congregational majorities voting to join the "Christians."

Landmark Baptists challenged this effort, while insisting that they had no need to restore anything, since they had remained faithful to the New Testament norms in an unbroken line since the first century. They were particularly distressed about the Restorationist emphasis on baptism and the implication that it was "essential" for salvation. Thus Landmarkists led a movement that affected Baptist life significantly through an emphasis on the symbolic rather than the sacramental nature of baptism. Baptists soon declared that "baptism is not salvific," or "baptism will not save you," assertions that led to innumerable Baptist-Restorationist debates in communities around the country.

Landmarkism shaped Baptist polity by rejecting infant baptism and requiring rebaptism of all the pedo-baptists who joined their churches. They even required the rebaptism of persons who had been immersed in non-Baptist churches (a practice they called "alien immersion"). For example, a person who had been immersed by Methodists, Presbyterians, or Restorationists would still have to be re-immersed if he or she joined a Landmark Baptist church.

Some Baptist denominations, such as the American Baptist Association, the Baptist Missionary Association, and certain Independent Baptist groups, are thoroughly Landmark in their theology. Other Baptist churches, while not Landmark, continue to promote Landmark approaches to baptism, requiring rebaptism of all unimmersed people who seek to join their number. Still others require rebaptism only of those baptized as infants. Some, however, maintain an "open" baptismal policy, receiving professing Christians into membership without requiring rebaptism but practicing immersion as the norm for new converts. Intermarriage, ecumenism, and denominational "switching" led many unimmersed Christians into Baptist churches, raising these questions in churches that had not dealt with them before.

### Candidates for Baptism: The Age of Accountability

Since they did not baptize infants, the early Baptists were compelled to deal with two important issues. The first involved the eternal state of unbaptized infants. Would unbaptized infants be saved? As noted, some Calvinistic Baptists believed that only *elect* infants would be saved. Non-elect infants, like non-elect adults, were totally depraved and cut off from Divine grace. Arminian Baptists, on the other hand, insisted that all infants were "under grace" and would receive salvation if they died in infancy. The assertion of infant innocence raised a second question: When are human beings morally responsible and therefore in need of salvation? When are they appropriate candidates for salvation and baptism?

Again, Baptists in the United States differ over the proper age and time for baptism. Some look to an "age of accountability" as that time when individuals move from the age of innocence to the beginning of moral responsibility. It is the period when one recognizes right from wrong and stands under the judgment of God. While few Baptists set a specific age for this moral transformation, it is generally thought to occur in adolescence, perhaps even childhood.

Likewise, while they do not baptize infants, Baptists give significant attention to the nurture of children, teaching Bible stories and Christian ideals. Some adults reared in Baptist churches confess that they never knew a time when they did not "love Jesus" or consider themselves a Christian. Thus many Baptist communions baptize adolescents or young adults who choose to profess faith in Christ. Some churches have lowered the age of baptism to middle childhood and younger. A significant number of Baptist congregations baptize children between the ages of eight and eleven. In some churches baptismal candidates are as young as five or six.

The baptism of preschool children illustrates the concern of some parents that their children at some mysterious moment might cross into the age of accountability, die without having made the necessary profession of faith, and be sent to hell. Those ministers who baptize preschoolers may insist that the biblical norm for faith and baptism is not limited to adults but extends to those who have an "experience of grace." They believe that children are capable of such an experience and are fit candidates for baptism and church membership.

Other Baptist communions do not rush to baptize children. Primitive and Old Regular Baptists seem less concerned about the age of baptism, since in their theology no one who is in the elect will depart this world without having been saved. Thus these traditions often extend the age of baptism to a much later time of life. The average baptismal age among Primitive and Old Regular Baptists is generally between twenty and thirty years of age.

The lowering of the baptismal age in some Baptist churches has produced another phenomenon, the rebaptism of Baptists who in adulthood concluded that they did not correctly understand what they had done as children. Thus they repudiate the earlier baptism as administered when they were not really Christians, "re-profess" their faith, and are again immersed. Some individuals have done this multiple times.

The baptism of children who are again baptized when they reach adulthood is a serious theological problem for the Baptist churches that permit the practice. It suggests that (1) Baptists need to revisit their theology of conversion, what it means, when it occurs, and how it is secured; (2) Baptists need to rethink their understanding of baptism and its relationship to the age of accountability; and (3) decisions to baptize children require extensive efforts to aid the baptized in understanding the nature of that commitment and nurturing a sense of Christian maturity. A "mediated memory" might be helpful, whereby the community of faith guides children in reflecting on the meaning of their baptism as they move toward adulthood. Simply rebaptizing those who were baptized as children is a serious problem for a believers' church.

## Baptists and the Lord's Supper

### *The Supper and Its Meaning*

The Lord's Supper is the second sacrament, or ordinance, practiced by Baptist churches throughout the world. Baptist approaches to the Lord's Supper (communion) generally mirror those of other Protestant denominations and involve a basic reenactment of Jesus' last meal shared with his disciples before his death. The observance is described in this passage taken from 1 Corinthians 11:23–26 (REB):

> For the tradition which I handed on to you came to me from the Lord himself: that on the night of his arrest the Lord Jesus took bread, and after giving thanks to God broke it and said: "This is my body, which is for you: do this in memory of me." In the same way he took the cup after supper, and said, "This cup is the new covenant sealed by my blood. Whenever you drink it, do this in memory of me." For every time you eat this bread and drink this cup, you proclaim the death of the Lord, until he comes.

When Baptist churches celebrate the Lord's Supper, these or similar passages are read. Prayers are then offered by a minister or a deacon, and deacons then distribute the "elements," the bread and a small cup of grape juice (seldom wine), to the waiting congregation. Unleavened communion wafers or pieces of bread, prepackaged or baked by members of the congregation, are commonly used. In most churches, trays are used to distribute individual glasses or cups containing a small amount of grape juice. Wine, used normatively in Baptist communion services until the late nineteenth and early twentieth centuries, has largely been abandoned in response to the temperance movement. While a limited number of churches in the Baptist family use wine in communion, most continue to use unfermented grape juice, a practice that emerged during the temperance movement of the twentieth century. One distributor has even developed a pull-tab package that contains both bread and juice and allows for easy preparation and distribution. Statistically, few Baptist churches administer communion every week. Most observe the ordinance on the first Sunday of the month or once a quarter.

Some Baptist ministers wear pulpit robes when communion is administered in their congregations, others wear business suits. In some churches, especially those related to African American communities, deacons and ministers alike often wear white gloves as a sign of reverence and dignity in the distribution of the elements. Some congregations use a common cup and invite participants to come forward to the communion table or chancel to receive. A few have begun to use both fermented and unfermented wine, offering recipients a choice of those elements.

As to the meaning of the Supper, Baptists deny the Roman Catholic view sometimes known as transubstantiation, the belief that through the words of institution offered at the altar during the celebration of the mass, the elements of bread and wine are miraculously transformed into the very body and blood of Jesus Christ. The *Second London Confession* (1688) stated specifically:

> That doctrine which maintains a change of the substance of Bread and Wine, into the substance of Christs [*sic*] body and blood (commonly called Transubstantiation) by consecration of a Priest, or by any other way, is repugnant not to Scripture alone, but even to common sense and reason.[28]

Most would reject Martin Luther's theology of "real presence," whereby the elements, while not transformed into Christ's very body and blood, are nonetheless evidence of Christ's physical participation in the bread and wine. In this view, Jesus' words "this is my body" were taken literally, and his physical presence was experienced in the Supper.

When it comes to a theology of the Supper, Baptists generally move between the theories set forth by the Protestant reformers John Calvin and Ulrich Zwingli. In Calvin's theology, Christ is "spiritually present" in the celebration of the Supper, a special means of grace made known in bread and wine. Early Baptists sometimes used the term *sacrament* to describe the experience of communion, while others prefer the term *ordinance*. Later Baptists used *ordinance* almost exclusively. The *Second London Confession* (1688) suggested that the bread and wine "represent" Christ's body and blood but "still remain truly, and only Bread, and Wine, as they were before." The confession concluded: "The Body and Blood of Christ, being then not corporally, or carnally, but spiritually present to the faith of Believers, in that Ordinance, as the elements themselves are to their outward senses."[29]

Ulrich Zwingli, the reformer of Zurich, differed from Calvin on the meaning of communion. Zwingli denied that Christ was present physically or spiritually in the elements of the Lord's Supper. He noted that Christ's language was metaphorical in speaking of his body even as it was metaphorical when he referred to himself as "the door." Zwingli insisted that the

Lord's Supper was a memorial in which the congregation of believers reflected on Christ's death and resurrection, with the bread and cup representing or symbolizing his body and blood. Christ's presence, therefore, was not in the elements but in the faith present in the hearts of the believing community gathered at the table.

Although generalizations are difficult, it is probably accurate to suggest that the prevailing theology of the Supper among Baptists in America reflects most aspects of the Zwinglian position. In other words, a large number of Baptist churches describe the Lord's Supper as a memorial that represents Christ's death and resurrection as recalled by the members of the community of believers. Communion tables in Baptist churches from coast to coast are engraved with the words *This do in remembrance of me.* Likewise, in most congregations, unbaptized children or adults are not permitted to receive the Supper when it is observed.

Some Baptists have popularized the theology of the Supper in such a way as to desacramentalize it beyond even the Zwinglian position. In this regard, ministers seek to assure the congregation that communion is "merely a symbol," with no magical, sacramental, or grace-communicating aspects. It is a command that the church must fill until Jesus returns. This radical deconstruction often leads churches to "tack on" the Supper to the worship service, streamlined for the sake of convenience and minimized in terms of its theological and spiritual significance. Certain congregations merely distribute the bread and juice at the end of worship, offer a prayer, sing a hymn, and depart with limited attention to the biblical, historical, or theological meaning of the event.

### The Lord's Supper: Open or Closed?

One of the enduring debates in Baptist life concerns the constituency for communion: who can receive it and who cannot. This raises the question of whether communion should be open or closed. Once again, Baptists have disagreed on that issue from their beginnings to the present day. Some early British and American churches included open communionists who invited all Christians to receive the Supper when it was celebrated. Others practiced closed communion and invited only immersed persons to the table. Some permitted only members of the specific congregation to receive the Supper. In that view, still common in certain (Landmark) Baptist churches, only local congregations have the authority to administer the Supper, and only members of the specific church can partake.

Landmark beliefs regarding communion are evident in a 1946 document written by Ben Bogard, one of the founders of the American Baptist Association, who was quite explicit in his description of the Supper. Bogard wrote:

> The Lord's Supper is a commemorative ordinance to be observed by the church in memory of the broken body and shed blood of the Saviour. I Cor. 11:24: "This do in remembrance of me." Only baptized believers have a right to partake of the Supper. The commission given by our Master commands that the newly made disciples be baptized and then "teach them to observe all things whatsoever I have commanded you." Matt. 28:19–20. One of the things the Lord had commanded was the partaking of the Memorial Supper. . . . To partake of the Supper before baptism is to violate this law, and if we encourage any to thus violate the law of the Lord on this subject we shall be partakers of their sin. To invite unbaptized people to partake of the Lord's Supper is a sin. Open Communion is therefore a sin—a transgression of the Master's law concerning the Supper.[30]

While the battle over open and closed communion still rages in some Baptist groups, during the last quarter century or more it has become less controversial, since an increasing number of Baptist churches have moved away from closed communion policies. Some churches still restrict communion to members only; others to those who have been immersed as Christian/Baptist believers. In certain churches the minister may invite all persons present who are of "like faith and order" to receive the Supper. "Like faith and order" generally refers to Baptists, although some interpret it to mean all Christians. Still other churches invite all baptized Christians present to receive, regardless of their specific church membership.

### Children and the Lord's Supper

One of the implicit issues in Baptist discussions of the Supper involves the participation of unbaptized children of church members. Since baptism is deferred, then "first communion" may also be delayed. This has sometimes created frustration for families who consistently attend church and whose older children and adolescents are not permitted to receive communion until they have been baptized. While this seems understandable on a purely intellectual level, it is sometimes confusing for children, who feel left out of or cut off from fellowship with the community. It may also have had some impact on the lowering of the baptismal age in some churches. Thus children often move toward baptism at an early age in order to be able to receive communion.

## Re-forming the Supper

As the twenty-first century began, a growing number of Baptist churches were using the Lord's Supper as a nurturing, communal event at other times than Sunday worship, particularly on retreats, at conferences, and in small-group gatherings. This still was resisted by those Baptists affected by the Landmark movement. Landmark proponents insisted that the Supper could be celebrated only when the duly elected pastors and deacons were present in the gathering of a specific congregation. They challenged attempts to practice communion in non-churchly settings where the proper administrators were not present and the constituency not properly monitored. The Landmark emphasis kept many Baptist-related schools from observing the Lord's Supper in their chapels or in other student-based contexts on their campuses.

## Congregational Polity: "Messy" Governance

### Baptist Polity

Baptists began and continue as a Christian communion grounded in a radical congregational polity. They are ever struggling with the tension between individual autonomy and corporate connectionalism. In a sense, Baptists are a people's movement, at the center of the so-called Free Church tradition. Their congregations move across a spectrum that runs from rabid localism and individualism to varying degrees of communal and denominational conformity. Their system of ecclesiastical order creates a dramatic sense of freedom for individuals and churches to determine their own directions, yet such populism ensures dissent, disagreement, and the potential for schism at every turn.

Baptists' radical congregationalism is based on the idea that Christ's authority is mediated not through bishops, presbyteries, or synods but through the congregation of Christian believers. The congregation bears the authority for administering the sacraments, preaching, ordaining, and determining the nature of its own ministry. Yet no sooner was the movement under way than individual congregations created associations with other like-minded churches for fellowship, mutual encouragement, doctrinal solidarity, and

other connectional interactions. Early associations in Britain and America developed extensive influence, exercising varying degrees of authority among
cooperating churches. Yet an uneasy tension often existed between local congregations and corporate associations, particularly when local autonomy was
threatened by authoritarian bureaucracies. To this day, Baptist polity retains
an elusive quality. Writing in 1947, Henry Cook observed: "Strictly speaking
there is no such thing as 'Baptist polity,' because Baptists by their own fundamental principle are committed to accepting the Church polity of the New
Testament, and no-one can really say with positive certainty what that actually is."Amid associational and denominational connections, local autonomy,
individual freedom, and congregational church government combined to
make schism, debate, and division an ever-present reality in Baptist life. In her
study of American frontier religion, Christine Leigh Heyrman described the
tendency of Baptist churches to split over a variety of issues and stated: "The
absence of any authoritative higher body left the Baptists with no means of
settling disputes among the clergy, generational or otherwise." Heyrman thus
concluded that when conflicts arose, "the Baptists could only wait and hope
for a resolution after the blood-letting over contested leadership engulfed and
then exhausted their churches. Given their abiding devotion to congregational independence, a veritable icon of lay adoration, the Baptists could not
have handled matters differently and still remained Baptists."[32] Congregational polity and its application in Baptist churches often mean that debates
and divisions are not only possible, they are probable.

## *Officers*

This congregational polity posited two officers, set aside by the laying on of
hands. These included pastors or elders, who shared in the ministry of the
Word, and deacons, who were responsible for responding to the physical
needs of the faithful. The *Amsterdam Confession* (1611) stated it clearly and
concisely: "That the Officers of every Church or congregation are either Elders, who by their office do especially feed the flock concerning their souls,
Act. 20.28, Pet. 5.2, 3. or Deacons Men and Women who by their office re-
lieve the necessities of the poor and impotent brethren concerning their bodies, Acts. 6.1–4."[33] That early statement generally reflects the nature of Baptist ministry into the twenty-first century.

   This concern for ministry among both clergy and laity led to differences
in congregational approach to the administration of the sacraments. Some
Baptist churches permitted any individual duly elected by the congregation,

ordained or not, to serve at baptism or the Lord's Supper. Others explicitly required only ordained persons to preside at those events. In 1693 the Western Assembly of British Baptists determined that "no private brother (however gifted) if not solemnly called to ministerial office and separated thereto ought to administer the ordinance of baptism or the Last Supper."[34]

## Associations

Baptists are deeply committed to the autonomy of the congregation, but they also developed associational relationships with other congregations. Baptist associations are gatherings of churches usually in a given geographic region, linked for fellowship, mutual encouragement, and extended ministries. Associations represent one of the earliest forms of Baptist connectionalism and "denominational" organization. British Baptist historian W. T. Whitley wrote: "Baptists from the beginning sought to maintain sisterly intercourse between local churches; they never thought that one church was independent of others."[35]

## Contemporary Baptists

In one sense, twenty-first-century Baptists share a common polity with their seventeenth-century forebears. Most continue to affirm the centrality of the local church, join in associational relationships, and, with some exceptions, form conventions, societies, or unions with like-minded Baptists in their regions or nations. Generally speaking, these unions or denominations are derivative in authority from local churches. Individual congregations elect their own officers, search for and select their own ministers, raise their own budgets, and pursue their own specific ministries. Governance is mediated by majority vote, with various lay committees charged with carrying out specific aspects of church life and governance.

All contemporary Baptist groups practice varying forms of congregational polity in autonomous congregations that ordain ministers, define ministries, relate to regional, state, and national bodies (or choose not to do so), and fund their own budgets. Currently, debates over the ordination of women, ministerial authority, biblical inerrancy, homosexuality, abortion, baptism, denominational participation, and other controversial issues divide individuals, churches, and denominations themselves. Congregational polity means that all members have voice (potentially) in church affairs and that

congregations can determine their own futures according to the consensus of the community. This polity means that individual churches can make choices on either side of controversial issues without *necessarily* dividing the entire denomination. For example, one Baptist church may choose to ordain women while another chooses not to do so, yet they remain in the same Baptist denomination. (This possibility is increasingly difficult to sustain.) However, problems arise. These include:

1. The absence of effective moderators for church disputes
2. The dynamics of clergy/laity power blocs
3. The difficulties of placement and personal trauma faced by ministers who have been terminated by one congregation
4. The difficulties of implementing collective ministry in a context of continued divisions and polarization
5. The threat to the role of the community in Baptist life posed by a growing emphasis on individualism in the church and in the society

These are but a few of the issues that are increasing the questions of identity among Baptists in the United States.

Walter Rauschenbusch wrote of this polity:

> Our churches are Christian democracies. The people are sovereign in them. All power wielded by the church's ministers and officers is conferred by the church. It makes ample room for those who have God-given powers for leadership, but it holds them down to the service of the people by making them responsible to the church for their actions. That democracy of the Baptist church is something to be proud of.[36]

This rather idyllic description of Baptist church government belies the difficulties of this democratic method. From the beginning of the movement, Baptists have been plagued by schisms, divisions, and intra- and interchurch feuds that led to new churches, associations, and groups. If each church is free to set its own directions and ministries, then associations and denominations are also free to dismiss those whose ideas and positions differ. While the will of the majority prevails, dissent by individuals or minorities is an ever-present reality. Being Baptist is messy, controversial, and divisive. It also has the potential to give voice to each member and each congregation in powerful, radically egalitarian ways.

# Baptists and Religious Liberty

## Citizenship and Freedom

Baptists are among the most outspoken advocates of religious liberty in modern Protestant history. Indeed, it is appropriate to suggest that Baptists were the first English-speaking religious communion to advocate complete religious liberty. They were not satisfied to receive the crumbs of mere toleration doled out by assorted state-supported religious establishments in England and colonial America. Rather, they demanded complete religious freedom for heretic and unbeliever alike. They have often identified themselves with religious freedom and a general support for the separation of church and state, the belief that government should not interfere in matters of religion. At the same time, Baptists have struggled with the way in which religious liberty affected issues of patriotism, citizenship, and the unending debate over America as "Christian nation."

Contemporary Baptists often differ as to the role of religious liberty in an increasingly secular nation. Many divide over the meaning of separation of church and state, the possibility that secularism represents a new religious establishment, the use of government funds for parochial schools, and the role of religion in the "public square." Indeed, at the beginning of the twenty-first century Baptists in the United States may have been more polarized by questions of religious liberty than by any other religious issue.

### Religious Liberty: Early Twentieth Century

By the early twentieth century, the rhetoric of many Baptist leaders offered eloquent support for the historic Baptist doctrine of religious liberty. Profes-

sor and Social Gospel advocate Walter Rauschenbusch insisted that "the ma-
chinery of church and State must be kept separate, but the output of each
must mingle with the other to make social life increasingly wholesome and
normal. Church and State are alike but partial organizations of humanity for
special ends."[1]

In 1920 George W. Truett, longtime pastor of the First Baptist Church of
Dallas, Texas, addressed a Baptist group on the steps of the United States
Capitol and touted the Baptist legacy of religious liberty for a new century.
Truett's widely quoted remarks included the assertion that "religion must be
forever voluntary and uncoerced, and that it is not the prerogative of any
power, whether civil or ecclesiastical, to compel men to conform to any religious creed or form of worship, or to pay taxes for the support of a religious
organization to which they do not belong and in whose creed they do not
believe."[2]

While the rhetoric of religious freedom has long characterized Baptists'
own sense of identity, the application or appropriation of those ideas has
been varied and even divisive in Baptist life. This vaulted language did not
mean that Baptists themselves were undivided on the nature of citizenship,
the role of the church in response to political issues, and the boundaries of
American pluralism.

Toward the end of the twentieth century, W. A. Criswell, Truett's successor at the First Baptist Church of Dallas, warned that secularism was a serious threat to the Christian roots of the American Republic. He even declared
that "this notion of the separation of church and state is the figment of some
infidel's imagination."[3] While Baptists may agree on the importance of religious liberty and their own heritage of support for such freedom, they differ
on its meaning and application in the church and in the world.

### Religious Liberty: A Baptist Legacy

Baptist concern for religious liberty was evident in the beginning of the
movement. As early as 1612, Baptist leader Thomas Helwys (ca. 1550 to ca.
1616) suggested that neither magistrate nor religious establishment could
judge the heretic or the atheist. All individuals were free, under God, to practice religions that were declared heretical or to believe nothing at all. God
alone was judge of conscience, and it was to God alone that the individual
was responsible. In a work addressed to King James I and titled *A Short Declaration of the Mystery of Iniquity* (1612), Helwys wrote:

Oh, let the king judge, is it not most equal that men should choose their religion themselves, seeing they only must stand themselves before the judgement seat of God to answer for themselves, when it shall be no excuse for them to say we are commanded or compelled to be of this religion by the king or by them that had authority from him?[4]

Helwys's views led to his arrest and imprisonment. He died in prison, probably in 1616. British Baptists continued to demand religious liberty from monarch and parliament.

In America, Roger Williams took up the cause in the 1630s, with his insistence on radical religious liberty, not mere toleration of sectarians by the majority. He demanded that the colonial government justly compensate Native Americans for the land they confiscated and challenged the prevailing idea that the Puritan experiment constituted a "Christian commonwealth." Exiled for his views, Williams fled into the "howling wilderness" of New England, where he was befriended by the Narragansett people from whom he bought land to found Providence Plantation in the colony of Rhode Island. Williams also helped to found the first Baptist church in America at Providence sometime between 1638 and 1639. Soon convinced that no existing church had the true revelation, Williams abandoned the Baptists and became something of an individual "seeker," carrying his expectations and hope with him. His contribution in the idea and practice of religious freedom remains a significant legacy for Baptists, however, even when they cannot agree on the benefits of that contribution. Williams insisted that "enforced uniformity confounds civil and religious and denies the principles of Christianity and Civility." He concluded that "a national church was not constituted by Christ Jesus. That cannot be a true religion which needs carnal weapons to uphold it."[5] Williams represented an important vision of liberty that Baptists in the United States have claimed throughout their history.

Williams was not alone. Dr. John Clarke (1609–1676), Baptist founder of Newport and author of the Rhode Island charter (1663), was another fearless advocate of religious liberty. His views are evident in that charter and its insistence that "all and every person . . . freely and fully have and enjoy his own judgements and conscience in matters of religious concernments."[6]

This concern for religious liberty was particularly important to Baptists, since their sectarianism and dissent brought them into continuing conflict with the two colonial religious establishments, Puritans in the East and Anglicans in the South. Baptist churches in those regions were frequently boarded up, their clergy and laity fined, and their beliefs attacked as heretical.

Many wrote, preached, and lobbied for religious liberty as the new Republic took shape.

Isaac Backus (1724–1806) a Congregationalist who joined the Baptists in 1756, was appointed by the Warren Association of New England Baptists to lobby the first Continental Congress on behalf of religious liberty. Backus believed that

> nothing can be true religion but a voluntary obedience unto God's revealed will, of which each rational soul has an actual right to judge for itself; every person has an inalienable right to act in all religious affairs according to the full persuasion of his own mind, where others are not injured thereby.[7]

Backus's own vision of America seems to have been as a Christian nation, providing freedom primarily for those anchored in New Testament faith and enabling them to work toward the Christianization of the nation. William McLoughlin wrote that

> Backus insisted that the United States of America was and should be a Christian nation. Thomas Jefferson [and other Baptists] said it was definitely not a Christian nation. Backus wanted friendly cooperation, not a rigid wall of separation between church and state, and he had a very fuzzy view of precisely where the civil enforcement of Christian morality ended and the religious freedom of Christ's kingdom began.[8]

Virginian John Leland (1754–1841) was a Baptist who represented some of the most radical positions on religious liberty of the colonial period. A son of the Enlightenment, Leland was adamant in his demand for complete religious liberty for all persons, including those outside the boundaries of Christianity. Eloquent to a fault, he articulated a religious pluralism that anticipated twentieth- and twenty-first-century religious diversity. In delineating the "evils" of religious establishments, Leland wrote:

> Uninspired, fallible men make their own opinions tests of orthodoxy, and use their own systems, as Procrustes used his iron bedstead, to stretch and measure the consciences of all others by. Where no toleration is granted to non-conformists, either ignorance and superstition prevail, or persecution rages. . . . These establishments metamorphose the church into a creature, and religion into a principle of state, which

has a natural tendency to make men conclude that *Bible religion* is nothing but a *trick of state*.[9]

With the Constitution and the Bill of Rights, Baptist concerns for religious liberty were reflected in elements of American democracy. Yet freedom brought new challenges. By the 1830s Baptists were no longer a tiny
movement but (with Methodists) had become one of the two largest Protestant denominations in America. Baptists then faced the challenge of whether
a newly privileged communion would continue to defend the right of all persons to religious freedom.

### Freedom of Religion—Freedom from Slavery

Among Baptists in the North and in the South, the debate over human slavery had implications for issues of religious liberty. It is ironic that Baptists in
the South who were fearless opponents of religious establishments and were
often fined or imprisoned for their refusal to conform to laws regulating religious practice and state control of religious minorities were in many cases
slave owners, stripping other human beings of their most basic rights to "life,
liberty and the pursuit of happiness." Some colonial Baptists were at once advocates of religious liberty and slave owners. John "Swearing Jack" Waller,
mentioned earlier, was such a Baptist. A prominent Virginian, Waller was
imprisoned for his opposition to the Anglican establishment and his stubborn
refusal to secure a preaching license from the state. He was also a slave
owner, buying and selling individuals as property. Waller's concerns for religious liberty did not extend to freedom for slaves.

The divisions over slavery were so pronounced that many Baptist groups
sought to avoid confrontation and potential schism by insisting that slavery
was a political matter, unrelated to the spiritual pursuits of the church. Some
suggested that Baptists should stay out of such political debates lest they
cross the line of church/state separation. In the name of religious liberty,
therefore, and in an attempt to avoid a split in their movement, they suggested that slavery be left to the jurisdiction of the state.

Abolitionist Baptists pressed the denomination to take a stand against
slavery, and Baptists in the South defended the rights of the states. As tensions mounted, Baptists in the South introduced a test case, the appointment
of a slaveholder as a missionary. When the mission board withheld its approval, the Southerners bolted and the Southern Baptist Convention was

formed in 1845. Other abolitionist Baptists supported the Northern cause and urged the government to emancipate the slaves.

Reconstruction and the evolution of the South's separate but equal society also raised issues for Baptists over matters of states' rights, government "interference," and Jim Crow laws. In those battles, biblical, ethical, and political issues collided. Again, many Baptists in the South hesitated to address the political issues. Baptist Walfred H. Peterson observed that "unquestionably, if by the middle of this [twentieth] century if a knowledgeable person felt her or his religious freedom was being denied, she or he would *not* hasten to the First Baptist Church to find support."[10] As with slavery, white Baptists in the South often insisted that racial issues were political, not religious, and therefore the church should not get involved in them because of the separation of church and state. African American Baptists, though not with complete unanimity, often took the opposite approach and insisted that the church could not keep silent on political issues that exploited the freedom of any group.

## Early Culture Wars: Baptists and Social Crusades

Baptist appreciation for separation of church and state did not mean that they were silent on matters related to the political implications of a variety of ethical issues. Indeed, many Baptists engaged in significant efforts to address social questions, from the voting booth to the bedroom.

Walter Rauschenbusch and later generations of Baptist ethicists and pastors were among those Baptists who sought to "Christianize the social order," bringing Christ's teachings to bear not simply on individuals but on economic and political practices as well. Rauschenbusch and others (Baptists and non-Baptists) organized the "Brotherhood of the Kingdom" to nurture scholarship, spirituality, and community action. Many participants hoped for a day when Christian socialism would create a new sense of community beyond economic exploitation of the working classes, and through legislation promote greater equality among all social classes. Rauschenbusch called the church of his day to "come out of its spiritual isolation." He observed that the church

> has often built a sound-proof habitation in which people could live for years without becoming definitely conscious of the existence of prostitution, child labor, or tenement crowding. It has offered peace and spir-

itual trinquillity [*sic*] to men and women who needed thunderclaps and lightnings [*sic*]. Like all the rest of us, the church will get salvation by finding the purpose of its existence outside itself, in the kingdom of God the perfect life of the race.[11]

A child of the Progressive Era, Rauschenbusch contributed to the church/ state divisions his concern that the government respond to issues of economic inequality and social justice by applying the principles of Jesus to the practice of democracy. His work as a pastor in the Hell's Kitchen section of New York City (near West Fortieth Street) convinced him of the need to address individual sins and also the corporate corruption that dehumanized individuals. J. M. Dawson wrote that Rauschenbusch "strengthened the American principle of church-state separation by helping to demonstrate the dependability of the [democratic] system when confronted with entrenched social evils or with conditions incident to radical social change."[12]

Debates abounded within the Baptist fold as to the extent to which Christians should become involved in the public sphere. On a basic level, some suggested, the church's calling is primarily evangelical—to convert individuals who will then seek to transform the society. These Baptists were "passive reformers," who were convinced "that conversion and one's faith would naturally produce desirable social change."[13] Others, like Rauschenbusch, believed that the Christian gospel had both individual and social ramifications. The society had to be changed in order to provide deliverance for those who were economically, spiritually, and politically exploited.

On a deeper level, however, Baptists addressed a variety of social issues, urging the state to intervene in certain matters, many of which related to personal moral issues such as alcohol use, prostitution, and gambling. During the early twentieth century, North Carolina Baptist women lobbied the government for child-labor reforms in order that these young people "be not completely stunted and crushed mentally, morally and physically." They expressed their desire to respond to the problems of "the unlovely people about us," including children and women in factories, African Americans, and others caught in a cycle of "poverty, ignorance, disease, and crime."[14]

The Woman's Missionary Union of the Southern Baptist Convention, founded in 1888, was at the forefront of early-twentieth-century reform efforts, calling on Baptists to encourage "those forces in our country which make for righteousness: patriotism working toward universal and permanent peace, prohibition, Sabbath observance, the sacredness of the home, the effort toward a more general re-establishment of the family altar, and the crusade against poverty, disease, illiteracy, vice and crime."[15] They, like other Baptists, tended to encourage "blue laws," legislation that prohibited business openings on Sundays, and "liquor laws," which regulated the sale of alcohol in local communities.

Baptists also worked toward legislation to limit gambling and the use of tobacco. Yet temperance crusades raised other theological and political dilemmas for male Baptists. In the late nineteenth century, many Baptist men supported the Women's Christian Temperance Union (WCTU) and its efforts to change liquor laws, until, as J. B. Hawthorne noted, they realized that Francis Willard, founder of the movement, called for women's suffrage and encouraged "women into the gospel ministry, as preachers and leaders."[16]

## Baptists and American Catholics: The Church/State Debates

Following the Civil War, Baptist support for religious liberty was tested with the arrival of Catholic immigrants from Europe and the British Isles. The growing Catholic presence in America stretched Baptist views on religious liberty to the limit. Baptist mistrust of Catholics was multifaceted. First, the Roman Catholic Church represented the ultimate religious establishment, with centuries of privilege and authority connected to European governments. Second, Roman Catholics were strongly anti-Protestant and were known to have promoted persecution of Protestants around the world, especially in so-called Catholic countries. Third, many Baptists and other American Protestants feared that Roman Catholic immigration would create voting blocs that would result in Catholic majorities across the nation, ultimately to the benefit of a foreign monarch, the pope. Finally, nineteenth-century Catholicism was on record in opposition to democratic reforms including religious liberty and the separation of church and state. The famous *Syllabus of Errors* compiled by Pope Pius IX in 1867 condemned Protestantism, religious liberty, freedom of the press, and public education. It concluded by condemning any suggestion that "the Roman Pontiff can, and ought to reconcile himself to, and agree with, progress, liberalism, and modern civilization."[17]

Some Baptists joined in the Nativist effort to claim America as a Protestant nation and protect the country from a papist takeover. Nativists often worked from an anti-Catholic, anti-immigrant position in questioning Catholic rights and motives.

Baptist concerns about the growing Catholic presence and influence in the United States began in the nineteenth century and continued into the twenty-first century, with several justifications from those who participated. First, critics said that Catholics could never fully become Americans because they were dependent on the Church for salvation and the Church was governed by those who accepted the *Syllabus of Errors*. Second, many Baptists not only denied that the Roman Church was the "one true church" but questioned whether it was a church at all.

Certain twenty-first-century Baptist groups and individuals continue to assert that Catholics have a faulty ecclesiology, built on papal supremacy, a doctrine that has no basis in Holy Scripture. They still insist that Catholic emphasis on "works" and external sacraments means that they cannot be considered truly Christian. Many Baptists—Independent, Separatist Baptists, for example—claim that Catholics who lack a "born again" experience are "unsaved" even if they are active participants in Catholic churches. (They would say the same thing about Baptists who lack the "born again" experience.)

This response to Roman Catholicism in America was particularly evident in the first two presidential campaigns involving Catholic candidates. When Al Smith ran for president in 1928, many Baptists opposed it, believing that a Catholic president could not protect and defend the constitution from enemies "foreign and domestic" since even the president was dependent on the authority of the pope to be in fellowship with the true church. Many preachers, including fundamentalist pastor J. Frank Norris, were vehemently opposed to Smith's candidacy. Norris took great pleasure in Smith's defeat and claimed credit for making that happen. He declared, "In the name of the American Flag and of the Holy Bible, I defy the Roman Catholic machine of New York."[18] Norris obviously feared that a Smith presidency could extend Catholic dominance of the entire American nation.

During the presidential election of 1960 many Baptists opposed the candidacy of John F. Kennedy for similar reasons. Baptists were among other Protestant clergy who suggested that Kennedy had an allegiance to the Roman pontiff that would be a threat to his oath to uphold the Constitution of the United States. They warned that since Kennedy's eternal salvation was dependent on Catholic commitments, he might be required to follow Catholic dictums rather than support the law of the land. In 1960 the Southern Baptist Convention adopted a resolution affirming the Constitution's denial of religious requirements for officeholders but also arguing "that no Roman Catholic should be elected president because his church's position on religious liberty, prenuptial marriage contracts, and state aid to church schools were in 'open conflict with our established and constituted American pattern of life.'" Catholics were "inescapably bound by the dogma and demands" of the Catholic Church.[19]

In response to Kennedy's candidacy, numerous Baptist leaders signed on to "A Statement on Religious Liberty in Relation to the 1960 National Campaign," calling Americans to stand by Article VI of the Constitution, which denies all "religious tests" as prerequisites for candidates for office. Baptist signers of the document included Clarence W. Cranford, pastor of Calvary Baptist Church, Washington, DC; Herbert Gezork, president of Andover Newton Theological School, Newton, Massachusetts; and Carlyle Marney, pastor of Myers Park Baptist Church, Charlotte, North Carolina. That same year, Baptists were among 150 Protestants who met Kennedy in Houston, Texas, and heard him repudiate the idea of federal aid to parochial schools, an ambassador to the Vatican, and any state support for religious institutions. Kennedy insisted that his was a vision for America where "the separation of church and state was absolute."[20] This meeting is often interpreted as a turning point for Kennedy's candidacy and Catholicism.

Even after Kennedy's election many Baptists continued to raise questions about the relationship between Catholicism and American citizenship. Various Independent Baptists were constant critics of Kennedy's politics and religion. Some even responded to the assassination of President Kennedy by insisting that it was Divine retribution against the Kennedy family and their ties to the "liquor traffic." Because his father, Joseph Kennedy, had made much of his fortune through business ventures involving liquor sales, they concluded that God "permitted" John and Robert Kennedy's deaths.[21] Underneath these bizarre charges was an implicit sense that these tragic events were the result of a Catholic's election to the presidency.

Other, more liberal Baptists reacted to the Catholic presence by establishing networks that fostered Baptist-Catholic dialogues. In North Carolina, for example, faculty members at the Baptist-related Wake Forest University and at the Benedictine-related Belmont Abbey founded the Ecumenical Institute in 1968. Its primary purpose was to further communication and understanding between members of the two religious groups. The institute continues, with additional participation from South Carolina institutions such as the Trappist Mepkin Abbey and Furman University, a school with a Baptist heritage.

Independent Baptists such as Jerry Falwell continue to differ with Catholics on theology and doctrine but to unite with them in certain moral crusades related to the political implications of abortion, school prayer, homosexuality, and vouchers for use in private schools. Falwell's Moral Majority organization readily welcomed Catholics to membership and participation in political action on behalf of conservative political-ethical causes. In

1994 various conservative Baptists joined with other conservative Baptists and Catholics in drafting "Evangelicals and Catholics Together: The Christian Mission in the Third Millennium," calling Christians to "resist the utopian conceit that it is within our power to build the Kingdom of God on earth" and contend "for the truth that politics, law and culture must be secured by moral truth."[22]

At the same time, many Baptist groups continue to view Catholic dogma with disdain, challenging its biblical and historical claims. The conservative American Baptist Association, based in Arkansas, challenges Catholic teachings regarding Scripture, papal authority, baptism, and other dogmas on its Internet Web page under the rubric "False Doctrines."[23] Catholics remain a target of evangelism for many Baptists, especially those actively involved in the burgeoning Latino communities in the United States. Separatist Baptists in the General Association of Regular Baptist Churches resist connection with any Baptist individuals or groups (Billy Graham, for example) who participate in any programs in which Catholics are involved.

## The Baptist Joint Committee on Public Affairs

In 1939 three separate Baptist denominations—the Northern Baptist Convention, the National Baptist Convention, USA, Inc., and the Southern Baptist Convention—each approved "A Pronouncement on Religious Liberty," which addressed historic Baptist commitments to freedom of religion. Officially published under the title *American Baptist Bill of Rights*, it warned that religious freedom was under threat because increasing numbers of people "are looking to the State to provide" their physical needs. It called on Baptists to protect "absolute religious liberty" for Jews, Catholics, Protestants, and "everybody else" and concluded that "Baptists condemn every form of compulsion in religion or restraint of the free consideration of the claims of religion."[24]

Rufus W. Weaver (1870–1947), executive secretary of the District of Columbia Baptist Convention, succeeded in getting representatives of the three denominations together in the Associated Committees on Public Relations. In 1942 the group became the Joint Conference Committee on Public Relations, with headquarters in Washington, DC. It became a full-time operation in 1946 under the leadership of Joseph Martin Dawson, who remained director until 1953. In 1950 it was renamed the Baptist Joint Committee on Public Affairs (BJCPA). This organization was intended to "enunciate, defend, and extend, issues related to religious liberty and separation of church and state." It brought together numerous Baptist denominations in cooperation for religious freedom in the Baptist tradition and continues that work as related to Baptist perspectives on religion and the public square. The committee's purposes include the following:

1. It seeks to inform Baptist groups and individuals as to significant public issues, with particular attention to matters related to church and state.
2. As permitted by time and staff, it seeks to provide "primary information" for Baptist organizations regarding public policy information.
3. It provides government committees and agencies with reports on Baptist actions on behalf of church-state issues.
4. While not part of direct litigation in church-state matters, it has frequently submitted *amicus curiae* (friend of the court) briefs in evaluating certain cases.[25]

During the years 1962–1963 the BJCPA supported the Supreme Court decisions regarding school prayer and challenged congressional efforts to create a constitutional amendment to respond to court action. During the 1970s, under the leadership of executive director James Wood, the committee challenged what it felt was inappropriate government interference in church-related matters. It opposed efforts to compel its staff to register as lobbyists and the Department of Labor's attempt to require churches to pay unemployment taxes. It proposed legislation that kept the Central Intelligence Agency from co-opting foreign missionaries in the acquisition of intelligence information. The BJCPA continued its long opposition to vouchers, tax credits, and other forms of direct or indirect aid to public education. The committee cooperated with numerous agencies in successfully opposing required chapel at the U.S. military academies and efforts of certain states to prohibit clergy from running for public office. It offered support for welfare reform, reaffirmed governmental integrity after the Watergate controversy, urged Congress to improve laws on child abuse and "sexual exploitation of children," and encouraged the "equality of all persons under law."[26]

Since its inception the BJCPA has occasionally addressed international issues, calling on the Soviet Union to respect religious liberty and to free dissidents such as Baptist leader Georgi Vins; opposed Israeli laws forbidding evangelism by Christian groups; and offered continued opposition to the appointment of U.S. ambassadors to the Vatican.

During the 1970s and 1980s the committee included representatives of a wide variety of Baptist groups, among them American Baptist Churches,

USA; Baptist Federation of Canada, Baptist General Conference; National Baptist Convention of America; National Baptist Convention, USA, Inc.; Seventh Day Baptist General Conference; and the Southern Baptist Convention. However, a controversy between the committee and the conservative leadership of the SBC intensified, particularly because of differences over approaches to various social and political agendas.

During the 1980s Southern Baptist conservatives expressed their concerns about the Baptist Joint Committee and its executive director, James Dunn. Many were distressed with the committee's opposition to movements to "bring prayer back to public schools," school vouchers, and Dunn's criticism of the New Religious Political Right. They were particularly angered in 1982 when Dunn labeled as "despicable demagoguery" a proposal by President Ronald Reagan to promote a constitutional amendment supporting public prayer. After the convention adopted a resolution supporting such a constitutional amendment, Dunn declared it "an incredible contradiction of our Baptist heritage."[27] Conservatives were not pleased, and as early as 1984 some attempted to cut funding to the BJCPA, but with little initial success.

In 1990, after years of negotiation and debate, the SBC voted to leave the BJCPA and establish its own Washington office related to the denomination's Christian Life Commission. Known as the Religious Liberty Commission, it continues to represent another Baptist presence in the nation's capital. The BJCPA is now composed of some thirteen Baptist "supporting bodies": Alliance of Baptists; American Baptist Churches, USA; Baptist General Association of Virginia; Baptist General Conference; Baptist General Convention of Texas; Cooperative Baptist Fellowship; National Baptist Convention of America; National Baptist Convention, USA; National Missionary Baptist Convention; North American Baptist Conference; North Carolina Baptist Convention; Progressive National Baptist Convention; and the Religious Liberty Council. It continues to work on behalf of religious liberty issues, often setting itself against more conservative groups associated with the Religious Political Right.

### Federal Aid to Baptist Schools

During the mid-twentieth century some Baptist groups divided over whether Baptist-supported schools should receive government funds for educational programs. In many states, Baptist colleges were founded by the regional Baptist state conventions that supported those schools directly or indirectly. In these states, the trustees of the schools were appointed by the conventions. The church-related schools were discouraged from pursuing or receiving state grants or funds. Some Baptists even opposed programs such as student ROTC lest they connect church and state unduly. Resolutions at denominational conventions called on schools to reject government monies, in keeping with Baptist concern for separation of church and state. Government grants, ROTC, loans for buildings, and other programs were attacked.

The approval of the National Defense Education Act of 1958 was one of several efforts that made state funds available to private schools for funding programs, buildings, and students that would aid the country in responding to issues raised by the Cold War. In 1963 the Southern Baptist Convention responded to these efforts in a resolution that read:

> Whereas, Baptists are committed to the principle of supporting taxation for public purposes only, leaving church institutions to the voluntary support of persons desiring to participate in the support of and maintenance of those institutions; and Whereas we see in these principles the meaning of the "no establishment" clause of the first Amendment to the Federal constitution as well as that of the "Free exercise" clause of that same amendment; it is recommended, now, therefore:
>
> 1. The Southern Baptist Convention strongly opposes all legislation, federal and state, which would provide public grants to church colleges and universities for the construction of academic facilities.[28]

Changes in Baptist response to public funding in the South were evident in 1968 when the Religious Liberty Committee of the Baptist General Association of Virginia proposed in a 6–3 vote that schools be permitted to secure education grants and recommended that the convention work toward a change in the Virginia constitution that would allow for "equitable participation by all colleges and universities within the State of Virginia, state supported and private, including those related to a church or church group" in order to secure government aid when needed. Among the reasons given for this change in opinion regarding government funding were the following: (1) some programs fund individuals rather than institutions; (2) some government monies are provided "for services rendered"; (3) there was evidence of government "innocence" regarding "control" of ecclesial communities; (4) and, most pressingly, many schools required government aid as "essential to survival."[29] The General Association asked the committee to revisit the matter, and it went no further at that time.

Separationists were concerned that federal funding would separate Baptist institutions from their denominational roots, link them with the state, and increase secular influences. The scene was set, however, for other, more successful efforts to move toward formal use of tax monies by Baptist schools. By the latter twentieth century a growing number of Baptist schools were accepting student aid funds from state and federal grants, welcoming ROTC units to campus, and utilizing various federal programs to fund building programs and research. Thus, many Baptist hospitals and universities have become self-supporting, distancing themselves from their parent Baptist bodies and receiving a variety of public funds for specific educational and medical projects.[30]

## Baptists and Parochial Schools

Fear of potential Catholic hegemony in American religious life often led Baptists to oppose any suggestion that public moneys would be used for what was sometimes labeled as "paroch-aid." This was particularly true during the 1950s and 1960s, when Baptists had few parochial schools of their own. The Baptist Joint Committee on Public Affairs has long been outspoken in its opposition to any effort to provide public funding for parochial education.

Baptists and others became particularly concerned when, in 1947, the Supreme Court released its decision in *Everson v. Board of Education* agreeing that New Jersey state funds could be used to provide transportation for parochial school students. In its ruling, the Court affirmed that Thomas Jefferson's "wall of separation" between church and state "must be kept high and impregnable. We could not approve the slightest breach. New Jersey has not breached it here."[31]

Concerns over the *Everson* development led Baptists and others to found another lobbying agency aimed at protecting the "wall of separation." Known as Protestants and Other Americans United for the Separation of Church and State (POAU), the organization was led by a variety of Baptists, including Edwin McNeil Poteat, professor at Colgate-Rochester Divinity School; Joseph M. Dawson of the Baptist Joint Committee; and Baptist congressmen Brooks Hays and Joseph R. Bryson.[32] Across the years the organization expanded its membership and is now known as Americans United for Separation of Church and State. The POAU and the BJCPA demonstrated particular concern about *Everson*, the appointment of a U.S. ambassador to the Vatican, and other Catholic-related political developments. They affirmed the Court's decision in *Meek v. Pittenger* (1975) against any "auxiliary aid" to parochial schools, except for the loan of textbooks and other teaching materials.[33]

As C. C. Goen has shown, Baptists in the pew often applauded when their lobbying agencies challenged Catholics, but they were less forceful when such challenges spilled over into the "Protestant consensus." When the Joint Committee filed an *amicus curiae* brief in support of *McCollum v. Board of Education*, in which an atheist questioned the "release-time" program in Champaign, Illinois, that permitted public schools to send students for religious instruction, some Baptists were not pleased. The Detroit Missionary Society passed a resolution that the Joint Committee's efforts had given "the impression" that the nation's Baptists "are standing with the alleged atheist mother of Champaign and other secularists whose aim is to destroy all religion." Goen concluded that whenever the Joint Committee "opposed Roman Catholics hankering to dip into the public till—and it do so often—it enjoyed the full backing of all Baptists. Whenever it stood against evangelicals clinging to the assumptions of the 19th-century Protestant consensus—and it did so fairly consistently—it suffered sharp criticism from many in its constituency."[34]

During the latter decades of the twentieth century, however, many Baptists softened opposition to state funds for parochial schools, particularly in matters of vouchers. Advocates pointed to the inadequacies of public education and the economic inequities that kept low-income families from even considering alternative education. Other Baptists (represented in the Baptist Joint Committee, for example) vehemently opposed vouchers as a direct violation of church/state separation and a detriment to the future of American public education.

Concerned about the changing shape of religious response to public issues, the General Board of American Baptist Churches, USA approved "An American Baptist Policy Statement on Church and State" in December 1986. It acknowledged that "in the last quarter of the twentieth century issues of Church-State relations have taken on new significance and it is urgent that we remember our historic commitment to a firm policy of separation of Church and State and renew our witness to this policy."[35] The document enumerated various illustrations of the "changing attitudes toward the role of religion in public life." These included: efforts to reinstate "designated periods of prayer" in public school classrooms; "a demand for tuition tax credits for parents with children in private . . . schools"; "government funds for textbooks . . . [used] in church-sponsored schools"; and efforts "to establish . . . doctrinal positions through legislation on such issues as abortion and capital punishment." It noted: "Some Baptists, and even some Baptist bodies, have reversed long-held historic positions regarding mandated prayer in public schools."[36]

The document expressed "explicit opposition" to "mandated prayers," tuition tax credits, "recognition of Church or religious entities by government" (i.e., a U.S. ambassador to the Vatican), government efforts to define religious language, and "government surveillance" of religious groups.[37] It concluded that "without religious liberty all other human rights are in jeopardy and in danger of being perverted or abused."[38]

The American Baptist statement illustrates one of the most serious divisions among Baptists in America during the last twenty-five years, pitting traditional Baptist separationists on church/state matters against accommodationists, who believe that government should accommodate religion as extensively as possible. Not to do so is to extend the hegemony of secularism as the dominant religion in American culture. Separationists continue to give attention to the boundaries between church and state regarding formal school prayer, aid to religious institutions, and the posting of religious symbols—Nativity scenes, the Ten Commandments—on state-related property. Accommodationists, however, are leery of impinging secularism, evident in limitations on school prayer, aid to parochial schools, and the use of religious symbols in the public arena.

### Baptists and the New Religious Political Right

The 1980 presidential campaign was a watershed in church-state issues, many of which had implications for Baptists. The Baptist president, Jimmy Carter, ran against the conservative icon, Ronald Reagan. Reagan intentionally courted evangelical-conservative religious leaders, who encouraged their constituents to participate in the political process, some for the very first time. Baptists were central to the founding of two political action agencies, Religious Roundtable and Moral Majority, aimed at conservative religious communities. Baptist laymen Paul Pressler and Ed McAteer urged Baptists to enter the political realm, and work for candidates who pledged to support conservative/religious social and ethical agendas. Although Jimmy Carter was the "born-again" candidate, Ronald Reagan was more successful in cultivating the evangelical vote. When addressing the Religious Roundtable in Dallas in 1980, Reagan acknowledged that while the nonprofit organization might not be able to endorse him officially, he would endorse them and the religious values they represented. Many Baptists chose to support Reagan rather than Carter, who some felt had "sold out" to the forces of secularism. Carter recalls that

> a high official of the Southern Baptist Convention came into the Oval Office to visit me when I was president. As he and his wife were leaving, he said, "We are praying, Mr. President, that you will abandon secular humanism as your religion." This was a shock to me. I didn't know what he meant, and am still not sure.[39]

Carter reports that in the early days of the "Christian Right," Baptist Jerry Falwell "condemned me because I 'claimed' to be a Christian." Carter notes that these were the beginning stages of a movement aimed at bringing conservative Christians into the political process and targeting specific conservative agendas for social reform.[40]

Baptists were among the earliest leaders of the movement that became known as the New Religious Political Right. Ed McAteer, a Republican operative, helped to found the Religious Roundtable in 1980. The organization "served primarily as an agency to coordinate and provide resources for conservative religious leaders."[41] Others included television preacher James Robison; Charles Stanley, pastor of First Baptist Church, Atlanta; Gary Jarmin, a founder of Christian Voice; and Jerry Falwell, a Lynchburg, Virginia, pastor and a founder of the Moral Majority. The last movement, initially built around the leadership of Independent Baptist pastors, sought to unite conservatives of various religious and social camps to "take back America" for moral values and patriotic loyalties.[42] McAteer was among those who sought to energize conservative Baptists and other conservatives to vote, run for public office, and take a larger role in addressing the nation's political and ethical future.

Many of these Baptists were convinced that something had to be done to stop the nation's moral and spiritual decline that was evident in the increasing sexual promiscuity, crime, and divorce rates, the disregard of Christian values, and the impact of religious pluralism on genuine faith. Secularism had become the real religion of the Republic and, unchecked, it would ultimately wear down every viable religious community. As conservatives understood it, they entered the public sphere in order to retain the dissenting tradition of the Baptists in their response to secularism, the de facto established religion in America. Some even believed that the idea of church-state separation was a vehicle for preventing Christians, particularly conservatives, from political activism. As many saw it, secularism was the real religious establishment, dominating every aspect of American cultural life. It was an assault on traditional values, creating an environment in which abortion, divorce, and homosexuality proliferated. The pluralism it engendered could easily become detrimental to the Judeo-Christian tradition. It undermined religious particularism and opened the door to universalism, relativism, and moral anarchy.

Baptist Tim LaHaye, who later authored the popular *Left Behind* novels on Christ's Second Coming, declared that through the New Religious Political Right the time would come when "the real American People will regain their country and culture." As Samuel Hill and Dennis Owen comment. "Thus it is that the NRPR represents itself as the true America, defending the nation from those who have led us away from our original calling and have sorely tried God's patience in so doing."[43]

Jerry Falwell pressed the case against secularism following the terrorist destruction of the World Trade Center on September 11, 2001. In an interview on *The 700 Club*, Pat Robertson's television program, Falwell commented: "I really believe that the pagans, and the abortionists, and the feminists, and the gays and the lesbians who are actively trying to make that an alternative life style, the ACLU, People for the American Way, all of them who have tried to secularize America. I point the finger in their face and say, 'You helped it happen.'" The attack, Falwell suggested, was the result of God's judgment for "throwing God out of the public square, out of the schools." He claimed that "living by God's principles promotes a nation to greatness, violating those principles brings a nation to ruin." Secularism and immorality had caused God to withdraw protection from America. Protests against these statements led Falwell to offer an apology, concluding that "I would never blame any human being except the terrorists."[44]

Independent Baptists (and other conservatives from various Baptist groups) composed a significant segment of the New Religious Political Right. They have become strong supporters of the Republican Party and have given particular attention to certain "hot-button" socioreligious issues. A brief survey of those issues is provided here.

### Prayer in Schools (and at Other Public Events)

Controversy surrounding prayer in public schools has divided Baptists and other Christian since Supreme Court decisions *Engel v. Vitale* (1962) and *Abington v. Schemp* (1963) ruled against the use of state-mandated or formal prayers in schools and at other public gatherings. For many Baptists, that decision was a classic illustration of the secularization of America and the loss of Christian values. For others, it was an appropriate boundary separating church and state.

When the initial *Engel* decision was handed down, the Baptist Joint Committee, which had filed an *amicus curiae* brief with the plaintiffs, declared:

> We concur with the decision of the Supreme Court in *Engel v. Vitale* that prayer composed by Government officials as part of a governmental program to further religious beliefs is and should be unconstitutional. We think along with the court, that the constitutional prohibition against laws respecting an establishment of religion, must at least mean that in this country it is no part of the business of government to compose official prayers for any group of the American people to recite as part of a religious program carried on by government.[45]

In response, crusades to "put God back into the schools" have echoed from churches and religious rallies for decades. Baptists of various stripes have participated in efforts to return public prayer to schools, graduations, and sporting events. They have also provided support for political candidates they believed would work to appoint judges to the courts, especially the Supreme Court, to reverse such practices.

Baptists such as Richard Land, director of the Southern Baptist Ethics and Religious Liberty Commission, insist that school-related public prayer is at the other end of the so-called Establishment Clause of the Constitution, that "Congress shall make no law concerning the establishment of religion or prohibiting the free exercise thereof." By permitting prayer in schools, the government is simply recognizing the rights of students to the "free exercise" of religion. It does not represent an effort by the state to establish religious requirements. Other Baptists such as Brent Walker, director of the Baptist Joint Committee on Public Affairs, contend that the argument is moot since prayer was never taken out of schools. All students are free to pray privately in their own way, but were not compelled to participate in "state mandated" prayers. Such prayers imply a religious establishment or create such a generic form of prayer that the result is devoid of specificity and spiritual benefit.

Disputes over prayer in schools have become important symbols of larger debates regarding religion in the public square. They reflect serious divisions among Baptists that create varying definitions of Baptists regarding the nature of religious liberty and the separation of church and state.

## Moral Issues and the State

The Supreme Court's decision in *Roe v. Wade* (1973) permitted "legalized abortion," based on the right of the mother to choose to terminate or continue pregnancy. It also united conservative Catholics and Protestants in a "pro-life" crusade. Baptists reflected these differences, dividing between "pro-life" and "pro-choice" positions.

The Southern Baptist Convention is a case in point. In the 1970s the convention, including many of its prominent conservatives, articulated a somewhat moderate approach to the issue, with reasoning based on voluntarism in religion. The convention's first public response to abortion came in 1971 in a resolution that resisted a completely pro-life position but urged legislation that would permit abortions so as to avoid the "likelihood of damage to the emotional, mental, and physical health of the mother."[46]

A 1976 SBC resolution noted: "The practice of abortion for selfish nontherapeutic reasons wantonly destroys fetal life, dulls our society's moral sensitivity, and leads to the cheapening of moral life." It called on Southern Baptists to "reaffirm" the "sacredness and dignity" of all, even fetal, life and to "encourage" people to reject abortion as a "means of birth control." It urged Southern Baptists to "reject any indiscriminate attitude toward abortion, as contrary to the biblical view."[47]

James E. Wood Jr., founder and director of the J. M. Dawson Institute of Church-State Studies at Baylor University, appealed to Baptist traditions on freedom of conscience as a basis for woman's right to choose in questions of abortion. He did so, he said, "out of concern that in our pluralistic society the state should not embody into law one particular religious or moral viewpoint on which differing views are held by substantial sections of the religious and nonreligious communities." Wood agreed with the actions of the Baptist Joint Committee in opposing legislative limitations to *Roe v. Wade* "out of its long tradition for upholding liberty of conscience and the separation of church and state." In those early days after the court decision, some conservatives, such as W. A. Criswell, affirmed this approach.[48] This was soon to change, as abortion became a major point of division between varying groups of Baptists.

The conservative resurgence in the SBC brought a change in the denomination's response to abortion. A 1980 resolution (not binding on churches) declared: "Our national laws permit a policy commonly referred to as 'abortion on demand'" and continued: "Be it resolved that we abhor the use of tax money or public, tax-supported medical facilities for selfish, non-therapeutic abortion." The resolution called for "appropriate legislation and/or a constitutional amendment prohibiting abortion except to save the life of the mother." This statement remains on record as the denominational approach to the abortion issue.[49]

In 1986 Southern Baptist leader Paige Patterson insisted: "We want an open, pro-life position in all our institutions and agencies, dealing with abortion and euthanasia. We want to be pro-family, pro-prayer anywhere."[50] Richard Land acknowledged in 1988: "I oppose abortion except where the mother's physical life is in danger." He noted that this view "puts me completely in line with resolutions [opposing abortion] passed by the convention in the last decade."[51] Land also expressed support for capital punishment "as part of the biblically mandated authority of the civil magistrates."[52]

Homosexuality, one of the most divisive issues confronting Baptists and other denominations, had implications for church and state. The ordination of gay ministers in Baptist churches, the conducting of "unions" between same-sex couples in Baptist churches, and the possibility of gay marriages raised concerns and divisions among Baptists.

Conservative Baptists have also opposed what many label the "homosexual agenda," an attempt by gay communities across the nation to change laws related to homosexual behavior in the culture. In 2003 the Supreme Court struck down a Texas law that made homosexual activity (oral or anal sex) a crime. Many conservative Baptists attacked the decision as an assault on "Judeo-Christian" moral teachings and as one facet of an effort to secure government approval of same-sex marriages. Some expressed concern that the court decision was yet another step in a "homosexual agenda" to move toward same-sex marriages that would be recognized by the state. Also in 2003 the Southern Baptist Convention announced a program to "redeem" homosexuals and turn them from their sinful lifestyle. It represented an effort to "hate the sin, but love the sinner," as articulated by Baptist leaders.

### America as "Christian Nation"

Perhaps the most volatile debate involved the question "Is America a 'Christian nation'"? In response, some Baptists vehemently denied that any country could be considered "Christian." James Dunn asserted that such a claim was historical ignorance at best and idolatry at worst. He appealed to colonial Baptists the likes of Roger Williams and John Leland, who denied such an idea in the earliest days of the Republic. Other Baptists, such as James Draper, executive director of the Southern Baptist Sunday School Board and at the other end of the ideological spectrum, asserted that "Christianity was assumed in everything that was undertaken in the founding of our country. The United States was to have not established Church, but it was to be Christian."[53] Still other Baptists disagree with Draper's position but affirm that Judeo-Christian principles were at the heart of American democracy and identity. They believe that those principles are steadfastly being undermined by liberalism, secularism, and the loss of the nation's moral compass.[54]

## Baptists and Religious Liberty:
## Separatists and Accommodationists

These questions have led many conservatives to distinguish between religious liberty—freedom for religious observances without government intervention—and separation of church and state—problematic attempts to keep religion out of the public sphere and promote secularism. Many liberal and moderate Baptists insist that conservatives have simply sold out to the Christian Right and its effort to perpetuate a Protestant establishment, implicitly or explicitly. They continue to assert a separationist position, drawing explicit boundaries to avoid implicit or explicit establishmentarianism.

This division has led to a distinction between Baptist separatists and Baptist accommodationists. Separatists claim a strict reading of the Constitution's Establishment Clause, that "Congress shall make no laws concerning the establishment of religion or prohibiting the free exercise thereof." They watch to see that the state in no way aids religious communities, lest it create de facto establishments, and they continue to press for separation of church and state. Accommodationists, as Barry Hankins notes, essentially believe that "government should take a friendly stance toward religion, accommodating it wherever possible," and "are willing to permit far more government support for religion under the Establishment Clause than are separatists, even to the point of supporting government funds for religious institutions so long as this is done on a nonpreferential basis. Generally, separationists want only as much accommodation as is required under the Free Exercise Clause."[55]

Hankins cites Albert Mohler, president of the Southern Baptist Theological Seminary, Louisville, Kentucky, as representative of those conservative Baptists who are hesitant to use the term "separation of church and state" in referring to relations between the two "kingdoms." While Mohler agrees that religious liberty is an important aspect of Baptist heritage, he believes that moderate/liberal Baptists "made a creed out of the amorphous idea of religious liberty, taking it out of all proportion to where it belongs in the whole

Baptist system and insisting that there is only one way to view all issues."[56]
Hankins concludes that Mohler finds that the extreme "separationist" Baptists are in error since their position "emanates from progressivism and . . .
this stance contributes to the secularization of American culture." He quotes
Mohler's observation: "I think the phrase 'separation of church and state' is
a very unfortunate statement."[57]

Baptist attorney and separationist Melissa Rogers responds that those
who "tie the doctrine of church-separation to the Establishment Clause and
link religious liberty with the Free Exercise Clause" are guilty of a "fundamental misunderstanding." She insists that both "clauses require the separation of church and state," since "the Free Exercise Clause commands church-state separation by ensuring that government takes care not to burden
religious with unnecessary regulation. The Establishment Clause commands
church-state separation by requiring the government to refrain from attempts to turn religion into a creature of the state."[58]

During the early twenty-first century, Baptist separationists and accommodationists collided over issues of "faith-based funding" proposed by the
administration of President George W. Bush as a way of providing government money for church-related ministries. The Baptist Joint Committee was
particularly outspoken in opposition to these efforts to permit churches to
apply for certain government loans while being exempt from requirements
related to hiring and other policies.

An accommodationist approach suggests that Baptists and other religious
groups had been "denied their rights" to tax monies because they were not
able to conform to bureaucratic requirements. Comments from President
George W. Bush reflect that approach in acknowledging that government
"has no business endorsing a religious creed. . . . Yet government can and
should support social services provided by religious people." He concluded
that "faith-based programs should not be forced to change their character or
compromise their mission."[59] Bush proposed that grants be distributed to
churches and other nonprofit agencies that would be permitted some exemption from certain requirements regarding hiring and use of funds.

Separationists, often represented in the Baptist Joint Committee, warn
that this is a way of bringing religious communities into the government
sphere and would compromise longstanding church/state divisions. Holly
Hollman, chief counsel for the Joint Committee, notes: "There is inherent
conflict between allowing religious social service providers to maintain their
distinctive character and complying with the Constitution's prohibition

against government funding of religious activities such as religious worship, instruction or proselytization."[60]

African American Baptists are particularly divided over these questions, some seeking to fund ministries with faith-based grants and others warning that such involvements are a compromise that would make religious communities beholden to government and the Republican Party. Some of their congregations have used or are seeking state funds for community housing or service projects.

The issue of public display of religiously based documents was played out in 2003 when Roy Moore, chief judge of the Alabama Supreme Court and a conservative Baptist, attracted national attention with his display of a stone engraving of the Ten Commandments in the Alabama statehouse in Montgomery. When the courts ruled that the obelisk be removed, Moore refused to comply. Both he and the commandments were subsequently removed from their positions. In response, conservative Christians from around the nation showed up in Montgomery to protest. Moore insisted that his effort was a battle between secularism and the religious foundations of the American Republic and that his opponents were attempting to remove all vestiges of faith from the American public square. His actions and the resulting court responses galvanized conservative Christians, especially Baptists from across the nation. The event served to punctuate the continuing divisions over the role of religion in public life and gave evidence of the diverse readings of history evident in American and Baptist communities. Reflecting on these divisions, William Brackney writes: "Unaware of their basically liberal heritage in matters pertaining to religious liberty, many modern Baptists are not as concerned about freedom as with their task to create a cultural Christianity."[61] In the end, Baptists will surely remain divided over which of multiple readings to give to their history within the church of Jesus Christ and the American Republic.

Fig. 1. First colored Baptist church, Savannah, Georgia. Church organized ca. 1788 by slave-preacher Andrew Bryan. Building erected in 1794. (Courtesy of Schomburg Center, Manuscripts, Archives, and Rare Books Division, the New York Public Library.)

Fig. 2. Mountain Mission School, East Tennessee, ca. 1920. These schools were often founded by home missionaries working in the Appalachian region. (Courtesy of Southern Baptist Historical Library and Archives, Nashville, Tennessee.)

Fig. 3. Exterior of Sardis Primitive Baptist Church, Charlton County, Georgia. The church was organized in 1819. This is the fourth or fifth building. (Courtesy of John Crowley.)

Fig. 4. Pulpit of Sardis Primitive Baptist Church, Charlton County, Georgia. (Courtesy of John Crowley.)

Fig. 5. Front view of the First Baptist Church, Charleston, South Carolina, probably the oldest Baptist church in the South, founded in the 1690s. (Courtesy of First Baptist Church, Charleston, South Carolina.)

Fig. 6. Interior of the sanctuary of First Baptist Church, Charleston, South Carolina, the chancel area. (Courtesy of First Baptist Church, Charleston, South Carolina.)

Fig. 7. Interior of the sanctuary of First Baptist Church, Charleston, South Carolina, view from the pulpit. (Courtesy of First Baptist Church, Charleston, South Carolina.)

Fig. 8. Dexter Avenue Baptist Church, Montgomery, Alabama, ca. 1975. In 1957, the Reverend Dr. Martin Luther King, Jr., 25 years old, became pastor of the church. (AP photo.)

Fig. 9. Reverend Dr. Martin Luther King, Jr., Baptist pastor and civil rights leader. (Oliver F. Atkins/Atkins Collection/George Mason University Libraries.)

Fig. 10. Nannie Helen Burroughs, National Baptist leader and Women's training school founder. (Courtesy Helen Burroughs School, Inc.)

Fig. 11. Dr. Howard Thurman, African American Baptist, mystic, preacher, and writer. (Courtesy of Morehouse College.)

Fig. 12. John Sherfey, preaching, Fellowship Independent Baptist Church, Stanley, Virginia, 1977. (Photo by Jeff Todd Titon.)

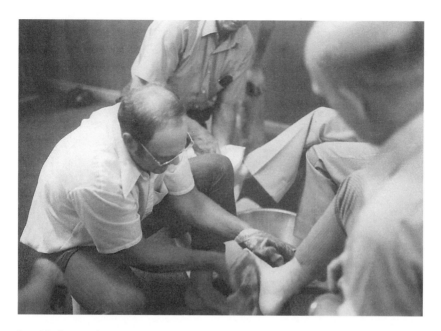

Fig. 13. Footwashing, as observed among various Baptist groups, usually in conjunction with the Lord's Supper. (Reprinted from *Foxfire, 7*, 1982, p. 367, with permission of the Foxfire Fund, Inc., Mountain City, Georgia. www.foxfire.org.)

Fig. 14. Ordination service, First Baptist Church, Savannah, Georgia. (© 1999 First Baptist Church, Savannah, Georgia.)

## CHAPTER EIGHT

# Ethnicity and Race in Baptist Churches

Baptist beliefs and practices are present among a variety of racial and ethnic groups in the United States. While the majority of Baptists reflect Anglo-Saxon lineage, many come from a variety of ethnic and racial communities, including African Americans, Germans, Swedes, Danes, Norwegians, Japanese, Latinos, and others. They developed churches and schools, as well as associational and denominational connections. Some were assimilated into various Baptist groups while others founded specific ethnically or racially based Baptist denominations. As noted previously, early immigration brought Europeans to America who brought Baptist beliefs with them or accepted Baptist views after their arrival.

## Baptists and Ethnic Communities

The mid-nineteenth and early twentieth centuries witnessed Baptist growth among Native American, African American, and immigrant communities in the United States, much of it instigated by the American Baptist Home Mission Society. From this came numerous associations related to ethnic minorities. These included conferences and unions related to Germans, Swedes, Italians, Poles, Portuguese, Hungarians, Danes, Norwegians, Czechs, Romanians, Latvians, and Russians. As one scholar writes, "With the tide of immigration shifting from northern Europeans to peoples from southern and eastern Europe in the late nineteenth and early twentieth century, many Baptists felt a double duty toward reaching them—not only to win them to

Christ but also to help save the nation from the impact of alien values which they brought with them."[1] Thus some evangelization efforts were also related to Americanization. At the same time, these new groups formed new Baptist congregations with their own approach to Baptist identity.

By the 1850s, Swedish immigrants founded the Baptist General Conference, a movement strongly influenced by Swedish pietism and its emphasis on religious experience and "heart religion." These churches retained the use of Swedish in worship service and other church gatherings well into the twentieth century. General Conference Baptists founded Bethel Seminary in 1871 in Chicago, Illinois. It moved to various locations and for a time was the Swedish Department of Baptist Union Seminary, which in 1892 became the University of Chicago Divinity School. Bethel Seminary moved to St. Paul, Minnesota, in 1914; there it was related to Bethel Academy, later Bethel College. Those of Swedish descent dominated church and denominational life until the latter twentieth century when the membership became less directly tied to its early ethnic heritage.[2]

During the 1850s German immigrants who accepted Baptist views helped to form the North American Baptist Conference among German-speaking churches in the United States and Canada. The American Baptist Home Mission Society was particularly active in work with Germans in the nineteenth and early twentieth centuries. Two significant waves of German-Russians immigrated to the United States in the 1920s and 1940s, many of them with Baptist connections. Some united with the North American Baptist Conference.

With the beginning of World War I, German Baptists increasingly abandoned the German language in worship and dropped German ethnicity in their denominational references, partly as an effort to assert their patriotism. In spite of this, some churches departed the German-oriented denomination lest they be thought to be too foreign.

During the latter twentieth century, the denomination extended missionary work among Hispanics in the United States and Mexico. Other urban congregations have developed ministries with Asian immigrants moving to Canada and the United States.[3]

Baptist missionary work with Hispanics began in California, New Mexico, and Texas in the nineteenth century. Southern Baptists and the American Baptist Home Mission Society were particularly active in the early work with Hispanics. In 1910 Mexican Baptists in Texas founded a separate convention, today known as the Hispanic Baptist Convention. It united with the Baptist General Convention of Texas in 1964. A Hispanic Baptist Theological Seminary was founded in San Antonio in 1947. Today, a Korean Baptist Convention also works with an expanding group of Asian Baptists in the United States.[4]

## Baptists and Race

Racial issues have divided Baptists in America since the time of slavery. In fact, in one of the great ironies of American history, Baptists have often found themselves at odds over racially related issues in their own churches and in the nation at large. During the civil rights movement some Baptists were staunch defenders of segregation and racial inequality while others were at the forefront of efforts to secure racial equality in the United States. One way to study the history of Baptists in America is to trace the relationships between black and white Baptists from the colonial period to the present. At the beginning of the twenty-first century racial segregation continued to characterize the majority of Baptist churches in the United States for a variety of complex reasons that are well worth exploring.

While the earliest concerted efforts at Christianizing slaves probably began with Southern Anglicans in the late 1700s, Baptists and other Protestants soon followed suit, initiating attempts to evangelize slaves, teaching them the rudiments of Christianity and encouraging them to trust Christ as Lord and Savior even as they remained true to their earthly masters. Many Africans responded by receiving baptism and admission to the membership of white Baptist churches. Slaves in frontier settings were taken to camp meetings and revival services, where many of them experienced dramatic conversions and were added to the church membership rolls. While blacks were admitted as members, they were often required to sit in designated areas or slave galleries in the back or in the balcony of the meetinghouse. Black preachers frequently traveled with white evangelists, preaching and exhorting sinners to repentance, conducting services in the slave quarters, and responding to the spiritual needs of the Africans. Slave owners were cautious about such efforts, and religious communities sometimes had to assure them that salvation did not affect the slave's earthly status of servitude.

Baptist church minutes give evidence of the presence of slaves and their interaction with churchly issues. Discipline was frequent in nineteenth-century Baptist churches, and slaves were frequently the objects of such actions. Occasionally the slaves could secure a hearing from the congregation in matters of cruelty or mistreatment by their masters. Cruelty to slaves could result in discipline, as illustrated by this notation from the minutes of the Forks of Elkhorn Baptist Church, Kentucky:

> Br Palmer complains against Br. Stephens and his Wife for not dealing with their Negroe Woman & bringing her before the Church and for putting her in Irons—Br. Stephens was Acquited [*sic*]. A second Charge against Sister Stephens for giving their Negroe Woman the lye—She was Acquited from both charges.[5]

In 1806 the same church took up an amendment that read: "Query: does this Church think that Baptist Preachers are Authorised from the word of God to Preach Emancipation of Negroe slaves, the above Query [was] voted out [defeated]."[6]

Other Baptists disagreed and formed antislavery societies in the early 1800s. For example, David Barrow (d. 1891), pastor of the Mount Sterling Baptist Church in Kentucky, was instrumental in gathering his church and eight other congregations into a new association called the Baptized Licking-Locust Association, Friends of Humanity in 1807. Thoroughly abolitionist, these congregations rejected any fellowship with Baptists or Baptist churches that supported slavery in any way and would not admit known slave owners to membership. One of its many antislavery resolutions declared: "There are professors of Christianity in Kentucky, who plead for it [slavery] as an institution of the God of mercy; and it is truly disgusting to see what pains they take to drag the holy scriptures of truth, into the service of this heaven daring iniquity."[7] Questions over slavery and the place of blacks in Baptist congregations were evident well before the Civil War and the Emancipation Proclamation.

At the same time, independent congregations were also evident among black Baptists, in the North and in the South. The first black Baptist church in the South was probably the Silver Bluff Church, on the South Carolina side of the Savannah River, near Augusta, Georgia. Records suggest that the slave George Liele (Lisle) organized the church between 1773 and 1775, but tradition places it as early as 1750.[8] Liele, who later immigrated to Jamaica and did Baptist ministry there, was also instrumental in the conversion of Andrew Bryan and Jesse Peters. These two slaves founded the First African Church of Savannah, probably in 1788. By 1800 there were as many as 25,000 black Baptists in the United States, approximately 150,000 by 1850, and 500,000 by 1870.[9]

Of the African congregations that arose in the South, many were led by self-ordained preachers who were slaves or "freedmen." One such slave preacher was Nat Turner (1800–1831), a slave of Methodist owners who had connections with Baptists. Turner's revolt against slaveholding society in Virginia in 1831 led to the death of fifty-seven individuals, including members of his own master's family. Turner and sixty other insurrectionists were arrested, and he was executed on November 11, 1831. The Nat Turner Revolt struck fear into the hearts of the slave-owning society, which had long feared slave uprisings, and led to increased monitoring of slave activities, including worship. Thus Miles Mark Fisher commented:

> A Negro Baptist church was somewhat independent in the North, although associations like those in Philadelphia and New York could appoint preachers for Negro churches. In the south a large congregation of colored people could lay no claim to sovereignty apart from the white people. This point is illustrated in the First African Baptist Church, Savannah, whose membership of seven hundred was divided into three churches by the Savannah Association in 1802. . . . Only after emancipation can complete autonomy be called a distinguishing mark of a Negro Baptist Church.[10]

As noted earlier, emancipation and the South's defeat in the Civil War led to a variety of responses from Baptists black and white. Baptists from the North, many acting through the American Baptist Home Mission Society, worked in "freedmen's relief," founded churches, and established schools throughout the South. At war's end, Northern Baptists sent numerous home missionaries into the South to work with churches and newly freed blacks and to found a variety of educational institutions, many of which became part of the United Negro College network. These included Richmond Seminary (Virginia), Atlanta Baptist Seminary (Georgia), Roger Williams University (Tennessee), Bishop College (Texas), Selma University (Selma), Spelman Seminary (Georgia), Hartshorn Memorial College (Virginia), Florida Institute (Florida), Indian University (Oklahoma), Benedict Institute (South Carolina), Wayland Seminary (Washington, DC), Jackson College (Mississippi), Seminole Female Academy (Oklahoma), and Tullehassee Manual Labor School (Oklahoma).

By the 1870s and 1880s a mass exodus of blacks from white churches North and South was under way, leading to the founding of a variety of new African

American Baptist congregations. Freestanding black Baptist churches were established in significant numbers throughout the nation, not only in the South. These churches then formed a variety of African American Baptist associations, missionary societies, state conventions, and national denominational groups.

The National Baptist Convention was founded in 1895 as several earlier associations and conventions came together. As Harvey Johnson, a Baltimore minister, saw it, the new churches were a sign that African American Baptists would stop "fawning, bowing, scraping, begging at the white man's feet for a few crumbs from his table." They would minister specifically to the needs of blacks rather than serve "merely as a means to an end for the white man's greater and stronger organization."[11] Another black Baptist concluded: "God had unquestionably linked the race on the religious world through the Baptist church and given each individual sufficient latitude for the utmost expansion of his possibilities."[12]

White Southerners soon aligned themselves with the prevailing segregationist policies of their region and with the prevailing belief in the racial inferiority of blacks. Near the turn of the century, Henry Holcombe Tucker (1819–1891), Baptist minister and president of Mercer University and the University of Georgia, articulated that position and even linked it with Christian orthodoxy in remarks published in 1883. Tucker wrote:

> We do not believe that "all men are created equal," as the Declaration of Independence declares them to be; nor that they will ever become equal in this world. . . . We think that our own race is incomparably superior to any other. . . . As to the Negro, we do not know where to place him; perhaps not at the bottom of the list, but certainly not near the top. We believe that fusion of two or more of these races would be an injury to all, and a still greater injury to posterity. We think that the race-line is providential, and that . . . any . . . great intermingling [of the races] must have its origin in sin.[13]

Tucker concluded by noting that these views were racially "orthodox," adding, "If we are not so, we should be glad for some one to point out the heresy."[14] This approach to racial differences serves to illustrate the deep divide that existed between black and white Baptists in the South and elsewhere well into the years leading up to the civil rights movement (and in some cases beyond). H. Shelton Smith commented that "Tucker's racial creed" became extremely important after emancipation because whites "could no longer employ the power of ownership to keep freedmen in 'their place,' and thus had to provide social sanctions (buttressed by laws) to produce the same result."[15]

As the twentieth century began and Jim Crow laws were solidified in what became the South's "separate but equal" society of racial segregation and inequality, black and white Baptists in the United States in general and the South in particular fell into various roles brought on by racial categories implicit or explicit throughout the culture. In his excellent study, *Redeeming the South*, Paul Harvey writes of this period:

> In the 1920s they [African Americans] entered a period of relative political dormancy until the flowering of the Civil Rights movement. White southern Baptist progressivism was defeated from within; black Baptist progressivism was defeated from without. The black Baptist story during the era of Jim Crow, then, is not one of triumph but of struggle, of small victories hard won and even harder kept.[16]

E. C. Morris, one of the early advocates of "black self-help," acknowledged that while there were "no color or racial lines" in God's kingdom, "race distinctiveness" was an ever-present reality. After World War I, Morris affirmed that black Baptists were loyal citizens of the United States, even after generations of slavery and the inequalities that they continued to experience. He declared that every time the American flag "has been placed in the hands of the ebony-hued sons of America its folds have not been allowed to trail in the dust."[17] Blacks had died for American freedom on foreign battlefields and deserved greater freedom themselves in their home country. He and many other black Baptist ministers encouraged their white counterparts to aid in the destruction of racism.[18] For most white Baptists, this was not a real possibility.

Harvey notes that for most white Baptists in the South, racial divisions were less an "American dilemma" than merely a "Negro 'problem' that could be managed successfully by judicious whites." Most tended to criticize or bemoan the inability of blacks to succeed as a race, develop effective leaders, and benefit from educational opportunities made available to them by the white majority. Harvey concludes: "Even racial 'liberals' among white southern Baptists were, at best, paternalists who proffered 'patience, persuasiveness, and helpfulness' as the answer to the race problem."[19] White Baptist leaders urged patience and hard work as a way of anticipating the possibility of greater strides toward freedom for blacks in the decades to come. They generally opposed lynching and other mob actions, while urging whites to practice "law and order, almost deliberately disavowing any sympathy for the victims of mob action."[20]

The early African American denominations and mission boards looked straight toward Africa as an object of their missionary imperative. Like their white counterparts, many black Baptists viewed African religion as pagan and Africans as in need of deliverance from disease and sin. Yet they were also suspicious of Anglo-Saxon missionary efforts, since they often were carried out in conjunction with the exploitation of the continent and its people. The genuine gospel would promote New Testament Christianity, not "the character of any nation of Europe, Asia, or America."[21]

Yet for white Baptists in the South, even missionary strategy had racial implications. For example, James Franklin Love, executive secretary (director) of the Southern Baptist Foreign Mission Board from 1915 to 1928, shaped missionary policy in light of racial attitudes. In 1890 Love declared: "Let us not forget that to the white man God gave the instinct and talent to disseminate His ideals among other people and that he did not, to the same degree, give this instinct and talent to the yellow, brown or black race. The white race only has the genius to introduce Christianity to all lands and among all people."[22] Love proposed a mission methodology that he believed would model that of the Apostle Paul and that would first evangelize Europe, since the Anglo-Saxon race had "the adventurous, the pioneer spirit essential to missionary advance and success. No yellow, brown, red or black race is thus constitutionally adapted to this task."[23] Racial attitudes shaped the theology and strategy for missionary outreach among Southern Baptists.

Yet missions also became a means for confronting Southern Baptist segregationist views. While many SBC churches approved policies that set membership boundaries to exclude black members, questions ultimately arose over whether churches could admit Africans who came to the United States, often to study at Baptist-related schools. The presence of African students at Baptist universities and colleges created a serious theological dilemma that led to fissures in numerous congregations. For many white Baptists, to admit Africans meant bending the color line in ways that could lead African Americans to pursue membership in the church. Thus some church members opposed admission of any person of color to all-white churches. Others countered that Africans were the object of Baptist conversionist efforts and the refusal to accept them as members in American churches had the potential to undermine the missionary endeavor itself.

Mercer University in Macon, Georgia, changed its admissions policies regarding blacks when African students sought to matriculate at the school.

This did not keep churches in the Macon area from refusing admission to African students because of their color. Many white churches in the South developed membership regulations that were specifically intended to keep blacks from joining the congregations. In certain instances, church leaders actually stood at the doors of the church to keep out African Americans who might attempt to enter the church building for Christian worship.

Many prominent Baptist preachers in the South developed particular ways of responding to the developing calls by blacks for a change in the "separate but equal" society. In *God's Long Summer: Stories of Faith and Civil Rights*, Charles Marsh documented such a response in the approach of Douglas Hudgins, pastor of First Baptist Church, Jackson, Mississippi, at the height of the civil rights movement. Hudgins, a Ph.D. graduate of Southern Baptist Theological Seminary in Louisville, Kentucky, was the epitome of the "gentlemen theologians" who led prominent Southern Baptist churches during much of the twentieth century. Hudgins achieved a certain degree of prestige by which he exercised leadership in a variety of organizations in the denomination and the community. His effort to serve as pastor of First Baptist Church influenced his own responses to the civil rights activities that confronted Jackson in the mid-1960s. Marsh observes: "The cross of Christ, Hudgins explained at the conclusion of a sermon in late 1964, has nothing to do with social movements or realities beyond the church; it's a matter of individual salvation. The congregation at First Baptist knew exactly what Hudgins meant."[24]

In 1963 church members had approved a resolution expressing regret at "the present social unrest brought about by agitators who would drive a wedge of hate and distrust between white and colored friends." It declared that First Baptist Church, Jackson would "confine its assemblies and fellowships to those other than the Negro race, until such time as cordial relationships could be established."[25] This resolution was not about admitting blacks to membership but was aimed at keeping them from simply attending services. The same attitudes and actions were multiplied throughout the South during the upheavals of the civil rights movement.

In an article titled "Southern Baptists and Desegregation, 1945–1980," Mark Newman identified three periods that characterized the Southern Baptist response to civil rights. Before 1950 the denomination and its people represented a strong segregationist stance, utilizing a variety of "biblical" and cultural arguments to undergird their views. In 1948 Southern Baptist leader M. E. Dodd touted the rapid development of Southern blacks due to the "efforts of Southerners" and noted: "The Jim Crow law is for the protection of the Negroes themselves. They have places reserved for them on trains and streetcars."[26]

After *Brown v. Board of Education* in 1954, Southern Baptists moved away from segregation, although hesitantly. With the Civil Rights Act of 1964, they increasingly repudiated segregation and mistreatment of blacks as "unchristian." Certain individuals related to the denomination's Social Service Commission (later called Christian Life Commission), the Woman's Missionary Union, and the Home Mission Board were early advocates of integration and a changing response to racial divisions in the South and among Baptists. During the 1951–1952 school year Southern, Southwestern, and New Orleans Baptist Seminaries opened their admissions programs to African American students.[27]

Professors at several Baptist schools confronted controversy when they spoke out against segregation and even participated in the civil rights movement. T. B. Maston, longtime professor of ethics at Southwestern Baptist Theological Seminary in Fort Worth, published his first call for racial equality in 1946 under the auspices of the Women's Missionary Union. In *The Bible and Race* (1959) and *Segregation and Desegregation*, published the same year, Maston set forth what he believed to be a biblical mandate for breaking down walls of racial division in the society and the church. Henlee Barnette, professor at Southern Baptist Theological Seminary in Louisville, was another ethicist deeply concerned that Baptists change their views on segregation and civil rights. Barnette wrote extensively on the subject and marched with Martin Luther King Jr.

Professors like Barnette and Maston influenced generations of Baptist students, some of whom carried their views into the churches. Others worked outside the academy, among them Clarence Jordan (1912–1969), a graduate of Southern Baptist Theological Seminary who founded Koinonia Farm, an interracial community near Americus, Georgia, in 1942. The farm was to offer a witness to racial justice, peace, and "fellowship," the English translation of the Greek word *koinonia*. Jordan and others who joined him were trailblazers for racial reconciliation in Georgia and a reference point for others responding to racial issues throughout the region. Koinonia Farm became a center of controversy and the subject of significant racist reaction, with acts of violence perpetrated against the community. In 1968 Jordan joined Baptist Millard Fuller in forming Koinonia Partners and extended its work to include the building of low-income housing.[28] Fuller later developed Habitat for Humanity, a program devoted to using volunteer labor to construct housing for the impoverished.

As the civil rights movement got under way, certain Southern Baptist–related segregationists urged the denomination to reaffirm support for Jim Crow laws, but denominational leaders generally sought to steer a middle course, refusing to advocate segregation and in many cases remaining silent on the issue. Those pastors who were outspoken advocates of racial integration were often silenced or fired outright. Many churches split over whether to admit blacks to worship and membership. As the movement intensified and produced significant white opposition, the SBC and many of its state conventions called for peace and reconciliation. A 1961 SBC resolution denounced mob violence as well as "unwarranted provocation" from outside forces.[29]

In 1964 the denomination's Christian Life Commission recommended that the SBC support a statement asserting, "We pledge to support the laws designed to guarantee the legal rights of Negroes in our democracy and to go beyond these laws by practicing Christian love and reconciliation in all human relationships." The convention resisted that more precise statement in favor of a narrowly approved resolution that ignored national legislation and asserted that the "final solution" to such matters would come only "on the local level" through churchly responses to the guidance of the Holy Spirit.[30]

The SBC Home Mission Board was also at the forefront of racial reconciliation during the 1960s and 1970s. Its *Home Missions Magazine* was the first SBC periodical to run "mixed race" photos depicting whites and blacks together. Even that photographic report of interracial connections created significant controversy within the convention.

During the 1970s the SBC increasingly identified itself with racial integration, openness, and dialogue, at least as its formal statements and the work of several of its boards would indicate. SBC-related churches with a majority of African American members increased 76 percent during the years 1973–1976, from 191 to 340. In 1980 predominantly black SBC churches numbered approximately 600. Yet most congregations in the SBC continued to be almost exclusively white.

During the 1970s the nation experienced trauma over the practice of busing students across school districts to achieve racial balance. Cities from Boston to Louisville had major outbreaks of violence associated with the practice. While many Baptist clergy and laity worked to alleviate the tensions, others opposed the actions. Out of those actions another generation of parochial schools, many founded by and in Baptist churches, appeared as alternatives to integration and busing.[31]

In 1995 a resolution was presented to the Southern Baptist Convention expressing repentance for the denomination's activities, implicit and explicit, in slavery and segregation. The resolution, written by numerous Southern Baptists black and white, was approved by messengers who recognized that it was impossible for the South's most prominent denomination to seek to appeal to African Americans without repenting for significant portions of the denomination's history. It acknowledged failures related to "the role that slavery played in the formation of the Southern Baptist convention" and the "bitter harvest" that "we continue to reap" because of "acts of evil such as slavery."[32] It concluded: "Be it further RESOLVED, that we apologize to all African Americans for condoning and/or perpetuating individual and systemic racism in our lifetime; and we genuinely repent of racism of which we have been guilty, whether consciously (Psalm 19:13) or unconsciously (Leviticus 4:27)."[33] Commenting on the importance and theological difficulties involved in such a statement, Barry Hankins observes: "This carefully worded section addresses the need for an apology and plea for forgiveness without the theologically problematic notion of repenting for the sins of others." In many respects, the resolution was essential to continued work between Southern Baptists white and black, and increasing demands from African Americans who could not in good conscience develop affiliations with the SBC so long as its participation in the South's slave and segregationist cultures remained publicly unacknowledged.

## Independent Baptists and Race

Independent Baptists seem to have maintained publicly segregationist and other racist positions longer than other Baptist groups. Even a brief survey of many of Independent Baptist–related periodicals such as the *Bible Baptist Tribune* (Springfield, Missouri), the *Fundamentalist* (Fort Worth, Texas), and the *Sword of the Lord* (Murfreesboro, Tennessee), give evidence of extensive attention, even diatribe, dealing with racial issues. These fundamentalists were associated with independent congregations whose pastors participated in networks or fellowships. Many, as noted earlier, were biblical separatists who sought to disassociate themselves from any groups or individuals who appeared to compromise the faith, create anarchistic responses to the state, or who themselves were associated with any vestige of secularism.

The civil rights movement posed difficulties for these Baptist fundamentalists for several reasons. First, it encouraged a "mingling" of the races that extended the possibility of racial intermarriage, a practice they believed to be a violation of biblical teaching. Second, it undermined the social order by perpetuating anarchy and social unrest. Third, at the very least it was a vehicle used by communists and socialists to promote their agendas in the society. At worst, it was a communist-inspired effort to destroy American democracy and Christian freedom. Fourth, civil rights leaders were infidels, liberals, and heretics whose views on the fundamentals of the faith put them outside orthodox Christianity. Underneath this rhetoric, however, was a powerful racism linking theology with segregationist ideology.[34]

John R. Rice, editor of the *Sword of the Lord*, responded to *Brown v. Board of Education* by noting that the "Supreme Court, largely influenced by the New Deal and left-wing thought, has changed its stand" from its earlier "separate but equal" rulings on race. Ever a segregationist, he acknowledged that "godly colored people, born again, would be in heaven," yet even there "we may prefer to be with those we know than with those we do not know."[35] Even heaven was separate but equal. Rice acknowledged that racial hatred was wrong "when stirred up in a church by a modernist infidel preacher in the North as it is stirred up in the south by an over-zealous defender of Southern white womanhood and the status quo."[36] Nonetheless, he feared that integration would mix the races in ways that undermined biblical teachings and violated the Divine order.

Rice was not alone; other Independent Baptists also had harsh words for civil rights activities and leaders. The American Baptist Association, an Independent Baptist group based primarily in Arkansas and Texas, passed a resolution at its 1963 conference that reaffirmed support for segregation "in social activities" as part of a "divinely inspired racial plan."[37] T. H. Masters, Baptist editor of the *Fundamentalist*, wrote that there were divinely ordained "mental" and "moral" differences between blacks and whites, and insisted, "If [President] Kennedy wants to help the colored people, why doesn't he urge them to raise their moral standard if they expect to be accepted in good society?"[38] Masters, a confirmed segregationist, equated racial differences with moral deficiencies in nonwhites.

Noel Smith, editor of the *Bible Baptist Tribune*, warned that African Americans were their own "worst enemy" and suggested that "the most strutting, merciless, brutal enemy the Negro ever had on this earth is the Negro." He asserted that Martin Luther King was "lying" when he "blamed" whites for the problems of blacks. Smith observed that, generally speaking, "self-discipline, responsibility, energy, persistency, sound judgment, and pride in their surroundings, are foreign terms" to African Americans.[39]

Many fundamentalist Baptists were highly critical of the religious observances practiced at some civil rights demonstrations. One preacher attacked the use of prayer at public demonstrations as "sham-praying." He concluded that the New Testament knew "no antics, no mob demonstrations, involving recalcitrant believers."[40] Others attributed the violence to the work of "modernists," "pinks," and socialists. Rice repudiated those preachers who he believed had abandoned evangelism for social action, and he called churches to return to "the old-fashioned gospel instead of the newfangled social gospels, the United Nations, the National Council of Churches, sit-downs, pickets, strikes and lawbreaking."[41]

While some of the contributors to Independent Baptist periodicals acknowledged the tragedy of Martin Luther King's assassination, many were quick to suggest that he had sown the seeds of his own destruction. In one of the harshest responses, an Alabama Baptist pastor lamented King's death but labeled the civil rights leader's movement "anti-Christian" since "Jesus Christ was not and is not a 'revolutionary.'" He concluded that Bible-believing Christians should mourn the fact that a martyr had been made of a liberal preacher who had "rejected the cardinal tenets of Biblical Christianity for the heathen philosophy of Mahatma Gandhi."[42] G. Archer Weniger, a California Independent Baptist minister, insisted that King was a "pro-communist" and "modernist" who denied that hell was "a place of literal burning fire." He concluded that "by this definition, Dr. Martin Luther King is an apostate."[43] Again, Baptist separatism shaped Independent Baptist response to King's assassination.

The civil rights movement created a serious hermeneutical dilemma for many Independent Baptists, since some had linked segregation with biblical authority and divine sanction of the separate but equal laws in the South. Efforts that challenged that interpretation of biblical texts, especially by other Baptists, were a potential threat to the veracity of all Scripture.

Some Baptists who wrote for Independent Baptist periodicals believed that African Americans were somehow morally deficient and that their integration into the dominant white society would be destructive to the American way of life. As conservative Baptists they rejected Martin Luther King's credentials as a Baptist because he was a theological liberal. Thus, if King was wrong on doctrine, he was surely wrong on racial issues and civil rights.

In fact, King's liberalism was a frequent target of Independent Baptist preachers and editors. Several acknowledged King's Baptist connections, his pulpit skills, and his thriving congregation in Atlanta but declared that his work could not be "of God" since he was a theological liberal who "did not believe the Bible." John R. Rice concluded that "although religious infidels boost him as a Christian, Dr. Martin Luther King has openly declared that he does not believe the Bible. He is not a Christian in the historic sense of holding to the great essentials of the Christian faith, he is a 'minister' who doesn't preach the gospel, doesn't save souls."[44] King's liberalism negated all other aspects of his ministry and activism.

Independent Baptists are an outspoken lot. In many respects, they transferred the rhetoric of the fundamentalist/liberal controversy of the 1920s to the civil rights movement of the 1960s. In those volatile years, many seemed to be servants of the Southern status quo, protecting segregation with the language of orthodoxy and social control. They tied the authority of Scripture to the social ethos of their times so that abandoning specific cultural practices meant relinquishing the inerrancy of the biblical text. As political conservatives, they linked the civil rights movement with aspects of communism and anarchy.

Later Independent Baptists distanced themselves from the more blatant attitudes of their forebears, extending relationships with those African American Baptists who could meet the doctrinal litmus tests. However, most of their churches remain predominantly Anglo-Saxon, with limited connections to African American Baptists, especially if they cannot pass the separatist tests.

### African American Baptists and Civil Rights

Innumerable Baptist leaders paved the way for Martin Luther King Jr. and the activities of the Southern Christian Leadership Conference and other civil rights organizations. Civil and religious dissent began well before Rosa Parks and the Montgomery bus boycott.

A 1946 gathering in Montgomery, Alabama, was called by Baptists such as J. Pius Barbour in response to continued efforts by the state to undermine black voting rights. In 1948 a group of African American Baptists, meeting in Birmingham, demanded an end to segregation and called on Christians everywhere to work to overcome the South's separate but equal society.[45] William Holmes Borders, a Georgia Baptist leader, noted in 1948: "The Negro preacher must take the lead in fighting for the civic rights of the southern Negro and he must not flinch before the Ku Klux Klan or any other race hating group. We must serve notice . . . that we will not be intimidated."[46] In assessing these developments, Andrew Manis concluded: "The racial milieu within the black community in general encouraged this burgeoning activity among black Baptists. The stirrings among National Baptists set the stage for the work of Martin Luther King, the Montgomery Improvement Association, and later the SCLC."[47]

As African American soldiers returned home from participation in World War II, black Baptist leaders insisted that their service to the country was yet another reason for the complete abolition of segregation. In testimony before a Senate committee in 1947, black Baptist pastor Sandy F. Ray insisted that with the war's end, "now, we hope for the real America. The America of the constitution. The America of the patriots' dream. The America which we are capable of becoming: 'One nation indivisible, with liberty and justice for all.'"[48] Before the civil rights movement got under way, numerous African American Baptists called for a change in American policy toward their race.

Not all Baptists agreed on the appropriate strategy, however. As noted earlier, National Baptists did not always support King and his agendas for securing civil rights. Joseph Jackson, longtime president of the National Baptist Convention, was an outspoken opponent of King's methods while affirming the need for greater freedom for blacks in the United States. In the 1980s, as he reflected on those earlier years, Jackson noted: "No one could be in step with the times, and not behold this revelation of freedom and feel the urgency and power of its thrust. To be on the side of the movement for freedom was no question: it was a certainty in the minds of all. The only question was methodology."[49] While historian Gayraud Wilmore suggested that the National Baptist Convention "simply refused to be identified" with King, other scholars, like Andrew Manis, insist that the response of National Baptists "was not quite as simple or as monolithic as Wilmore suggests." Jackson's voice was powerful, but it was not the only one present in the convention. Not only did individual churches and ministers in the NBC offer support to King, but, Manis notes, "one can argue that King enjoyed fairly strong institutional support from the National Baptist Convention despite the strong criticism he sometimes received from its president."[50] The NBC gave significant support to the National Association for the Advancement of Colored People (NAACP), and that was generally extended to the Southern Christian Leadership Conference (SCLC) after it was founded by King. Joseph Jackson wrote with anticipation shortly after the SCLC was founded of his hopes that

> we, of the National Baptist Convention, would have within our reach a
> group dedicated not only to civil rights but to America and to the Chris-

tian point of view. We believed that now the Convention . . . has brought
into existence a group of young men who understand the visions of the
founders of their convention and who were willing to make a sacrifice . . . to make the Christian ideals of brotherhood a practical reality in
the United States of America.[51]

Jackson apparently believed that King's methods of nonviolence and
civil disobedience went too far. They violated those constitutional boundaries that permitted the right of assembly for the purpose of addressing government response to citizens' grievances. Jackson warned that "unknown
conspirators in pseudo-patriotic cloak" could participate in King's efforts
less to secure human rights than to destroy the American government itself.
He challenged any suggestion that "lawlessness can be substituted for law
and thereby bring to pass an ordered society."[52]

As noted earlier, divisions over civil rights methodology divided the National Baptist Convention during the 1950s and 1960s, leading to the formation of the Progressive National Baptist Convention. At the 1956 convention
meeting, Martin Luther King Jr., fresh from the Montgomery bus boycotts,
preached a sermon titled "Paul's Letter to American Christians," in which he
urged black Baptists to reject "gradualism" and work toward immediate ces-
sation of segregationist practices. Although the crowd was deeply moved
and responded enthusiastically, President Jackson reclaimed the microphone
and was said to have declared: "We must not crown our young heroes too
quickly." King and others began an effort to challenge Jackson's leadership
in the convention. The result was the formation of a new denomination in
1960–1961.[53]

From its inception, the Progressive National Baptist Convention understood itself as unashamedly Baptist and a proponent of civil rights advocacy
in the American nation. After the death of Martin Luther King Jr., Gardner
Taylor, another of the new convention's leaders, acknowledged: "Progressive Baptists may take justifiable pride in the unassailable fact which must
now forever be true, that when he had no spiritual (denominational) resi-
dence. You provided him with an address in the community of Black Baptists. Let angels record that truth and let succeeding generations bring their
gratitude to your tent door."[54]

Progressive National Baptists claim numerous leaders of the continuing
movement for civil rights in America, among them Jesse Jackson, Benjamin
Hooks, William H. Gray III, Walter Fauntroy, William Booth, and Evelyn
Brooks Higginbotham. Writing at the turn of the new century, PNBC leader

Wallace C. Smith observed that the denomination was continuing to work as a "model of decentralized authority" and against "hierarchies, top down decisions and centralized authority." He noted that the denomination was "postured for future cooperative initiatives" with other Baptists and non-Baptist groups. He also observed that many of the PNBC churches are "dually aligned," with connections to multiple Baptist denominations, especially the American Baptist Churches, USA.

The PNBC continues to provide leadership for and commitment to civil rights issues in the United States and elsewhere. For example, National and Progressive Baptists have worked together on the Revelation Corporation, a collective endeavor to promote "economic development issues" in African American communities.[55] Some churches maintain credit unions, housing agencies, and other social services in their respective communities.

Writing of the legacy of the National Baptist Convention, USA John Kinney suggests that black Baptists have made numerous "theological contributions" to "the Christian family and the Baptist fellowship" in general. Their "methodological contribution" involves the "recognition of the legitimacy of personal and cultural experience" and the realization "that faithfulness to God does not require negations of one's particularity."[56] The life and faith of African American Baptists was shaped by the Baptist context inside the larger African American context from slavery through segregation to the civil rights movement and into the present day. The "hermeneutical contribution" (method of biblical interpretation) of black Baptists led them to "an approach to scripture that affirmed the primacy of the word without destroying the life of the word." Black Baptist preachers have been the particular vehicles of this effort to move beyond the crude literalism that led to biblical justification of slavery and segregation to "truth that sets free and . . . transforms."[57] African American Christians in general and black Baptists in particular have made unique "liturgical contributions" to the nature of worship. This is evident in music, preaching, and the "answering congregation" in which members of the audience speak spontaneously throughout the worship service. The spirituality of black preaching and worship unites rhetoric, heart religion, evangelicalism, and music and audience interaction in dramatic ways. Kinney comments: "The National Baptist Convention has helped recover the balance in Baptist life and preserve the 'soul' of Baptist praise."[58]

Concerning the nature of the church (ecclesiology), black Baptists link worship and service, belief and practice in ways that distinguish "faithfulness" as "an incarnational issue not a doctrinal discussion." This, Kinney believes, grew out of their effort to distinguish the liberating power of Christ from "slaveholding piety and racist religiosity that was doctrinally pure but essentially corrupt." Thus, "holistic ministry" was characteristic of black Baptist life from the beginning of the movement.[59] In terms of anthropology, a concern to affirm "the value of Black personhood" remains "an essential message of Black Baptists and the Black church." Likewise, the eschatological contribution of black Baptists involves not "otherworldly escape" but the promise of justice that inspires struggle, "power and purpose" for African Americans and all God's church here and now.[60]

One of the continuing questions regarding Baptists and race involves the segregation of churches black and white in Baptist and other Protestant congregations in the United States. Some still quote a statement attributed to Martin Luther King Jr. that "eleven o'clock on Sunday remains the most segregated hour in American life." While this assertion is certainly true and remains characteristic of Baptist churches across the nation, it requires greater investigation and additional responses involving multiple options. The segregation of the churches must be addressed from a variety of perspectives.

On one hand, integration of churches is an important goal that already occurs in a variety of Baptist congregations that have intentionally sought to include persons of multiple races and ethnic communities. Open membership policies, long opposed in many white congregations especially but not exclusively in the South, were hard won by those who at least hoped to extend the possibility of integration to all races. On the other hand, much segregation remains, for varying reasons. To view interracial relations as only or even primarily measurable by integration of churches may be important but not the exclusive method for forging relationships between black and white Baptists. In fact, many opportunities are being developed between various churches:

1. Some Baptist churches are working to achieve integrated membership evident in welcoming blacks to predominantly white churches and vice versa. This is increasingly true of congregations that place emphasis on charismatic aspects of worship and spirituality. Such integration may occur as churches confront changing racial configurations in specific communities. Others have achieved degrees of integration because they have made an intentional effort to do so, hiring staff, developing worship styles, and reaching out to specific constituencies.

2. Other Baptist communions are attempting to establish new congregations that are intentionally interracial from the beginning. Racial inter-

marriage and integrated neighborhoods also facilitate possibilities for great diversity in congregations old and new.

3. Some Baptist congregations have developed relationships with churches in which another racial group is dominant. They are attempting to move beyond tokenism of "pulpit exchange" or occasional joint services to genuine dialogue between members who engage in shared ministry together.

4. As noted earlier, American Baptist Churches in the USA have made a concerted effort to extend their leadership and membership to a broad range of ethnic groups in the Baptist family. While their leaders acknowledge that they have a long way to go, they have been reasonably successful in these endeavors.

5. A major challenge for Baptist communions involves additional ways in which denominations that are predominantly black or white can work together while retaining their own identities and interchurch relationships.

Baptist leader John Kinney acknowledges that African American–based congregations create significant heritage and space outside the white-dominant American cultural setting. He observes: "I fear that as more and more Black churches are 'absorbed' into the mainline that many of these rich distinctives will be lost, the liberating heritage will be dishonored, and the power of holistic transformation will be diminished. This comment and the general nature of this reflection are intended to be suggestive with the hope that they will engender meaningful discussion and serve as an entrée for further constructive effort."[61]

## CHAPTER NINE

# Women in Baptist Life

Women have shaped Baptist identity and practice since the Baptist movement began in the seventeenth century. In the believers' churches women are equal candidates with men for conversion and baptism. Some of the early Baptist communions had women deacons or deaconesses, who carried out particular ministries especially related to women and children. Women were active in the first congregations founded in the United States. Yet in many of these communions they were not permitted to vote or to speak in public gatherings of both sexes. Women were instrumental in founding mission societies, and they went out as missionaries, married and single, from the beginning of the Baptist missionary movement. Yet women's participation in the ordained ministry of Baptist churches was for the most part a long time coming. At the beginning of the twenty-first century among many Baptist denominations and churches women's ordination and related issues remained a matter of controversy and division. Questions regarding women's participation in Baptist churches produced extensive debates regarding Scripture and tradition in Baptist congregations, often pitting biblical literalists against those who pointed to conversion and baptism as the great equalizers of all people, male and female.

The role of women in Baptist life reflects the development of the "women's sphere" that defined the boundaries of women's activities in church life. It also indicates the evolution of efforts to secure greater participation of women in Baptist ministry and mission.

## The Women's Sphere

In one sense, women represent the core membership of every Baptist church, whether that church is conservative, moderate, or liberal in its theological orientation. In most, perhaps all, Baptist churches, women are in the majority Sunday to Sunday and provide a major element of the weekday ministry of the congregation. Yet in many segments of Baptist life, their activity is proscribed within what is sometimes known as the "women's sphere." Rooted in the early days of the Baptist movement, the women's sphere has become increasingly defined and debated as some women have sought to break out of it. In his study *Religion in the Old South*, Donald Mathews observed that the women's sphere became "a model of behavior and ideals which was peculiarly the possession of women and was based on their unique contribution to the ideal community."[1] The idea of a women's sphere meant that females were permitted to participate in church life in particular ways that included teaching children and other women, nurturing their children in the faith, providing hospitality, engaging in prayer and Bible study, attending worship, and funding church events. This domestic and spiritual role of women in church and family life received significant emphasis among Baptists and other evangelicals. Indeed, because women "were assumed to be more emotional and affectionate than men," they were thought to have a greater capacity for personal piety. Mathews concludes: "It was almost as if men willingly conceded the moral superiority of women in order to prevent active female participation in worldly [and larger churchly] affairs."[2] Women were exalted as paragons of virtue, spirituality, nurture, and motherhood, yet they were also reminded to be submissive to husbands at home and to the male leadership in the church. They often gained significant but indirect power and authority by learning how to "work the system" by which certain boundaries were set for them.

Among Baptists, women were converted, baptized, and admitted to membership in the church. They consistently attended church services in greater numbers than men, a characteristic that continued into the twenty-first century. Women have been and remain in the majority as active members of Baptist churches in the United States. In fact, most Baptist churches could not function were it not for the presence and work of women in the daily and weekly life of the congregation. Yet well into the twentieth century in many Baptist congregations women were not allowed to speak or vote in business meetings, teach men or boys (after they reached adolescence), or receive ordination as deacons or pastors. Within the prescribed context of the sphere, however, they often developed broad networks of mission and ministry and various types of implicit, indirect power. While the women's sphere has been enlarged in many Baptist contexts, it continues to shape the way in which churches view and understand the role of women as members, laity, and clergy. Some insist that the women's sphere is simply an outgrowth of biblically sanctioned roles set for members of both genders in the family and in the church. By following these biblical mandates the church fulfills its divinely appointed tasks. To do otherwise would be to undermine the teaching of Scripture and step outside the "chain of command" connecting people to one another and to God's plan for church and society.

Other Baptists insist that the Christian gospel involves a liberation that brings with it an equality of people that frees all individuals to follow divine callings wherever they might lead. If women are capable of being redeemed in Christ, they are therefore freed to participate in all facets of ministry and leadership in the church and in the world. Debates over the role of women in Baptist churches compel Baptists to confront the way they interpret both the Bible and the traditions of a Christian and Baptist heritage.

## The Bible and Women's Roles

In their efforts to define women's roles in the church, Baptists looked to the Bible for guidance. In *Women's Place in Baptist Life*, Carolyn Blevins sets out various traditional biblical responses to women's issues in the church. She notes that in 1905 Baptist leader W. P. Harvey, editor of the *Western Recorder*, a Baptist periodical, expressed opposition to women's preaching or teaching activities in churches. His biblical citations included the following:

Joel 2:28/Acts 2:17
*After this I shall pour out my spirit on all humankind; your sons and daughters will prophesy, your old men will dream dreams and your young men see visions.* (The Acts text parallels the Joel text.)

As Harvey saw it, "prophecy did not mean preaching." Women could exercise the gift of prophecy in public but could not preach lest they violate specific biblical passages related to women's silence in the church.[3]

I Corinthians 11:5–9 (REB)
*But a woman brings shame on her head if she prays or prophesies bareheaded: it is as bad as if her head were shaved. If a woman does not cover her head*

*she might as well have her hair cut off; but if it is a disgrace for her to be*
*cropped and shaved, then she should cover her head. A man must not cover his*
*head, because man is the image of God, and the mirror of his glory; whereas*
*a woman reflects the glory of man. For man did not originally spring from*
*woman, but woman was made out of man; and man was not created for*
*woman's sake, but woman for the sake of man.*

Harvey believed that during the apostolic age women did have some Spirit-filled inspiration but were to cover their heads to reflect their place in the church as subject to God and male authority.

### I Corinthians 14:34–35
*As in all congregations of God's people, women should keep silent at the*
*meeting. They have no permission to talk, but should keep their place as*
*the law directs. If there is something they want to know; they can ask*
*their husbands at home. It is a shocking thing for a woman to talk at the*
*meeting.*

Harvey suggested that these instructions required the silence of all women in public church services.[4]

### Acts 18:26
*He now began to speak boldly in the synagogue, where Priscilla and Aquila*
*heard him; they took him in hand and expounded the way to him in greater*
*detail.*

From Harvey's perspective, Priscilla only instructed Apollos in private and in the presence of her husband.

### I Timothy 2:11–15
*[Women's] role is to learn, listen quietly and with due submission. I do not*
*permit women to teach or dictate to the men; they should keep quiet for Adam*
*was created first, and Eve afterwards; moreover it was not Adam who was de-*
*ceived; it was the woman who, yielding to deception, fell into sin. But salva-*
*tion for the woman will be in the bearing of children, provided she continues*
*in faith, love and holiness, with modesty.*

Harvey insisted that "teaching and even praying in mixed assemblies were public ministries and were forbidden to women."[5]

By way of contrast, Blevins compares Harvey's views to those of his contemporary Adoniram Judson Gordon, a prominent New England Baptist who offered alternative readings to similar verses.

> Joel 2:8/Acts 2:17. Gordon insisted that the coming of the Holy Spirit created equality of gifts for men and women alike. It opened the door to women's full participation in the church and its ministry.
>
> Acts 21:9 and 1 Corinthians 11:5. These texts refer to the role of women as preachers in the early church. They are able to preach and minister along with men.
>
> 1 Timothy 2:11–15. As Gordon saw it, this was simply a list of instructions related to the "orderly" form of prayer in the church. It was not a prohibition against women's activity in a general sense.[6]
>
> 1 Corinthians 14:34–35. Gordon read these words—"if women want to know something, they should ask their husbands at home"—to be a simple recommendation for preserving order amid communal confusion. They did not limit women's participation in the work of the church, however.[7]
>
> Acts 18:18, 26 and 2 Timothy 4:19. Unlike Harvey, Gordon believed that the woman Phoebe was a teacher who provided significant instruction for the popular preacher Apollos and who worked closely with Paul in the work of the ministry.

Blevins concludes: "Gordon and Harvey stated clearly the diverse ways Baptist students of the Bible interpreted the same scriptures."[8] Their individual interpretations remain today as divisions between Baptist individuals and groups over specific ways of interpreting specific biblical passages that refer to the activities of women in the church past and present. This particular debate occurred in the late nineteenth and early twentieth centuries and illustrates how early were the divisions over how to read biblical texts regarding women's ministerial roles in Baptist churches. Harvey and Gordon were equally orthodox in their theological positions. They simply read the same texts with different interpretations. The debate they precipitated more than a century ago continues. Indeed, in some Baptist communions the traditional women's sphere remains intact, with few if any modifications. Among other Baptists women are offered full participation in church offices, leadership, and ordination. Still others, however, continue to struggle with just how far to go in expanding or abolishing the sphere of women's work in the church and its implications for interpreting Scripture and tradition. This is particularly evident in the evolution of events related to the actual ordination of women in Baptist churches.

## Women and the Churches: Early Ordinations

Women were among the duly baptized members of the first Baptist churches in Providence and Newport, Rhode Island, in the 1640s. Among them was Catherine Scott, the sister of the infamous dissenter Ann Hutchinson, who, as John Winthrop noted, was "infected with Anabaptistry," another name often associated with the early Baptists. She later moved toward the Society of Friends (Quakers).[9]

With the Great Awakening of the eighteenth century, Baptist women moved with their families to the "frontier" areas of the South and the West. Martha Stearns Marshall and her sister-in-law Sarah Johnston Stearns went with their husbands, Daniel Marshall and Shubal Stearns, into Virginia and North Carolina, where they founded churches, among them the Sandy Creek Baptist Church, the first Baptist congregation in North Carolina, in 1755. All were committed to the "enthusiastical" religion of the Separate Baptists with its emotional preaching and religious experience. As John Sparks notes, "After 1747 Marshall and his young wife began a phenomenally active joint ministry that would endure through nearly forty years of labor together, the births of several children, and countless ups and downs."[10] The Marshalls worked together in organizing churches and in ministry to certain Native American tribes. When Daniel Marshall was ordained in Virginia one local Baptist chose not to participate because the Separate Baptists, the Baptist group to which the Stearns and the Marshalls belonged, allowed women to offer public prayer in gatherings where men were also present. As one early commentator observed, Martha Marshall, "being a lady of good sense, singular piety, and surprising elocution has, in countless instances, melted a whole concourse into tears, by her prayers and exhortations."[11]

In Virginia in 1770 a woman named Margaret Meuse Clay was among a group of Baptists put on trial for "unlicensed preaching." The men in the group were convicted and whipped, while a man appeared out of nowhere and paid Margaret Clay's fine so that she would not be beaten. She apparently preached widely.[12]

Baptist women were also part of the Second Great Awakening, which spread across the new settlements on the western frontier—Indiana, Kentucky, Illinois, and other regions west of the Alleghenies. As Christine Leigh

Heyrman has shown, women received conversion in the camp meetings and revivals of the early nineteenth century. Some were baptized without their husbands' permission, a clear break with contemporary protocol. Heyrman writes that in the early years of the Awakening, Baptist and Methodist preachers affirmed that "women of all ages and races might exercise their gifts by speaking before public, sexually mixed, religious gatherings. Thereby the clergy endorsed the view that acceptable forms of female spiritual expression went beyond fulfilling their private roles as dutiful wives, mothers, and sisters."[13]

Heyrman concludes that while the preachers rejoiced in the enthusiasm of the women for evangelical religion, "they bristled when the sisters came forth too often or too forcefully. . . . In other words, early Baptist and Methodist preachers knew that they depended on women a great deal, but perhaps wished that they needed them a good deal less."[14] She shows how many of the revivalist ministers, concerned that they were losing influence with males, turned away from women's public proclamation in churches. Baptist and other Protestant ministers minimized the egalitarian and radical nature of conversion in order to attract men to the faith.

Nonetheless, some women pursued public ministry and even secured ordination in nineteenth-century Baptist churches. The Free Will Baptist General Conference seems to have been the earliest Baptist group to give women greater voice in governance and pulpit. Some Free Will Baptists seem to have licensed women to the ministry relatively early in the nineteenth century. One of the earliest was Ruby Knapp Bixby, licensed by 1846. She married a minister, N. W. Bixby, in 1842. At her death in 1877 her obituary noted: "She was not a subordinate, secondary helpmate, merely, but an independent, self-reliant preacher. Her discourses were characteristically persuasive, and she was more than ordinarily successful. She preached much with churches as pastor, and much as an evangelist."[15]

As early as 1874 Free Will Baptists were admitting women as delegates to their local and regional meetings. In 1877 the denomination's General Conference suggested that "devoted men and women should be encouraged to engage in gospel work, especially in destitute places." By 1886 they decided that "suitable women may be ordained to the Christian ministry, provided there are no objections to such indorsement [sic] other than the matter of sex."[16]

During the years 1876–1885 Bellevernon Free Will Baptist Church in Pennsylvania listed a female named M. A. Brennan as an ordained minister (though not pastor) in the church. Lura Maines was similarly noted in the

Burlington Free Will Baptist church in Michigan, 1877–1879. She also served as pastor of two churches in the state during the years 1880 and 1881. Another woman, Luissa M. Fenner, was reported as minister and pastor of Free Will Baptist churches in Rhode Island during the late nineteenth and early twentieth centuries.[17] Many of these congregations accepted women as ministers but not as pastors. Others called them to the pastorate as well.

Northern Baptists ordained May C. Jones at the Baptist Association of Puget Sound, on July 9, 1882. Much controversy surrounded the event, and critics charged that the vote to ordain was possible because all the opponents had departed in protest. She served as pastor of several Baptist churches in the state of Washington, including First Baptist Church, Spokane, in 1891.[18]

Among the Seventh Day Baptists, the first ordained woman was Experience (Perie) Fitz Randolph, who was graduated from Alfred Theological Seminary in the mid-1880s. By 1895 she had been ordained and was serving Seventh Day Baptist churches in Otselic and Lincklaen, New York. She married Leon D. Burdick in 1888 and helped support him while he went to seminary. The two then served as ministers in various churches. At the time of her death in 1906 she was pastor of the Seventh Day Baptist Church in Cartwright, Wisconsin.[19]

## Women and the Missionary Movement

Women have long served Baptist churches in various capacities, formal and informal. Women served as Sunday school teachers, fund-raisers, hospitality organizers, and general participants throughout Baptist church life. They have worked with children and youth, participated in the music program and cared for the dying, the aged, and the infirm in ways that modeled Christian devotion and commitment in Baptist churches across the United States.

One of the most prominent roles evident among Baptist women was that of missionary. Women were among the earliest American Baptist missionaries and played an important part in facilitating Baptist missionary endeavors across two centuries. Likewise, women were important leaders in efforts to raise money for missionary support. Among the Baptist women who founded a variety of missionary societies from the early nineteenth century was Mary Webb (1779–1861), who established the Boston Female Society for Missionary Purposes in 1800. A person with serious physical disabilities, she epitomized the concern of women to participate in the mission enterprise in whatever way might be open to them. The society funded some of the earliest Baptist female missionaries.

Ann Hasseltine Judson (1789–1826), with her husband, Adoniram, was the earliest female missionary supported by American Baptists. As noted earlier, the couple went out to India under sponsorship of the American Board of Commissioners for Foreign Missions (Congregational). Converted to Baptist views while aboard ship, they requested and received support from Baptists in the United States. Ann Hasseltine Judson, though unordained, was a fully functioning participant in the teaching, writing, and evangelizing work of the missionaries in Burma, their ultimate destination. She mirrored the contribution of many female missionary-spouses who, appointed with their husbands, understood their own ministry as part of a missionary calling. She also demonstrated another tragic side of the missionary calling, particularly characteristic of women, for she died in childbirth while her husband was away on a preaching mission. Adoniram Judson subsequently married two other women, Sarah Boardman Judson (1803–1845) and Emily Chubbuck Judson (1817–1854), each of whom died in missionary service.

Ann Judson's sacrificial life and death became mythic in Baptist churches north and south as a model both for women who went as missionaries and for those who stayed at home. She articulated her own sense of "calling" to the missionary task, in comments such as these, written in 1812: "I desire no higher enjoyment in this life, than to be instrumental of leading some poor, ignorant heathen females, to the knowledge of the Saviour."[20]

Judson's statement illustrates an important emphasis of the early Protestant and Baptist missionary movement with regard to the ministry of women, an approach known as "woman's work for woman." Dana L. Robert describes it thusly: "The proponents of 'Woman's Work for Woman' assumed that non-Christian religions led to the degradation of women, while Christianity provided not only salvation but 'civilization,' the nineteenth century term for social liberation, albeit in western dress."[21] Thus women were acceptable candidates for missionary service if they accompanied their husbands or, as single females, gave themselves to work with other women on the field. In one sense, this approach simply extended the women's sphere by offering a certain kind of missionary work for women but also restricting their work. Paradoxically, however, by giving women the opportunity to minister to other women, Baptists opened the door to women that enabled them to move toward more explicit aspects of Christian ministry.

Northern women formed the Woman's American Baptist Foreign Mission Society in 1871 and the Woman's American Baptist Home Mission Society in 1877. The Foreign Mission Society had organizations in the East and the West until they merged in 1914. Helen Barrett Montgomery, one of the society's leaders at the time of the merger, was a licensed Baptist minister who preached frequently. In 1910 Montgomery wrote a book titled *Western Women in Eastern Lands*, in which she surveyed the half century of women's missionary work in the United States.[22]

The Woman's Missionary Union, Auxiliary to the Southern Baptist Convention, was formed in 1888. The Woman's Convention of the National Baptist Convention was founded in 1900 by African American women. All these organizations soon funded and sent out women as missionaries at home and abroad. Their benevolent work extended to immigrants, freedmen, women, hospitals, inner-city ministries, and other activities. Blevins observes that "they could not vote and could not speak [at Baptist public gatherings], but they could work and make a difference."[23]

Yet even these efforts were met with suspicion from the male-dominated Baptist leadership, some of whom feared that permitting Baptist women to organize their own missionary societies would lead to a violation of biblical boundaries dictating the roles of women and would ultimately produce the most dreaded possibility—women preachers. If some Southern males were outspoken opponents of such efforts, certain Northerners were not far behind. Nineteenth-century New Jersey Baptist males rejected women delegates to their associational meetings out of concern that such a small step would lead to other demands for "perfect equality with male delegates."[24]

In 1888 the Baptist Convention of Virginia forbade women in their state to join the newly formed Woman's Missionary Union, Auxiliary to the Southern Baptist Convention, with the following rationale:

It is to be feared that a separate and distinct organization of the women of the churches for independent mission work might have a tendency, in its ultimate results at least, to compromise that womanly reserve and modesty, and as Paul styles it, that "shamefacedness," which is, in our esteem . . . beyond all price. Not only so, but we further fear that such an independent organization of women naturally tends toward a violation of the divine interdict against [a woman's] becoming a public religious teacher and leader—a speaker before mixed assemblies, a platform declaimer, a pulpit proclaimer, street preacher, lyceum lecturer, stump orator.[25]

Others were even more graphic, noting: "The only four things any Christian can do for missions are to pray, to give, to talk, to go. . . . Three of these are open to women. . . . They may give and pray and go to their heart's content."[26]

It took some time before Baptists agreed on whether to appoint single females to mission fields, but gradually all the boards acquiesced. Women's missionary societies were among the first to send out and fund the work of single females. Indeed, the first Swedish Baptist missionary from the United States was a female named Johanna Anderson, appointed to Burma in 1888 by the Woman's American Baptist Foreign Mission Society.[27]

Southern Baptists appointed their first single woman missionary, Harriet Baker, for work in China in 1849. In 1872 the Richmond (Woman's) Missionary Society sent Edmonia Moon to China, soon followed by her sister Charlotte, known to history as Lottie Moon, perhaps the most famous missionary in Southern Baptist history. Edmonia Moon did not remain long in China, but returned to United States, where she became one of the South's first female physicians. The Woman's Missionary Union, Auxiliary to the Southern Baptist Convention, began in 1888. Its auxiliary status meant that women were permitted to develop their own organization but within a separate "sphere" from the official denomination system. The same was generally true with all Baptist women's mission groups. Many began as auxiliaries or as freestanding societies.

In her history of the WMU, Catherine Allen writes:

> The first generation of WMU officers firmly believed in keeping silence before men. Many sincerely believed this rule was required by the Scriptures; others adopted the custom as politically expedient. . . . Lottie Moon hesitated to speak or to lead worship before men, even unconverted Chinese. . . . One of WMU's earliest guidance manuals for women's societies stated that public meetings might be held. . . . But reports must be read by the pastor or some other gentleman friend.[28]

In some ways women's missionary societies are classic illustrations of the power of the women's sphere in Baptist life. Women were encouraged to promote and finance missions but discouraged from extending that leadership into the larger ecclesiastical systems. Yet missionary societies and mission service extended the work of women as ministers long before official recognition of their move toward ordination and full participation in church affairs was made possible. As Mary L. Mild wrote of those women missionaries:

> The women took their call very seriously. Many gave up opportunities for marriage and family because the one who proposed to them did not have the same sense of ministry. Others married people they hardly

knew in order to be part of a joint venture in ministry. Above all, they understood their call as a call to bring the gospel to other women. They went as teachers, as evangelists and as nurses and doctors.[29]

Women's missionary societies and auxiliaries were significant resources for the Baptist mission movement. Most were highly committed to specific denominations, while developing their own organizational structures and women's networks. The network moved from local church women's societies to associational and state organizations with connections to the national organization. Women's societies often published their own instructional materials, which were made available to grassroots women's study groups in the churches. The literature provided educational materials for the churches and allowed the societies to become self-supporting. These funds and special offerings helped to support specific Baptist groups in their missionary efforts.

Yet one of the major challenges facing women's mission societies today is sustaining membership into a new generation. Declining denominational identities, competing evangelical organizations, women's work outside the home, and diverse schedules have taken their toll on membership in Baptist women's mission societies. Efforts to attract new constituency have involved extensive ministries, reorganization of age-group programs, and additional resource literature.

## Baptists and the Ordination of Women

The ordination of women to the Baptist ministry began in the nineteenth century but did not become a significant movement in most Baptist communions until after the Second World War. Ordination was a major theological issue for Baptist congregations and denominations, with implications for biblical interpretation and church polity. Opponents of women's ordination pointed to the important role of women in the church and their specific "callings" as spiritual guides, nurturers, and church workers. Ordination for women was seen as a violation of biblical mandates regarding women's voices in the church and other texts that indicated the centrality of men in the New Testament communities. Conservatives insisted that the Bible was clear in its delineation between the roles of women and men in "Bible-believing" congregations. They cited a variety of texts that they said showed that:

1. Women were to keep silent in the church.
2. The description of the offices of both pastor and deacon provided reference to men.
3. Women had a particular place in the church because of the actions of Eve, the first woman, in bringing sin to the human race.
4. Jesus called only males to be his disciples.
5. Baptist churches that ordained women were violating biblical teaching and therefore deserved to be disciplined, or even expelled from Baptist associations or other denominational groups.

Those who encouraged the ordination of women also pointed to a variety of biblical mandates and spiritual callings.

1. The apostle Paul acknowledged that barriers between males, females, and other divided groups had been broken down in Jesus Christ.
2. Many women were active in the community that surrounded Jesus and in the early Christian communities.
3. Women received the same gift of the Spirit that was given to men on the day of Pentecost.
4. Conversion and baptism were the great "equalizers" between men and women, freeing both to follow the callings and gifts that God had given them.
5. Baptist churches are autonomous and can choose to ordain those whom they believe to be called to ministry, even if that action stands outside the majority opinion of other Baptist churches or denominations.

Divisions over the ordination of women affected denominations and churches in the Baptist family. Generally, conservative Baptist groups continue to reject the ordination of women, for many of the reasons listed above. Some churches affiliated with conservative Baptist groups completely dismiss the practice. Baptist communions and fellowships such as the Independent Baptists, the Conservative Baptist Convention, the Baptist Missionary Association, the General Association of Regular Baptist Churches, Primitive and Old Regular Baptists, and large segments of the present Southern Baptist Convention oppose women's ordination as deacons or pastors, viewing it as an inappropriate, even unbiblical, action. Churches in the African American–based National Baptist Convention bodies (Incorporated and Unincorporated) are for the most part hesitant to ordain women to ministry. Other groups, such as the Progressive National Baptist Convention, the American Baptist Churches USA, the Alliance of Baptists, the Cooperative Baptist Fellowship, Free Will and Seventh Day Baptists, and General Conference Baptists, affirm ordination or accept the fact that their member churches may choose to ordain women if they wish. At the same time, numerous churches that do ordain women still hesitate to call them as senior ministers. The "stained-glass ceiling" that holds women back from full participation in pastoral leadership is evident among those Baptist groups that affirm the ordination of females. Local church autonomy and denominational order created significant divisions in many Baptist churches and denominations with respect to this issue.

## Women and the Ordination of Baptist Deacons

One of the early conversations regarding women's expanding role in Baptist leadership involves the question of women as deacons. As noted earlier, deacons are one of the two ordained offices in most Baptist churches. Deacons are lay leaders chosen by the congregation. They often act as "servants" of the community, caregivers to the membership. Some Baptist churches use deacons as the chief governing board of the church. In many Baptist groups they, like ministers, are ordained in a service that involves the laying on of hands.

Some Baptist churches have elected women as deacons since at least the nineteenth century. In the latter nineteenth century a growing number of congregations in numerous Baptist denominations began to elect women as deacons, a practice that was not without controversy in the denominations and in the churches. Conservatives insisted that the admonitions regarding women's silence in church and the passage stating that the deacon should be "the husband of one wife" were mandates to prohibit women from becoming deacons. Nonetheless, the number of female deacons surely increases annually in many Baptist communions.

## Women's Ordination in the American Baptist Churches, USA

In 1965 the American Baptist Convention (later ABC, USA) adopted a statement on the status women that encouraged increased emphasis on education for women and asserted that "there should be no differential treatment of men and women in the church, family or society and that there should be equal opportunity for full participation in the work of our God."[30] The statement urged Baptists around the world to promote women's rights, encourage

"full participation" in community and public life, "equalize job opportunities" for women, improve educational opportunities, work toward laws for
equality of males and females, and "secure full participation of women in the
life and work of the church (including pastorates) in all countries."[31]

Four years later the ABC passed another resolution encouraging churches
and agencies to work toward reversing the decline in positions held by women
in church and denominational staffs and developing "policies and practices"
that ensured "adequate opportunities for women" and to "give equal status to
women in positions of major responsibility (deacons, moderators, trustees,
etc.) within the local church."[32]

In 1974 the denomination established the American Baptist Churches
Task Force on Women to serve as a "channel for creating a climate in which
each person has the opportunity to take the risks to become the full person
God intended to use fully her or his god-given gifts." It urged denominational boards to work to "eliminate institutional sexism and empower
women" in all areas of ABC life.[33]

In 2003 American Baptist Women in Ministry reported some 1,392
women on their "professional registry mailing list," a figure that represented
21 percent of all American Baptist ministers. When combined with non-
ordained women in professional ministry the number reached 2,045. The organization reported that of 1,069 women serving in local churches, some 410
of them were women. This represented 9 percent of the pastors serving
American Baptist churches. Female associate pastors numbered 201, or 32
percent of all ABC associate pastors.[34]

## Women's Ordination and the Southern Baptist Convention

The Southern Baptist Convention, the largest Protestant denomination in
the United States, is a case study in the evolution of women's role in the
church and the ordination of women in Baptist life. In June 1973 the SBC approved a resolution on the "place of women in Christian service," acknowledging that "there is a great attack by the members of most women's liberation movements upon scriptural precepts of woman's place in society." In
response, the SBC messengers "reaffirmed God's order of authority" in the
church and in the home. It stated that Christ is head of "every man," "man
the head of the woman," and children subject to their parents "in the Lord."
It concluded that men and women were "dependent on one another."[35]

Resolutions passed at the 1980 and 1981 SBC annual meetings acknowledged the "need or want" of certain women to work outside the home and

urged "fairness for women in compensation, advancement and opportunities for improvement." They also reaffirmed "the biblical role which stresses the equal worth but not always the sameness of function of women" and did "not endorse the Equal Rights Amendment."[36]

The first Southern Baptist woman to receive ordination was Addie Davis, ordained in North Carolina in 1964. By the 1970s numerous efforts were being made to raise the consciousness of Southern Baptists regarding the possibilities of and need for the ordination of women. The denomination's Christian Life Commission held a conference in 1974 on women and the church. Its proceedings were published under the title *Christian Freedom for Women—and Other Human Beings*. The book served as a resource for churches studying the matter. In 1978 a volume titled *Women in the World of Jesus*, written by Southern Baptist educators Frank and Evelyn Stagg, was used as the centerpiece for a conference on "women in church-related vocations," another signal of extended interest in addressing issues related to the leadership of women in church life. By the mid-1970s there were fewer than a dozen ordained women in SBC churches.[37]

At the 1983 conference "Theology Is a Verb," dealing with "issues affecting women," a group of SBC-related women agreed to begin to develop a formal network for support and encouragement of women in the denomination. At a meeting in Louisville, Kentucky, that same year, Nancy Hastings Sehested, another ordained Baptist woman, called women in the SBC to extend their work and witness in the following ways:

> 1) to encourage women to fuller ministries in the life of our churches and denomination; 2) to provide an avenue for the sharing of the joys and struggles as disciples of Christ so women could gain courage, insight, strength, and challenge from each other; and 3) to explore, discuss, and form new paradigms of leadership in the Church, paradigms that empower, not control people.[38]

From these deliberations, the initial meeting of Women in Ministry, SBC, was convened at the annual meeting of the Southern Baptist Convention in Pittsburgh in June 1983. The new coalition approved a statement of purpose that it would "provide support for the woman whose call from God defines her vocation as that of minister or that of woman in ministry within the SBC and affirm her call to be a servant of God." Membership was extended to all women in ministry and to other females and males who supported their efforts. A new periodical, *Folio*, was initiated to provide "communication, support, and affirmation among Southern Baptist women ministers."[39]

During the 1980s two Southern Baptist seminaries, in Louisville, Kentucky, and Wake Forest, North Carolina, were centers of general affirmation for Baptist women in ministry. A number of local churches in proximity to those schools moved to ordain women to ministry during this period. However, as the SBC moved increasingly to the theological right, trustees at those schools came to challenge the ordination of women and their pastoral roles in the church. At the Southern Baptist Theological Seminary, Louisville, this concern over women's ordination reached a crucial point in 1990, when Molly Marshall, a professor in the school's theology department, was presented to the board of trustees as a candidate for tenure. Marshall, an ordained Baptist woman, was an outspoken supporter of women's ordination and equality in Baptist churches. Her tenure was subsequently approved, but not without great controversy among the trustees and in the SBC at large. Marshall remained at the seminary until Albert Mohler, an outspoken conservative, became president of the school in 1994. Mohler soon decided it was time for Marshall to move on and essentially bought out her contract. She moved to Central Baptist Theological Seminary in Kansas City, Kansas, as a professor of theology and Christian spirituality. She subsequently departed the Southern Baptist Convention for congregations related to the American Baptist Churches in the USA.

The Southern Baptist Convention has not been silent regarding the role of women in Baptist life. In 1984 conservative messengers to the denomination's annual meeting passed the first of what would be numerous responses to these matters. While resolutions passed at the SBC are not officially binding on any member churches, they carry a certain weight and give evidence of the opinions of the majority in attendance at Baptist meetings. This particular resolution noted that "women fulfilled special church service-ministries," but insisted that "the New Testament does not mandate that all who are divinely called to the ministry be ordained."[40] It stated:

> WHEREAS, The Scriptures attest to God's delegated order of authority (God the head of Christ, Christ the head of man, man the head of woman, man and woman dependent one upon the other to the glory of God), distinguishing the roles of men and women in public prayer and prophecy (1 Cor 11:2–5); and WHEREAS, The Scriptures teach that women are not in public worship to assume the role of authority over

men lest confusion reign in the local church (1 Cor 14:33–36); and
WHEREAS, While Paul commends women and men alike in other roles
of ministry and service (Titus 2:1–10), he excludes women from pastoral
leadership (1 Tim 2:12) to preserve a submission God requires because
the man was first in creation and the woman was first in the Edenic fall
(1 Tim 2:13ff.).[41]

The resolution concluded that

we not decide concerns of Christian doctrine and practice by modern
cultural, sociological, and ecclesiastical trends or by emotional factors;
that we remind ourselves of the dearly bought Baptist principle of the
final authority of Scripture in matters of faith and conduct; and that we
encourage the service of women in all aspects of church life and work
other than pastoral functions and leadership roles entailing ordination.[42]

Moderate Southern Baptists opposed the resolution, but it was a sign of
things to come as the convention was increasingly dominated by conservatives. The Baptist General Association of Virginia, the state's Baptist body
in affiliation with the SBC, denounced the action, as did other churches and
agencies. Others were unfazed. Conservatives even made an unsuccessful attempt to oppose seating messengers from First Baptist Church, Oklahoma
City, because that church ordained women as deacons.[43]

At the beginning of the new millennium, the leadership of the national
Southern Baptist Convention continued to oppose women's ordination and
made it more formal by amending the denomination's confession of faith,
the *Baptist Faith and Message*. Revised in 2000, the article on the church acknowledges that women may serve in the church, but not as pastor of a local
church.[44] The statement does not specifically forbid the ordination of
women, but insists that only men can serve as pastors. While many Southern
Baptists may oppose the ordination of females altogether, the denomination's confession of faith does not explicitly forbid the practice.

By 2003 moderate and conservative Southern Baptists had essentially
separated themselves either implicitly or explicitly over women's ordination
and other issues. Local churches and new coalitions such as the Alliance of
Baptists and the Cooperative Baptist Fellowship continued to ordain women
and call them to various positions in the church. (Even moderate/liberal
Baptists seem hesitant to call women as senior pastors, and relatively few
have actually done so.) While no statistics are available, there is no doubt that

many women reared in Baptist churches in the South have left those congregations for other denominations where there are greater prospects for females in pastoral ministry.

## Independent Baptists

Like their conservative Southern Baptist counterparts, a large majority of those who are associated with Independent Baptist churches oppose women's ordination and affirm various traditional roles for women in the church and the home. They generally acknowledge that the ideal is for women to remain in the home as nurturers and caregivers, but they are often forced to acknowledge that women are driven by issues of economics and family needs to work outside the home. Some preachers have even suggested that the changing role of women was a further sign of the "last days," a prelude to the Second Coming of Christ. As intense biblical literalists, most Independent Baptists adhere to a strict reading of the "silence" texts and other passages in the New Testament referencing women in the church. Many clergy and laity believe that women have a concrete role in family and church from which they cannot stray without violation of the divine order.

As separatist fundamentalists, Independent Baptists promote a conservative approach to women's role in local congregations. The Statement of Faith of the Bible Baptist Fellowship International declares:

> We believe that men and women are spiritually equal in position before God but that God has ordained distinct and separate spiritual functions of men and women in the home and in the church. The husband is to be the leader of the home and men are to hold the leadership positions (pastors and deacons) in the church. Accordingly, only men are eligible of licensure and ordination for pastor by the church.[45]

In this view, God has developed a plan of authority in the home and the church. In it, men are the primary authority figures who represent the will of Christ in both church and the family. This is sometimes known as the "chain of command" or chain of authority, the source of divine order in the world. Women thus relate to God directly for salvation, but through their husbands or pastors in matters of discernment, as well as spiritual and family order. Women's ordination is not simply a violation of biblical mandates; it creates potential chaos in the divinely ordained order of society and can only lead to ruin.

One Independent Baptist church warns of that ruin in words that no doubt resonate with many representatives of that sentiment in Baptist churches across the United States. In an article titled "Eve Is Again Listening to the Voice of the Serpent," the author insists: "A nation rises or falls with the virtue of its women. The degeneracy of women marks a nation's fall." The essay concludes:

> It is exceedingly dangerous for a woman to get out of her orbit. God never created woman to rule man. His whole Word is against it. Because of this broken law the curse of God is on the home, church, society, and nation. About fifty years ago a spiritual writer prophesied that one of the sins of the last days would be women striving for mastery over men. This has come to pass, and with it ruin; for woman must fight God to gain this place.[46]

Thus, many Independent Baptists affirm traditional roles for women and warn of dire consequences if they step outside the boundaries that God has set for them. The mere attempt to broaden those margins is detrimental to the entire society and constitutes a direct attack upon God.

## African American Baptist Women

The centrality of women in African American Baptist churches is beyond measure. Women occupy important roles of influence as teachers, financiers, worshipers, musicians, and, implicitly or explicitly, as leaders in every African American Baptist church. Yet in many of those churches the women's sphere is thoroughly intact. In some black Baptist congregations women occupy offices as deaconesses, nurses, "mothers of the church," and participants in a variety of women's groups. Some also recognize women's roles as "evangelist-preachers" who can proclaim the gospel in the church. In other congregations, however, ordination to the official ministry is another matter.

### Women in Church and Community Activism

As with other Baptist groups, African American women were active in the missionary movement from the time those agencies began. Nannie Helen Burroughs (1883–1961) led the Women's Convention of the National Baptist

Convention for almost fifty years. During that time the organization not only raised funds for the church's mission but spoke out on "lynching, disenfranchisement, stereotyping of blacks in the media and entertainment industries, and segregation in public transportation, as well as on women's suffrage and sexism of black men."[47] Burroughs also directed the National Baptist Convention's own National Training and Professional School for Women and Girls, located in Washington, DC. Baptists were in on the founding of the Fraternal Council of Negro Churches, an ecumenical African American organization begun in 1934. However, in keeping with Baptist practices of "walling off" women from leadership, the council, like the denominations, promoted women's auxiliaries that were the realm of women.[48]

Mary R. Sawyer writes that even the Southern Christian Leadership Conference (SCLC), founded by Martin Luther King Jr. and others, "was a Baptist-dominated and therefore male-dominated organization, which accounted for the establishment of a 'women's auxiliary' known as 'SCLC women.'" Nonetheless, several Baptist women, such as Ella Baker and Septima Clark, exercised significant leadership to the SCLC. Baker (1903–1986) was born in Virginia and was graduated from Shaw University, a Baptist-related school in Raleigh, North Carolina. Never ordained, she worked extensively with the NAACP and the SCLC, helping to organize the famous lunch counter boycotts in Greensboro, North Carolina. Sawyer states that "throughout her tenure [in the SCLC] Baker had serious philosophical disagreements with King over leadership styles, arguing for a more participatory and less Baptist model. She lost, of course."[49]

Marion Wright Edelman, director of the Children's Defense Fund (CDF), is another Baptist woman whose impact has had national significance. Through Edelman's leadership, the CDF has worked on behalf of families and children in lobbying efforts, community organizing, and other programs. She led her organization in developing a network of churches, community agencies, and other constituencies in working toward improved services for those on the margins of American society.

### Women's Ordination Among African American Baptists

Mechal Sobel writes: "Black women found much room for involvement, expression, and leadership in the Baptist churches, which was in keeping with both the Southern Separatist tradition and earlier African traditions. . . . Women were given formal roles as deaconesses and served on committees to work with women who had violated Baptist ethics. . . . Southern black women even attended the meetings of the American Baptist Missionary Convention in the North."[50] As the African American denominations took shape, ordination of women was not specifically forbidden, but it was not easily secured.

The National Baptist Women Ministers Convention, established in 1981, claimed approximately 250 members in 2000. In 1999 Carolyn Knight, a professor at the Interdenominational Theological Center, Atlanta, noted that in the entire NBC only about 100 women occupied the pastoral role. Knight, ordained in the NBC in 1978, commented: "Women are leaving the Baptist denomination for others that are accepting them in pulpits."[51]

Sociologists C. Eric Lincoln and Lawrence Mamiya developed a survey of women pastors in African American denominations and found that "among the Baptists, the Progressive National Baptist Convention tended to be only slightly more progressive on this issue of women pastors than the other conventions. PNBC had a total approval rate of 42.7 percent and a total disapproval rate of 57.3 percent."[52] The survey found that the National Baptist Convention, USA, Inc., reflected a general disapproval of women ministers, as confirmed by 43.9 percent of respondents. Approval from respondents was 26.5 percent. In the NBC, Unincorporated, the 25.4 percent approved of women ministers, while 74.6 percent disapproved.[53]

Amid this hesitancy, a growing number of African American women are receiving ordination in Baptist churches. Some have found more immediate ministry in the American Baptist Churches, USA and the Progressive National Baptist Convention, but others were ordained in the other more traditional groups (NBC, Inc; NBC, Uninc.). Some of these women have founded new congregations since so few African American congregations will call women as pastors.

## Women's Ordination and Baptist Polity

Congregational autonomy is an important element in the response of Baptist groups to the ordination of women. It means that while denominations may be opposed to the ordination of women implicitly or explicitly, local churches may choose to ordain women and call them to ministry. In fact, the progress that has been made toward incorporating women into ministry has been accomplished because of the autonomy of local churches. Yet while a growing number of Baptist congregations are ordaining women, few seem willing to call a woman as senior pastor. For pragmatic reasons, this situation may change sooner rather than later. As fewer male ministers choose to enter the ministry, congregational search committees may be compelled to move toward females. Polity and pragmatism affect theology whether that dynamic is recognized or not.

CHAPTER TEN

# Baptists and American Culture

## "In the World but Not of It"

When it comes to American culture, Baptists often seem to be opponents of "worldliness" wherever it appears, ever dissenting against the corruptions of the "present evil age" (Gal. 1:4). Outside observers may suppose that Baptists are unfailingly puritanical in their opposition to anything that is really fun. Many Baptists, past and present, insist that they have a dual citizenship in this world and the next and are called to live according to the "narrow way" (Matt. 7:14) of the gospel. They understand the rigorous ethical standards of Christianity as evidence of the cost of discipleship required of all who are truly "born again" (John 3:3). Many lament the decline of morality in America, evidenced in the general culture and in those churches that have compromised with the world. These Baptists see themselves as representatives of the forces of orthodoxy in their assertions that biblical teachings on specific moral issues are clearly delineated and are enduring mandates for those who would call themselves Christians.

Other Baptists affirm the costliness of faith, but steer clear of what seems an excessive legalism often associated with popular Baptist life. They suggest that the gospel demands strong personal and corporate morality, with prophetic implications for American economics, politics, racism, and other communal concerns. These Baptists often are listed among the "progressives" who advocate particular social reforms, ever challenging the moral and economic status quo. Baptists themselves divide over the ethical rigor of the gospel and its relationship to a variety of cultural and social phenomena. Indeed, representatives of Baptist orthodoxy and progressivism have often sought to be "in the world, but not of the world" in their efforts to live above the values and distractions of society. They frequently differ, however, on what actually constitutes worldliness.

## Baptists and the "Culture Wars"

In examining the relationship between church and culture, many turn for definitions to Clifford Geertz's work, *The Interpretation of Cultures*, and his assertion that culture "denotes an historically transmitted pattern of meanings embodied in symbols, a system of inherited conceptions expressed in symbolic forms by means of which . . . [individuals] communicate, perpetuate, and develop their knowledge about and attitudes toward life."[1] Through culture, communities establish norms for behavior, meaning, values, and other aspects of common life. As M. J. Herskovits writes, "a society is composed of people; the way they behave is their culture."[2]

For Baptists and other religious groups, the relationship to culture is difficult to determine and changes from generation to generation. One era's moral and spiritual nonnegotiables may be negated, ignored, or renegotiated in another time and place. Definitions of worldliness vary from church to church and individual to individual. For example, some Baptist churches reject dancing in any form, while others hold dances in their church halls. Some Baptist ministers refuse to perform marriages for previously divorced couples lest they violate biblical mandates, while others conduct such weddings as part of their pastoral care for families. Certain Baptist churches resist any action that might be seen as "affirming" homosexuality, while others seek to be "open and affirming" toward homosexuals in their midst. Certain churches utilize television as a way of bringing the gospel into the public marketplace, while others refuse to do so lest the medium corrupt the message.

In their efforts to confront American culture, Baptists no doubt reflect several of the categories delineated by H. Richard Niebuhr in his classic work *Christ and Culture*. Some Baptists clearly seem to be "against culture," convinced that as Christians they must distance themselves from the sinful ways of a corrupt society. This response is evident in Independent Baptists, Southern Baptists, certain African American Baptists, and other conservative Baptist groups. Others illustrate the "Christ of culture," affirming Christ's presence in the world and seeking to re-form society as the realm of God's rule and reign. Segments of the American Baptist Churches, USA, the Alliance of Baptists, and other liberal Baptists might be represented in this approach. In reality, as conversionists, most Baptists would concur with the "Christ transforming culture" motif, acknowledging that transformation of individuals and society is an imperative of the Christian gospel.[3] Few Baptists would deny the need for transformation of people and culture even if they differ on how that might be achieved.

More recent analysts go beyond Niebuhr and accentuate other ideas and possibilities. James Davison Hunter coined the phrase "culture wars," by which he meant that Christians in America often divide between the polarities of opposition and accommodation in response to changing cultural mores. In the last decades of the twentieth century, a variety of Baptists entered those "wars" that divided a nation on moral, political, and racial issues. As might be have been anticipated, Baptist individuals and groups covered a wide spectrum of support for and opposition to many of these issues.[4]

Contemporary Baptists divide over these issues even as they did over fundamentalist/liberal issues in early 1900s. While some churches (conservative/evangelical) have drawn various lines in the sand in opposition to cultural hegemony, others (liberal/progressive) demonstrate "the tendency to resymbolize historic faiths according to the prevailing assumptions of contemporary life."[5]

Hunter suggested that there were two distinct "visions of what kind of nation America ought to be" and that religious issues were central to these visions.[6] In the conflicts between the two visions, Baptists divided over theological and ethical issues that shaped their identity in American culture. For many conservatives, the problems of secularism had come home to roost, creating a moral anarchy that undermined ecclesial traditions, biblical authority, and family values. For Baptist moderates and liberals, the realities of this social and moral upheaval were challenges to the gospel and the church, requiring new paradigms that mandated serious responses to the realities of the modern era. The "wars" pitted Baptists against other Christians and non-Christians, and often against themselves, all played out in a variety of public concerns.

Other scholars challenge this analysis as too simplistic, yet many Baptists have latched on to it as a battle cry for responses to what they believe to be the capitulation of American society in general and religious communities to rabid amoral secularism and cultural compromise. Baptist preachers such as Jerry Falwell and Pat Robertson (Robertson began his ministry as a Baptist) frequently use the language of culture wars to characterize their battles against humanism, secularism, "the homosexual agenda," the "Clintons" (Bill and Hillary), abortionists, and other liberal endangerments.

Still other Baptists redefine the nature of the culture warfare, calling the people of God to address questions of environment, racism, gender inequality, economics, and sexism as signs of corruption in the society and the church. These congregations often challenge political establishments on issues like the death penalty, war, and racial profiling.

At times conservative and liberal Baptists alike seem "against culture" in their antiestablishment skirmishes, their moral crusades, and their desire to live untainted by the world. At other times they seem a most worldly people, succumbing to marketing techniques, captivated by consumerism, and employing a variety of other culture-based methods to promote their programs and package their versions of the Christian gospel. Indeed, many contemporary Baptists deplore compromises with culture while at the same time importing cultural agendas into their daily lives and their religious communities.

### Historic Baptist Sectarianism:  Class Consciousness

The earliest Baptists in America distinguished themselves from the world by their concern for a regenerate church membership, their practice of church discipline, their support for radical religious liberty, and their opposition to religious establishments. They were a sectarian people's movement, easy prey for critics who were scandalized by their baptismal immersion, their brash theological assertions, and their lower-class status. One colonial critic attacked Baptists for their ignorance and the audacity of their attempts to address serious theological questions. Traveling through the "Carolina backcountry" of eighteenth-century America, Anglican parson Charles Woodmason described the Separate Baptists he found there:

> And a gang of them getting together and gabbling one after the other (and sometimes disputing against each other) on abstruse Theological Questions . . . such as the greatest Metaph[ys]icians and Learned Scholars never yet could define, or agree on—To hear Ignorant Wretches, who can not write . . . discussing such Knotty Points for the Edification of their Auditors . . . must give High offence to all Intelligent and rational Minds.[7]

Clearly, these early Baptists were perceived as outside the mainstream of cultural and religious life. Certain critics were willing to challenge their right or their ability to address questions in any serious manner.

In truth, Baptists in America reflect several different strains of influence and response to issues of education, economics, and class. Some of the colonial Baptists were represented in the Regular Baptist tradition born in New England and transported south to Charleston, South Carolina. These Baptists valued and promoted education and were more orderly in their response to worship and church life. They were often found among the upwardly mobile classes of the developing American society. Another group, known as Separate Baptists, was born of the Great Awakening, given to emotional conversion, and mistrusted education as detrimental to "the Spirit"; this group attracted the working and farming classes of frontier society. Regulars tended to identify with the culture more than did the dissenting Separate Baptists.

By the nineteenth century, however, the sect had become a majority, one of the largest denominations in the United States. In words that could apply to Baptists throughout the Republic, David Stricklin describes the changes that this new majority status brought to Southern Baptists:

> They became more respectable and more powerful as they became more numerous. . . . Baptists preserved their determination not to allow government interference in matters of faith. But now, instead of conflicting with the power structure as they had during the colonial period, in many communities they constituted its core. They abandoned virtually any trace of their former critical stance toward coercive political and economic forces and instead focused their criticisms of society on untoward personal behavior.[8]

As Baptists' majority status expanded, they gave increasing attention to issues of personal morality, an emphasis that characterized many Baptist churches well into the twentieth century. Indeed, the divisions and distinctions between Baptist groups are evident in their responses to various ethical agendas set for and by them.

Issues of class related to economics and education were also a part of the Baptist confrontation with culture. The College of Rhode Island (later Brown University), founded in 1764, was the first Baptist-related school in America. Other schools soon followed, most in the nineteenth century. These included Colgate (1819), Bucknell (1845), Franklin College (Indiana,1834), University of Richmond (1830), Wake Forest University (1834), Morehouse College (1867), and Baylor University (1845). These schools and others like them were often founded before state colleges and universities.

They offered Baptist-based education aimed at ministers and other youth who sought to improve their lot in society. On the one hand, Baptist clergy and laity welcomed this effort. On the other, many were concerned that academic rationalism and skepticism would be detrimental to faith. As one Baptist preacher is alleged to have said: "We don't favor an educated ministry. We saw what it did to the Presbyterians!"

During the twentieth century some of the fiercest controversies to overtake Baptist communions related to their educational institutions. From evolution to biblical authority, Baptists divided over the purpose and mission of their schools. From the 1920s through the end of the twentieth century, professors at Baptist schools were frequently charged with heresy or teaching outside doctrinal norms. Indeed, significant controversies over the boundaries of Baptist education erupted throughout the century.

This led many schools to break their direct Baptist ties, distancing themselves from economic or administrative control by Baptist denominations. Others remained connected and committed to a direct Baptist connection. Some Baptist schools continue to have required weekly chapel; others have made it an option, while still others have abolished it all together. Some Baptist schools require faculty—at least those teaching religion classes—to sign or affirm certain doctrinal ideals, while others (probably a majority) make no such demand. In certain Baptist-related schools professors know that their orthodoxy could readily be challenged (and reported) by students or parents. Others struggle with what a Baptist heritage means at an increasingly diverse educational institution centered in pluralism and having an ever diversifying faculty and student body.[9]

### Baptists and Personal Morality: Developing Issues

Baptists' concern for personal behavior extended through many areas of individual morality. The "sin-list" included alcohol, illicit sex, gambling, card playing, dancing, motion pictures, tobacco, tattoos, rock music, and assorted other public and private evils. As noted earlier, Baptist churches in America did not hesitate to mete out varying degrees of discipline for ethical transgressions when they were discovered, in the hope that true repentance would occur and the evil would be forsaken. Recalcitrant members were often "churched," excluded from taking communion or put out of membership altogether, if they failed to conform to the moral rigors demanded by the community of faith.

## *Alcohol*

Ultimately, use of alcohol became a particularly heinous offense. Early on in Baptist history, many adherents, including ministers, manifested little or no opposition to the moderate use of "spirits." In certain frontier churches, barrels of liquor were pledged for support of the minister, who (one hopes) would sell them as a ready cash crop. By the late nineteenth century, however, serious social problems related to alcoholism combined with the populist appeal of the temperance movement to raise the consciousness of Baptists and other Protestants regarding the use of liquor. Converts were often asked to accept Jesus as savior and to take the temperance pledge immediately thereafter. As one Baptist editor commented, "The right of prohibition is based on the inherent evil of intoxicating liquor, and fundamental Bible teaching both as to this evil and as to human relations and principles of government."[10]

One important example of the fight against "demon rum" was the transition from wine to unfermented grape juice in the celebration of the Lord's Supper in Baptist churches. Many (though not all) Baptist communions made that change by the early twentieth century. For some, this crusade against alcohol in communion challenged a literal reading of the Bible and required supporters to develop arguments showing that the references to wine in the New Testament did not necessarily mean fermentation. Others refused to abandon the use of wine lest it violate biblical literalism. One enduring story tells of the venerable Baptist Sunday school teacher and teetotaler who was reminded by one of her students that Jesus himself had turned water into wine at the marriage feast in Cana as described in John 2. "Oh, yes," she replied. "He did turn water into wine, but I would have respected him a lot more if he hadn't!"

Like their Methodist counterparts, Baptist preachers often called sinners to "take the pledge" and refuse to use liquor under any circumstances. Some questioned the validity of conversion in those who were unable to "gain the victory" over alcohol use, especially those who made no effort to cease. In certain cases, churches also took action against individuals whose business practices involved the sale of liquor in any direct or even indirect way. Certain church covenants included abstinence as the sign of a valid church membership. During the 1980s a prominent North Carolina Baptist businessman was refused membership on the trustee board of a Southern Baptist agency when it became known that he owned property that was leased to a grocery chain that sold alcohol. Even indirect support of liquor was not acceptable.

In various regions of the country, Baptists have been at the forefront of efforts to promote liquor by the drink in counties and municipalities. Increasingly, those battles have been lost, especially in urban and suburban regions as tourist, tax, and restaurant concerns have prevailed to bring liquor to previously "dry" regions. At the same time, a growing number of middle-class Baptists admit to the moderate use of alcohol even as conservatives continue to denounce it as inappropriate for Christian disciples.

Some analysts conclude that the Baptist conviction regarding liquor was supported in part "because they have so sadly neglected other social problems." Rather than confront the power structures of urban and rural politics, North and South, they challenged "liquor interests" that were often of "marginal status and limited power." These cultural subgroups could thus "be attacked with impunity."[11] At the same time, the Baptist response to alcohol use has implications for serious social problems related to alcoholism, family abuse, and drunken driving. In fact, some Baptist advocates of the Social Gospel looked beyond the sale and use of alcohol, particularly in slum or tenement settings, to the economic exploitation of workers, conditions that might drive people to drink. As many Baptists understand it, the breech of biblical teachings regarding temperance has clear social implications.

### Tobacco and the "Tobacco Church"

The use of tobacco has long provoked strong responses from many Baptists in America who objected to it long before it was fashionable to do so. They insisted that it "defiled" the human body, which was the "temple of the Holy Ghost," and that Christians had no business using it. The West Association of New Jersey Baptists voted in 1877 "that in consideration of the wicked waste of money expended for tobacco, as well as from its offensive, injurious and demoralizing effects, and its tendency to lead to strong drink, we discountenance its use." For these Baptists, tobacco was a double fault. It wasted funds and could lead to the worse evil of liquor.

Such admonitions did not mean that Baptists had no business growing tobacco, however. Indeed, anti-tobacco sermons were often preached in churches in Virginia, Kentucky, and the Carolinas, states where tobacco was the chief "money crop," funding Baptist families and offerings in the collection plates.

Yet in spite of these warnings, many Baptists use tobacco. (It was not unheard of for preachers themselves to indulge in smoking or chewing from time to time.) Visitors to rural Baptist churches across the nation often found Baptists grabbing a quick smoke, a chew of tobacco, or a dip of snuff before Sunday morning worship.

When it came to attacking the excesses of tobacco, Baptists were ahead of their time, but their rhetoric did not keep Baptist farmers from producing tobacco and using a portion of the revenues to support their local Baptist churches. "Tobacco churches," as one scholar writes, "are any congregation, rural, small town or county seat, where the economy supporting that church and community gains its primary energy from growing, processing and/or marketing tobacco."[12] They illustrate the relationship between economics and ethics in local Baptist congregations in certain regions of the United States.

## Gambling

Gambling has long been ethically unacceptable to large numbers of Baptists, even to the point of renouncing any type of gambling from playing cards to lotteries to bingo. Some forbade the use of playing cards altogether, lest gambling become a temptation. In the past, many Baptist preachers inveighed against cards as an instrument of the devil for which there were no innocent uses. Gambling for money was particularly anathema for many Baptist congregations; those who indulged in it faced a potential discipline and even expulsion from the church. Betting on sporting events from football to horse racing has frequently been denounced by Baptist preachers.

More recently, Baptist groups have worked diligently to oppose state-based gambling programs such as lotteries or casinos in which revenue is used to supplement community educational or benevolent programs. While often unsuccessful, even in so-called Bible Belt states, these efforts bring together Baptists of varying theological sentiments who see gambling as unethical and exploitative, particularly among the poor. The increasing approval of lotteries and other state-based forms of gambling has served to divide Baptists who continue to oppose gambling in any form and those who support gambling when the funds go to education, public welfare, and other good causes.

In 1996 the General Board of the American Baptist Churches, USA approved a resolution on gambling that addressed the "disturbing reality" that "local and state governments see gambling as a source of income and become primary promoters." It urged churches and ministers in the ABCUSA to "help people understand that gambling can be unethical even if a portion of the revenue is used for socially needed programs."[13] Similar statements have been released by other Baptist groups.

*Sexual Immorality*

Preachers and evangelists have long deplored worldliness in its many forms, often singling out "Hellywood" (Hollywood) as the prevaricator of pornography, false values, and sexual immorality. Generations of Baptist pastors and evangelists attacked the sexual attitudes promoted in movies, books, and television as detrimental to Americans, particularly families and youth. Baptist parents are admonished to protect their children from the corruption of the culture that is evident in the mass media and more recently on the Internet. Indeed, adolescents have long been a target of warnings from teachers and preachers regarding the dangers of cultural compromise.

Dancing is an early illustration of the changing mores of American and Baptist life. Throughout much of the twentieth century dancing was characterized as a particularly dangerous activity, since it inflamed the passions in ways that could lead to aberrant sexual contacts and because dances were often held in settings that were not conducive to spiritual growth and nurture. At many Baptist youth camps, retreats, and other outings "mixed swimming" (boys and girls swimming together) was forbidden lest it contribute to inappropriate sexual arousal. (Other Baptists were less precise about this practice.)[14] Revival meetings, Sunday school classes, and denominational literature past and present challenge young people to practice sexual abstinence until marriage. Baptist ministers often differ over whether to perform marriages for Baptist couples in which premarital pregnancy is involved.

Along with these admonitions, Baptists are forced to acknowledge that pastors and laity are not immune from sexual scandals. Many churches, both liberal and conservative, have had to deal with issues related to illicit sexual activity, sexual harassment, and other improprieties on the part of their ministers. Scandals involving prominent public figures who are also Baptists are well known, among them the events related to Democratic president Bill Clinton and White House intern Monica Lewinsky, and the announcement that longtime Republican senator Strom Thurmond had fathered (at the age of twenty-two) a mixed-race daughter by a sixteen-year-old African American servant in his South Carolina family home. Clinton and Thurmond, politicians at both ends of the political spectrum, were lifelong Baptists. Sexual exploitation of male and female church members by Baptist ministers has become a particularly important matter for congregations in the last decade as more of these experiences have been made public and some have even led to lawsuits against ministers and churches.

Seventh Day Baptists mirrored other Baptist groups in affirming sex as "a God-given drive through which we participate in a continuing creation, and [which] is a mutually enriching blessing within the bonds of matrimony." They insist that "sexual intercourse outside the bonds of matrimony is wrong, and . . . any contraceptive to control pregnancy does not change this basic concept."[15]

Baptist denominations have consistently passed resolutions denouncing pornography and the exploitation of women and children in movies and magazines. For example, the American Baptist Churches, USA noted in a 1998 resolution: "American Baptists join with their sisters and brothers in other faith groups to condemn the presence of pornography in our society." It acknowledged: "The sexual disinformation that is prevalent in pornography prevents many persons from understanding that sex is a gift from God." The resolution concluded: "Any portrayal of sex as an unloving, violent, coercive event is clearly a defamation of God's gift."[16]

Concerned about the prevailing emphases on sexual activity rampant in American society, some Baptists have developed programs to promote abstinence among the young. Beginning in 1993, certain Baptist churches and groups sought to stem the tide of sexual experimentation outside marriage by promoting a practice known as "true love waits," a pledge taken by single males and females whereby they agree not to engage in sexual intercourse until after marriage. In 2003 advocates claimed that some 2.4 million young people had signed such a covenant. The pledge and related training courses are promoted by LifeWay Christian Stores, owned and operated by the Southern Baptist Convention. The pledge states: "Believing true love waits, I make a commitment to God, myself, my family, those I date, and my future mate to be sexually pure until the day I enter marriage."[17] Single adults are encouraged to sign the brief statement and use it as a guide for their premarital behavior. Likewise, they are urged to avoid sexual promiscuity because it is a violation of biblical directives, it extends the chance of contacting HIV or other sexually transmitted disease, and abstinence is evidence of their Christian commitment.

At the beginning of the twenty-first century, efforts to stem the tide of sexual promiscuity among young people seemed to be a formidable task. Baptist youth, like others around them, were reexamining or ignoring classic moral codes in ways that made dancing and "mixed swimming" seem a bit tame. On the other hand, there were still Baptists in America who insisted that when churches compromised on those and similar mores, they set out on the slippery slope leading to moral deterioration.

*Divorce*

In the post–World War II era, divorce statistics rose dramatically in America, and Baptists, like other Christian groups, were forced to come to terms with a new reality that had a significant effect upon most Americans, including those with traditional family structures. As divorce invaded Baptist churches and homes, it became necessary to reexamine Baptist rhetoric, theology, and practice regarding the nature of marriage and the meaning of family. Biblical references on divorce are at once explicit and complicated. In Matthew 5, Jesus himself says: "But what I tell you is this: If a man divorces his wife for any cause other than unchastity he involves her in adultery; and whoever marries her commits adultery" (Matt. 5:32 REB).

For many Baptists, these dictums are clear authorizations, to be followed to the letter. Divorce is thus permissible only when one party has been wronged by marital infidelity. Remarriage for or with a divorced person is the moral equivalent of adultery. Certain Baptist ministers refuse to participate in weddings if one or both of the parties has been divorced, since to do so would be to sanction a relationship that is contrary to the divine command. Other ministers are perhaps less literal, looking to Jesus' teachings on forgiveness and reconciliation. Many perform marriages of divorced people, ideally after the couple has had extensive marital counseling.

Yet the burgeoning divorce rate also affects ministers themselves. Throughout much of the twentieth century, divorce essentially meant that Baptist ministers were no longer able to function in their chosen career. Well into the 1970s certain Baptist-related theological schools refused to admit people who were divorced, since it seemed that they would never qualify for ministry among Baptists. While this remains the case in some conservative Baptist denominations and educational institutions, much has changed regarding divorced ministers. Many continue to serve parishes, even after their own remarriage.

American Baptist Churches, USA approved a policy on families affirming that "God intends marriage" to be "a monogamous, life-long, one-flesh union of a woman and a man." However, the document also states: "In God's grace remarriage for divorced Christians is appropriate where issues which ended the earlier marriage have been addressed and the new marriage shows promise of fulfilling God's intention for the marriage relationship."[18]

Divorce among church members continues to raise questions regarding their participation as active laity in individual congregations. Many moderate or liberal Baptist churches encourage divorced people who wish to serve as deacons, Sunday school teachers, or in other leadership roles to do so freely. Others permit certain types of service but would not, for example, allow divorced church members to serve as deacons.[19]

More-conservative Baptist churches exclude divorced people from any or all leadership roles, unless of course the person was wronged through a spouse's adultery.[20] Some have made clear their belief that the rising divorce rate in the United States (one in three marriages ends in divorce) is yet another illustration of the loss of religious values, the breakdown of family structures, and the indifference of Americans to their marriage vows.

### Homosexuality

Perhaps no single issue has been as divisive for American religious groups in general and Baptists in particular as homosexuality and the role of homosexuals in the church and the culture. In many ways these issues became the line in the sand, dividing churches that received self-identified homosexuals and their partners in an "open and affirming manner" from those that insisted that homosexuality is a sin requiring repentance and reformation.

**SOUTHERN BAPTISTS AND HOMOSEXUALITY** As early as 1976 the Southern Baptist Convention addressed homosexuality, noting in a nonbinding resolution that the convention "affirmed the biblical truth regarding the practice of homosexuality," but it did not offer specifics. It concluded that the convention, "while acknowledging the autonomy of the local church to ordain ministers, urge[s] churches and agencies not to afford the practice of homosexuality any degree of approval through ordination, employment, or other designations of normal life-style."[21]

A year later another resolution was much more specific regarding a "campaign" "to secure legal, social, and religious acceptance for homosexuality and deviant moral behavior at the expense of personal dignity." Success of this effort would "have devastating consequences for family life in general and our children in particular." It noted that "the radical scheme to subvert the sacred pattern of marriage in America has gained formidable momentum by portraying homosexuality as normal behavior." The resolution reaffirmed the previous year's action regarding homosexuality and affirmed "compassion for every person . . . regardless of lifestyle."[22]

In 1988 the resolution identified homosexuality as "a manifestation of a depraved nature" that "has wrought havoc in the lives of millions" and is "glorified in our secular media." It asserted that "homosexual activity is the primary cause of the introduction and spread of AIDS in the United States which has not only affected those of the homosexual community, but also many innocent victims." The convention declared homosexuality "a perversion of divine standards," "nature and natural affections." While noting the possibility of redemption for all persons, the document labeled homosexuality "not a normal lifestyle" and "an abomination in the eyes of God."[23]

Additional resolutions from the denomination condemned homosexuality in the military (1993) for reasons including "exposure to sexually transmitted diseases" and the danger of "tainted blood" on the battlefield. The same document condemned "acts of violence" committed by and against homosexuals, while noting that "homosexual politics is masquerading as 'civil rights,' in order to exploit the moral high ground of the civil rights movement," an effort with which it had "nothing in common."[24]

In an elaborate 1996 resolution the SBC condemned every aspect of homosexual marriage in no uncertain terms, concluding that "any law, or any policy or regulation" supporting homosexual marriage is "thoroughly wicked according to God's standards revealed in the Bible" and stating that therefore "we do most solemnly pledge our decision never to recognize the moral legitimacy of any such law." Thus, it insisted, "we will never conform to or obey anything required by any governing body to implement, impose or act upon any such law. So help us God."[25] This resolution affirmed a dissenting response to any governmental actions that promote homosexual marriage.

In 1996 the SBC called for a boycott of Disney-related products and promotions in response to the "Gay Pride Day" held at Disney World in Orlando, Florida. The "Disney Boycott" apparently had limited effect on the corporation but raised significant concern among conservative Baptists.

Homosexuality seems to be a defining issue for the Southern Baptist response to changing cultural practices and values. In the mid-1990s, the convention required that all messengers to its annual meeting sign a statement assuring that the congregation from which they came gave no support to homosexuality in any form whatsoever.

**THE COOPERATIVE BAPTIST FELLOWSHIP AND HOMOSEXUALITY**   The Cooperative Baptist Fellowship (CBF), founded in 1991 as an organization of churches and individuals that moved to distance themselves from the Southern Baptist Convention, confronted issues related to approaches to homosexuality through a statement approved at its annual meeting in 2000. The group, based in Atlanta, Georgia, funds a variety of Baptist-related projects, including missionary and educational endeavors, the Baptist Joint Committee on Public Affairs, the Associated Baptist Press, and the Baptist

Center for Ethics, among others. Difficulties over the issue of homosexuality arose when the Baptist Peace Fellowship of North America, a group with an affiliate relationship to the CBF, proffered statements that were considered "open and affirming" to homosexuals in Baptist communions and when certain divinity schools that received CBF scholarship funds were known to have open admissions that did not exclude homosexuals.[26]

Some felt that their churches could not in good conscience support CBF if it continued to contribute to organizations that were in any way (even by admissions regulations) supportive of homosexuality. Thus the CBF leaders felt compelled to address the issue, and they produced a document that clarified the organization's response to homosexuality in the churches and related agencies.

The statement declared that the new organization would not "knowingly" employ staff members or missionaries who demonstrate homosexual behavior, or fund organizations that "condone, advocate or affirm homosexual practice."[27] It noted that the large majority of CBF-related Baptists "believe that the foundation of a Christian sexual ethic is faithfulness in marriage between a man and a woman and celibacy in singleness." The statement declared that "leaders should be persons of moral integrity whose lives exemplify the highest standards of Christian conduct and character." Daniel Vestal, coordinator of the CBF, insisted: "This statement is not intended to force conformity or stifle debate on homosexuality," nor was it "intended to offend our gay and lesbian brothers and sisters in Christ." Leaders of the organization suggested that the document meant that CBF was "welcoming but not affirming" of homosexuals in Baptist churches.[28]

**AMERICAN BAPTISTS AND HOMOSEXUALITY** American Baptist Churches, USA (ABCUSA) have also addressed the issue of homosexuality. In October 1992 the General Board of the American Baptist Churches, USA approved the following basic statement: "We affirm that the practice of homosexuality is incompatible with Christian teaching."[29] That resolution remains as a guide for the ABCUSA. A 1993 resolution called "Dialogue on Issues of Human Sexuality" acknowledged "that there exists a variety of understandings throughout our denomination on issues of human sexuality such as homosexuality."[30] Several ABC-related churches across the country have been dismissed from their respective local associations because they chose to become "welcoming and affirming" toward homosexuals. Some have ordained homosexuals to the ministry or celebrated "commitment services" with homosexual couples.

American Baptists Concerned for Sexual Minorities was founded in 1972 as a resource to offer "support, education and advocacy for lesbian, gay, bisexual and transgender Baptists." A second supporting group, the Association of Welcoming and Affirming Baptists (AWAB) was organized in 1993 out of American Baptists Concerned. The groups began conversations for reunion in 2003 as the Association of Welcoming and Affirming Baptists.[31] The AWAB offers to churches that are "open and affirming" toward homosexuals a nongeographic association of churches engaged in similar commitments and ministries. It seeks to unite churches and individuals to "assist sexual minority people and their families and friends" in addressing specific needs and offering intentional support. It also aims "to persuade the ABC/USA to face honestly, aggressively and forthrightly" the needs of sexual minority persons inside and outside the church.[32]

**INDEPENDENT BAPTISTS AND HOMOSEXUALITY**   Independent Baptists are among the most outspoken Baptist opponents of what they often call the "homosexual agenda," publishing extensive criticism of the sin of homosexuality and the warning of the dangers that homosexuals and their supporters pose to "family values" in the American Republic. They insist that gays claim "rights" to which they are not entitled and are determined to secure laws that permit same-sex marital unions.[33]

Perhaps the most dramatic, controversial, and public response to homosexuals from a Baptist group during the last decade comes from the independent Westboro Baptist Church of Topeka, Kansas, and its pastor, Fred Phelps. Phelps and members of his small congregation gained national attention through their attacks on gays, their attendance at funerals of AIDS victims, and their outspoken charges that "God Hates Fags." Convinced that homosexual behavior is the ultimate abomination and that the Bible offers no quarter for those who practice it, Phelps insists that he has a duty to warn Americans of the judgment that awaits individuals and nations that tolerate it, saying: "You can't make that Bible subject any different than it has always been. It [homosexuality] is a monstrous sin against God that will destroy people, destroy their lives, damn their souls, doom the nation. Any nation that tolerates it has a short time to go in its national life as far as any dominance is concerned and that is what I am preaching."[34] Phelps and his supporters believe that homosexuality is so unacceptable that it has cosmic significance. He declared:

This sin is so insidious by its nature, and those who commit such things so abominable by their nature, that it serves as the litmus test for a society. When God has turned his back on a people, sodomites rule the land. America is on the cusp of that condition, and only by an abundance of mercy will God forebear the utter destruction of this country.[35]

Phelps's response represents the extreme of Baptist and Christian views on homosexuality. Other Baptists, even conservatives, have either condemned his views or sought to distance themselves from his actions. Phelps's church is an independent congregation with no formal connections to other Baptist denominations.[36]

**BAPTISTS RESPOND TO HOMOSEXUALITY**   Given Baptist concerns for local autonomy, many churches can retain the Baptist name while implicitly or explicitly becoming open and affirming to "sexual minorities" including gays and lesbians. Congregational autonomy has led a variety of Baptist-related churches to welcome homosexuals in a variety of public ways, among them baptism, ordination, and union ceremonies. These actions have also led associations or other connectional organizations to "deal" with these churches through disciplinary action. In Baptist polity, churches are free to act autonomously in matters of polity and practice, and the associational bodies with which they have "fellowship" are also free to respond accordingly.

In 1992, for example, two North Carolina churches were expelled from their respective associations, the North Carolina Baptist Convention and the Southern Baptist Convention, as a result of their actions regarding homosexual members. The Pullen Memorial Baptist Church in Raleigh facilitated a service of union for two gay men who were members of the congregation. That same year the Binkley Memorial Baptist Church in Chapel Hill performed an ordination for a gay divinity graduate. In response, the state Baptist convention approved a policy excluding "any church which knowingly takes, or has taken, any official action which manifests public approval, promotion or blessing of homosexuality."[37] Similar issues arose in 2003 when the McGill Baptist Church, a 101-year-old congregation in Concord, North Carolina, baptized two gay men and accepted them into membership. The North Carolina Baptist Convention dropped the church from its membership rolls, not because of that action, but because the church chose not to "repudiate homosexuality." James Royston, the convention's executive director/ treasurer, stated: "The basic issue that appears to be in violation of our policy is that by having openly gay members, the church sanctions or approves of homosexuality. The traditional interpretation of Scripture would call an openly gay lifestyle unbiblical and therefore un-Christian."[38] These divisions will surely continue as other congregations respond to homosexuals in ways that associations or conventions find to be morally compromising. They also raise questions as to how far Baptist groups are willing to extend discipline and over what issues. Would Baptist bodies renew disciplinary action against churches that appear to sanction other vices in the church and in the world? Controversies over homosexuals and homosexuality promise to divide Baptists well into the new century.

## Social Conscience: Against Culture

Numerous Baptists black and white have pressed churches to respond to the culture by addressing various social inequities, whether segregation, corporate greed, war, capital punishment, or other issues. Edwin Theodore Dahlberg (1893–1986) founded the Baptist Pacifist Fellowship (now Baptist Peace Fellowship) and also served as president of the National Council of Churches. Paul R. Dekar states that Dahlberg condemned "doleful expenditures by governments for social needs in contrast to military spending. He urged Christians to follow the model of churches in St. Louis, Missouri [where he was a Baptist minister] to achieve reconciliation in race, religion, economics and other areas."[39]

As noted earlier, Martin Luther King Jr., Ralph Abernathy, Clarence Jordan, and Millard Fuller challenged the prevailing racism in black and white cultures, in the North and the South. Vincent Harding concludes: "So can we begin to understand why the Black religious expressions of the freedom movement participants were often so threatening to their sisters and brothers in the southern white churches, parishes and synagogues. Perhaps we can also help each other to understand some of the reasons why there should have been such turmoil in the northern-based religious institutions when Brother Martin Luther King, Jr., moved into their precincts to challenge urban poverty, American militarism, some of the northern varieties of white racism—and the acquiescence of religious people in all these betrayals of human community."[40] These responses were also "against culture," in response to the calling of the redeemed.

## The Church "Culture": A Regenerate Church

Baptist response to culture is closely related to the nature of individual conversion and its implications for life in the world. In some sense, Baptists understand the world in light of their understanding of the church. Baptists begin with a concern for a "regenerate church membership," a belief that a "profession of faith" in Christ is a prerequisite for baptism and membership in the church. Regeneration involves a change of life made possible in the life of the sinner by the saving work of the Holy Spirit. Regeneration makes the person "a new creation" who is spiritually "born again." It demands a reformation of life and a commitment to live according to the demands of the gospel. The statement used at baptism in many Baptist churches declares that the new convert is "buried with Christ in baptism, raised to walk in newness of life." Thus conversion requires a new way of looking at the world and its charms, many of which are detrimental to the Christian.

This understanding of conversion leads to a view of the church as a "believers' church," composed only of those who have accepted the grace of God and the demands of the gospel. Only "baptized believers" are able to receive the Lord's Supper and participate officially in the governing life of the faith community. Baptists are able to make demands on members because members have chosen to accept the covenant of faith that binds them to God and to one another. The church, therefore, is another world within the world. It evaluates all the world's values in light of the life and teachings of Jesus Christ. While it is often impure and imperfect, its goal is to be re-formed into the image of Christ. The church may affirm God's presence in the world while seeking to avoid the agendas set by those whose commitments lie elsewhere.

As noted earlier, Baptists have often described conversion as a dramatic event that brought a radical change in the life of the new believer. Converts speak of being saved from hell, changed in their inner being, and called to a life of Christian discipleship. This radical event induces people to seek forgiveness of those they have wronged or otherwise make amends for old failures and hurtful actions. They sense that they are newly reborn and contrast it with their old life and outlook. Many people in Baptist churches claim a mystical experience of divine grace that overtook them, drew them toward God, and immediately transformed their lives. This kind of conversion may occur in public or private, when people are at the "end of their rope" in the world and desperate for an experience beyond themselves.

Some Baptist groups are highly evangelical about the need for radical conversion and transformation of life. Their preachers remain influenced by nineteenth- and twentieth-century revivalism that paints dramatic pictures of hell and the threat of eternity there. Laity and clergy in these groups may give public witness by going door-to-door or by preaching on street corners.

They literally go into the world to present the "plan of salvation" in hopes of winning souls to faith in Jesus. This plan takes many forms but essentially insists that:

1. All have sinned and fallen short of God's glory.
2. Sin brings every individual under the judgment of God.
3. God sent Jesus Christ into the world to die for the sins of the world.
4. All who have faith in Christ will experience God's grace and be saved for all eternity in this world and the next.
5. Those that do not receive Christ, who die in their sins, will go to an eternal hell.
6. Faith in Christ brings the demands of Christian discipleship and "separation from the world."
7. The truly saved will receive eternal life in heaven.

When the plan of salvation or one like it is presented, the sinner is then asked if he or she would like to "invite Jesus into your heart." If the answer is in the affirmative, the individual may be asked to pray the "sinner's prayer," a somewhat formalized confession of faith that literally invites Christ in. It generally follows this outline:

Lord Jesus, I know that I am a sinner and that you have died for my sins. I accept you as Lord and Savior, acknowledge my sins, and ask you to save me. I receive you into my heart right now and commit my life to living according to your will. Thank you for receiving me and forgiving me of my sins. Amen.

In certain Baptist congregations, the new convert is then encouraged to "walk the aisle" of the church as soon as possible to make a public confession of faith and request baptism. If and when that is done, then the individual is given the "right hand of Christian fellowship" and baptism is scheduled. In most Baptist churches, some type of new convert or "new member" class is encouraged in order to begin training the members in the history, ministry, and discipleship of the church. These methods would be evident in many Baptist groups, including Independent Baptists, General Association of Regular Baptist Churches, Southern Baptists, and various African American Baptist churches.

Those Baptists with particularly strong Calvinist leanings are less immediate in their demands for conversion. They hold that since God is the author of salvation, the sinner must wait for God to infuse grace in the heart of the elect individual. Prayers and invitations are a form of "works righteousness" whereby sinners think that they can coax God into saving them. In God's own time the elect will be delivered from the world's evil and regenerated by divine grace. Conversion will occur, but it will come from God. God alone, and not the sinner, is sovereign.

This response to conversion is evident in the Primitive, Old Regular, and United Baptists of central Appalachia. As noted earlier, in those churches it is not uncommon for individuals to be baptized between the ages of thirty and forty, as they wait on Christ to offer them salvation. The idea that one could simply kneel and pray a prayer and immediately receive divine grace is blasphemous to certain Calvinist Baptists. This tendency toward late baptisms is in sharp contrast to the Southern Baptist Convention, where the median age for baptism is somewhere between nine and ten years of age.

After conversion comes "discipleship," the growth and maturity of Christians in the faith. Christians are thus encouraged to study the Bible, to develop a life of prayer, and to participate in the life of the church. They are also instructed in the moral imperatives of Christian living. These may well differ from church to church and from Baptist communion to communion.

Evangelism is a major tenet of a variety of Baptist groups in the United States. Many churches and individuals are deeply committed to the practice of "witnessing" to their faith, encouraging persons who are "lost" (without evangelical salvation) to "accept Christ." Members are urged to give witness to their faith in every life setting; churches engage in evangelistic campaigns that may include traditional revival services and/or "seeker-oriented" efforts to attract people to faith. Baptist attempts to reach people for Christ have often compelled them to employ elements of the culture that they otherwise claim to disdain.

### Baptists and Culture: Evangelism and Pluralism

*Confronting Culture: Baptists and Seeker Churches*

A concern to reach America for Christ has sometimes led Baptists to embrace aspects of the very culture they disdained. This was evident in the frontier days when revivals and camp meetings brought multitudes of new converts into Baptist churches in nineteenth-century America. This movement led Baptists and other Protestants to use a variety of techniques—sometimes actually known as "new measures"—for reaching the unchurched populace. Among such methods were folksy hymnody, spontaneous, less formal services, impassioned appeals for conversion, and emotion-laden religious experiences. Churches sometimes divided over departure from the traditional religious forms, with conservatives insisting that the new measures were at once worldly and destructive to orthodoxy. Supporters responded that they were simply using those resources to get the attention of the sinner and that the eternal salvation of one soul was entirely worth the effort.

Twentieth-century Baptist revivalists also found that a variety of worldly methods were effective in getting the attention of sinners and would-be converts. Evangelists might sponsor pizza parties, offer prizes, or participate in outlandish events in order to accomplish their goals. It was (and sometimes still is) not uncommon for churches to enlist evangelical wrestling teams, clowns, sports celebrities, Christian rock groups, or other popular figures who help "pack the pews" to the max. J. Frank Norris and other Independent Baptist preachers illustrated great creativity in these methods. On one infamous occasion, when Norris baptized a well-known rodeo cowboy, he permitted the performer's trick horse to stand in the back of the church and watch the baptism.

Some contemporary churches include laser shows coordinated with Christian music or bring drama and images to wide screens above the worshiping congregation. These efforts are aimed at "seekers" who, like their twentieth-century counterparts, remain cut off from traditional religious exercises and outside the church.

In a study of "seeker churches," Kimon Howland Sargeant references several Baptist-related congregations, including Saddleback Valley Community Church, Orange County, California, and Second Baptist Church, Houston, Texas. Sargeant notes that H. Edwin Young, pastor of the Houston church, advised "his staff to make the church more 'user-friendly' by studying the strategies of theme parks like Disney World." Young intentionally uses "successful secular models" in shaping the church's approach to ministry, declaring "I take what is worldly, and baptize it."[41]

Sargeant writes that these "marketing techniques are clearly paying off," since the church has 22,000 members with a $16 million annual budget. He insists that the church's success is not simply in its packed Sunday services but in the varied options it provides for members. These include multiple sports teams and a family life center that features "six bowling lanes, two basketball courts, an indoor jogging track, racquetball courts, and weight and aerobics rooms, as well as a music wing for its orchestra and five-hundred-member choir."[42] These and other activities are vehicles for reaching people with the Christian gospel and then keeping them in the church. As one staff member explained, "People think because we're a church, maybe we shouldn't market. But any organization, secular or otherwise, if [it's] going to grow, [it's] got to get people to buy into the product."[43]

Saddleback Valley Community and its pastor have Southern Baptist roots but have minimized their denominational connections considerably. With more than 15,000 members, the church has become another model for what is sometimes known as the megachurch movement in American religious life. Its worship services are "lively, upbeat and contemporary," a trend that is having a powerful influence on Baptist churches large and small. Rick Warren, pastor of the Saddleback Valley Church, has also become a popular teacher on the nature of "the purpose driven church," as he calls it, exporting his methods across denominational lines through books and teleconferences beamed throughout the nation and the world.[44] Warren's book, *The Purpose Driven Church*, published in 1995, sold more than a million copies and was translated into twenty languages. More than 180,000 pastors have participated in seminars on purpose-driven churches.[45] Warren later published *The Purpose Driven Life*, a book that has sold more than 4 million copies. Warren suggests that the book's intention is to "help people develop a heart for the world," to move them beyond fixation on personal ambitions in order to follow God's purpose for life.[46]

The megachurch movement is changing the nature of churches in the United States, and many Baptists are right in the middle of it. A megachurch is a congregation of several thousand members, led by a chief-executive-officer-pastor-authority-figure, providing specialized ministries for target groups, and organized around intentional marketing techniques.[47] These churches seek to anticipate cultural trends, Christianizing them where possible as a way of evangelizing and addressing the culture itself. Leaders insist that they are not bringing the world into the church as much as they are attempting to extend the influence and ministry of the church into an increasingly secular world. These methods have led churches to develop elaborate programs for Bible study, youth, families, missionary outreach, and athletics. Most have family life centers that provide a variety of sports activities for members and friends. Some have developed movie theaters, food courts, and other "full-service" facilities. They have also made extensive use of the Internet in connecting with members and telling their story to the general public.

For example, Fellowshipchurch.com, an Internet address for Fellowship (Baptist) Church in Garland, Texas, was perhaps the first congregation in the country to become an official dot-com on the Internet. Its senior pastor,

Edwin Young Jr., is an innovative second-generation megachurch minister whose sermons deal with issues of practical living, from sexuality to gluttony. He calls the faithful to eschew marital infidelity and Texas-size chicken-fried steak dinners because their bodies are "temples of the Holy Spirit."[48] Fellowship Church, affiliated with the Southern Baptist Convention, has a 4,000-seat auditorium that accommodates 18,000 people at multiple services each week and is one of the most technologically sophisticated worship centers in America. The church baptizes more than 2,000 people each year, approximately 70 percent of them adults.[49]

Churches like Fellowship Church are having an important effect on Baptists for several reasons. First, they represent a concerted effort to evangelize the unchurched in America. These "seekers," as they are called, are persons who have no religious background or who have chosen to opt out of previous affiliations. "Seeker-sensitive" ministry is a primary evangelical method of megachurches, an effort to bring sinners to faith and enlist them in the church.

Second, in their effort to reach seekers, megachurches have reshaped the nature of Christian worship in ways that have affected a variety of congregations large and small. Seeker-oriented worship is often predicated on the idea that the non-affiliated may well be "turned off" by the traditional or be uncomfortable with services that use elaborate liturgies, hymnbooks, vestments, and other religious accoutrements. More-contemporary forms employ brief hymns, sometimes known as "praise choruses," that are displayed on screens and accompanied by "praise bands" using guitars, drums, and pianos. Some churches even facilitate music related to "Christian rock" or "Christian heavy metal" format. Ministers may wear sport clothes rather than suits or robes, in order to communicate informality and openness. Services often include skits or other dramatic presentations along with the sermon, which is directed toward practical implications of biblical texts and principles. "Contemporary" worship experiences have become so successful that many churches have added them to their weekly schedule. Indeed, megachurches have had a major impact on the changing nature of worship in American churches in the early twenty-first century.

Third, megachurches are raising issues of denominational identity for Baptists and other Protestants in the United States. Many of these churches are either nondenominational or generally minimize any denominational affiliation they maintain. They reflect the fact that fewer religious Americans think of their primary identity in terms of a denomination. People tend to identify with a particular congregation for the ministry it provides and the energy it elicits rather than the "brand name" it represents. Thus megachurches may appear to be mini-denominations, providing in one congregation many of the services—publishing, education, and mission—previously facilitated by denominational organizations. This approach to religion is forcing Baptist churches to reexamine their own history and theology to determine what they wish to pass on to another generation of churchgoers who claim the name Baptist.

Finally, implicitly or explicitly, the megachurch phenomenon raises continuing questions about the relationship between church and culture in America. How far can churches go in appropriating elements of the culture without irrevocably changing their own theology and identity? When does the church employ cultural agendas for a Christian purpose and when is the Christian purpose compromised by such worldly methods?

### *Embracing Culture: The Challenge of Pluralism*

By the end of the twentieth century, Baptists, like other religious communions, confronted a rampant pluralism that extended questions that had long been present in American life. The growth and proliferation of a variety of non-Christian groups, including Muslims, Hindus, and Buddhists, as well as "New Age" expressions of popular spirituality, compelled Baptists to revisit issues of religious liberty and theological particularity. That is, Baptists were forced to reexamine their heritage as defenders of conscience and liberty and their commitments to a believers' church, with its assertion of the uniqueness of the Christian revelation. Pluralism and religious liberty mean that all communions are free to practice and promote their views in the religious market. While recognizing that freedom, many Baptists insist that they must declare that Christianity is the only "way" and that all other religions are false.

"I knew my God was bigger than his," Lieutenant General William G. Boykin said of his Muslim opponent. "I knew that my God was a real God, and his was an idol." He concluded, "I am neither a zealot nor an extremist, only a soldier who has an abiding faith." Those remarks, recently delivered in a Baptist pulpit by an American army officer, himself a Baptist, raised issues of religious pluralism and particularity that even secular journalists could not resist addressing. Writing in the *Boston Globe*, reporter James Carroll commented:

> The general's critics are right to deplore the denigration of the faith of Muslims, but the problem goes deeper than a crudely expressed religious

chauvinism. In point of fact, the general's remarks do not make him an extremist. It was unfashionable of him to speak aloud the implications of his "abiding faith," but exclusivist claims made for Jesus Christ by most Christians, from Vatican corridors to evangelical revival tents, implicitly insult the religion of others. When Catholics speak of "salvation" only through Jesus, or when Protestants limit "justification" to faith in Jesus, aspersions are cast on the entire non-Christian world.[50]

Amid terrorism and another war in another Arabic nation, Baptists and other Americans confront a new internationalism centered in a new pluralism. The mission fields are no longer foreign or distant. They can be reached by air in a day or so. Likewise, non-Christians in significant numbers have found their ways to the United States. Pluralism forces Americans to deal with new questions of religious exclusivism and inclusivism. Christians are becoming Hindus and Muslims; while persons from divergent religions are marrying into American families. Globalism/internationalism is now neighborliness, and pluralism compels Americans to relate to religions that are no longer "over there" but next door.

In the face of these cultural transitions, some refuse to open the doors to greater dialogue lest they compromise the true faith. Certain Baptists continue to denounce the untruth of non-Christian faiths. As Southern Baptist leader Jerry Vines declared in 2002:

> I'm here to tell you, ladies and gentlemen, that Islam is not just as good as Christianity. Christianity was founded by the virgin born Son of God, the Lord Jesus Christ. Islam was founded by Muhammad, a demon possessed pedophile that had 12 wives, and his last one was a 9 year old girl. And I will tell you, Allah is not Jehovah, either. Jehovah's not going to turn you into a terrorist that'll try to bomb people and take the lives of thousands and thousands of people.[51]

In light of such comments, other Baptists seem to consider the following: First, coming to terms with global pluralism does not mean losing Christian identity or relinquishing an unashamed commitment to a specific faith tradition. In a truly pluralistic environment, every religion has the right to propagate and promote its views. Where all religions assert their unique identities, there will be many conversions and re-conversions, switching and re-switching from group to group. Pluralism need not compel capitulation to syncretism. Indeed, Baptists will continually struggle with the tension between specificity and relativism, religious rigor and syncretistic pabulum. Interfaith dialogue that ignores genuine distinctions between faiths can degenerate into paternalism.

Second, religious liberty requires that divergent, even contradictory, religious voices will be heard in the public square. Some Christians, Muslims, Jews, and Baptists are compelled by conscience to insist that theirs is the only true religion and that all others are false. And they are bound to declare those beliefs even when they sound like bigots in the public square.

Pluralism means that Baptists like General Boykin and Reverend Vines have every right to speak their consciences in matters of religion. And because they do, religious liberty is absolutely essential, for them and for everyone else. For it is only a step from asserting that all other religions are false to insisting that since they are false the state must protect the innocent ones from such false doctrine and write legal sanctions against them. Without religious liberty, particularism can become persecution in an instant.

Third, some Baptists are bound to struggle with the unceasing paradox of conversionist particularism and pluralistic libertarianism, knowing that many people in other religions will struggle to do the same. This effort will require a certain theological and cultural messiness that involves continued reflection on the nature of faith and interfaith relationships. Contemporary globalism brings foreigners to America, while intermarriage links families amid diverse religious communities. Likewise, Christianity itself is thriving outside the West, confronting pluralistic environments that are sometimes open and sometimes closed to the idea of a believers' church. Pluralism may well be the door, not the death knell, to spiritual vitality for all religious groups. But Baptists will surely divide over the meaning of pluralism in light of Christian particularism and the centrality of Christian revelation.

| | |
|---|---|
| 1609 | John Smyth and Thomas Helwys constitute first (General) Baptist church, Amsterdam |
| 1612 | Thomas Helwys and other Baptists constitute first Baptist church in England |
| 1638 | First Particular (Calvinist) founded (by this time) in London |
| 1638/9 | First Baptist Church founded in Providence, Rhode Island |
| 1641 | Baptismal immersion becomes normative for Baptists |
| 1663 | John Clarke writes *Ill Newes from New England* |
| 1665 | First Baptist Church, Boston, organized |
| 1670 | General, Six Principle Baptists founded in Rhode Island |
| 1699 | First Baptist Church, Charleston, South Carolina, founded by this time, first in South |
| 1707 | Philadelphia Baptist Association founded |
| 1727 | Free Will Baptists founded |
| 1728 | First Seventh Day Baptist Church in America founded in Pennsylvania |
| 1740 | Separate/Regular Baptist divisions occur amid First Great Awakening |
| 1742 | *Philadelphia Confession* (*Second London*) adopted by Philadelphia Association |
| 1764 | Rhode Island College (Brown University) founded by Baptists |
| 1780 | Free Will Baptists begin in New Hampshire |
| 1812 | Adoniram and Ann Hasseltine Judson become Baptists on the way to India |
| 1814 | Triennial Convention (mission society) founded in Philadelphia |

| 1824 | Baptist General Tract Society founded (later became American Baptist Publication Society) |
| 1825 | Newton Theological Institute founded in Massachusetts |
| 1831 | Baptist William Miller organizes early Adventist movement |
| 1832 | American Baptist Home Mission Society founded |
| 1835 | First Primitive Baptist organizations begin in New York and Pennsylvania |
| 1843 | Abolitionists found American and Foreign Free Baptist Missionary Society |
| 1845 | Southern Baptist Convention founded in Augusta, Georgia |
| 1846 | Ruby Knapp Bixby licensed to ministry by Free Will Baptists |
| 1859 | Southern Baptist Theological Seminary founded in Greenville, South Carolina |
| 1871 | General Conference Baptists found Bethel Seminary |
| 1877 | Women's Baptist Home Mission Societies of the East and the West founded |
| 1882 | May C. Jones ordained by Northern Baptist Association |
| 1888 | Woman's Missionary Union, Auxiliary to the SBC founded |
| 1895 | National Baptist Convention founded |
| 1905 | Baptist World Alliance founded |
| 1907 | Northern Baptist Convention established |
| 1911 | Free Baptists unite with Northern Baptist Convention |
| 1915 | National Baptist Conventions, Inc. and Unincorporated formed |
| 1922 | Harry Emerson Fosdick preaches "Shall the Fundamentalists Win?" |
| 1925 | Southern Baptists approve *Baptist Faith and Message* as confession of faith |
| 1932 | General Association of Regular Baptist Churches founded |
| 1939 | Baptist Joint Committee on Public Affairs founded |
| 1942 | Baptist Clarence Jordan founds Koinonia Farm in Americus, Georgia |
| 1943 | Conservative Baptist Foreign Mission Society founded |
| 1948 | Conservative Baptist Home Mission Society founded |
| 1950 | Northern Baptist Convention becomes American Baptist Convention |
| 1957 | American Baptist Convention offers opposition to segregation |
| 1960 | Southern Baptist seminary professor Ralph Elliott fired over "Genesis" controversy |
| 1961 | Progressive National Baptist Convention founded |
| 1963 | Southern Baptists revise *Baptist Faith and Message* |

1964    Addie Davis ordained to ministry in a Southern Baptist church

1968    Baptist pastor Martin Luther King Jr. assassinated in Memphis, Tennessee

1972    American Baptist Convention reorganized, becoming American Baptist Churches, USA

1979    Conservatives elect Adrian Rogers as SBC president to promote biblical inerrancy

1980    Religious Roundtable founded, involving many Baptists

1986    Alliance of Baptists founded by SBC "moderates"

1991    Cooperative Baptist Fellowship founded by SBC "moderates"

2000    Southern Baptists revise *Baptist Faith and Message*

**Chapter 1**

1. Shaped-note singing is a form of hymnody in which each note has a distinct shape in order to indicate its tone on a "fa-so-la" range. It was a method for teaching people to sing who could not read music in a formal way. The church and others like it are profiled in the film *In the Good Old Fashioned Way*, produced by the Kentucky-based documentary film company Appalshop,

2. Bill J. Leonard, "Good News at Wolf Creek," *Christian Century*, March 14, 1984, 277–278.

3. See www.Saddleback.com.

4. Bob Smietana, "Megashepherd," *Christianity Today*, February 2004, 31.

5. Walter B. Shurden, *The Baptist Identity: Four Fragile Freedoms* (Macon, GA: Smyth and Helwys, 1993), 3. Shurden notes a survey in *U.S. News and World Report*, May 14, 1984, that listed Falwell, Jackson, and Graham as numbers 7, 8, and 9 on a list of most-influential Americans.

6. Albert W. Wardin, ed., *Baptists Around the World: A Comprehensive Handbook* (Nashville: Broadman and Holman, 1995), 473.

7. Walter B. Shurden, *Not a Silent People* (Nashville: Broadman, 1972).

8. Bill J. Leonard, *God's Last and Only Hope: The Fragmentation of the Southern Baptist Convention* (Grand Rapids: Eerdmans, 1990), 1.

9. For many years, it was common for Baptist churches to present elementary-age children with Bibles that had a zipper joining the two outside covers. Black leather Bibles were normally given to boys, white leather Bibles to girls. The Sunday school "Quarterly" was so called because it included Bible lessons for three months and was issued each quarter of the year. The tithe was and in many churches remains the preferred biblical guide or mandate for financial contributions to the church. Each member is asked to contribute one tenth of his or her earnings to the ministry of the

church. These practices were common in Baptist denominations such as the American Baptist Churches, USA, the Southern Baptist Convention, the Seventh Day Baptists, and certain African American Baptist congregations. Independent and other less denominationally based churches resisted the use of printed Sunday school materials because they distracted from the direct study of the biblical text alone.

## Chapter 2

1. H. Leon McBeth, *The Baptist Heritage* (Nashville: Broadman, 1987), 30.

2. A. C. Underwood, *A History of the English Baptists* (London: Baptist Union of Great Britain and Ireland, 1970), 37, cites W. T. Whitley, *The Works of John Smyth*, 1:xciii.

3. McBeth, *The Baptist Heritage*, 42–44.

4. William L. Lumpkin, *Baptist Confessions of Faith* (Valley Forge, PA: Judson, 1974), 120.

5. T. Dowley, "Baptists and Church Discipline," *Baptist Quarterly* (October 1971):158; Bill J. Leonard, *Baptist Ways: A History* (Valley Forge, PA: Judson, 2003), 56–58.

6. Leonard, *Baptist Ways*, 104–105.

7. Ibid., 76.

8. J. M. Dawson, *Baptists and the American Republic* (Nashville: Broadman, 1956), 75, citing "Backus Collection," Andover Newton Theological School.

9. H. Leon McBeth, ed., A *Sourcebook for Baptist Heritage* (Nashville: Broadman, 1990), 180.

10. Some believed that education was detrimental to genuine "heart religion." Many Separate Baptists also rejected the idea that clergy should be paid or hired for their services.

11. Ann Hasseltine Judson, "Letter to a friend about becoming a Baptist," in McBeth, *Sourcebook*, 207.

12. McBeth, *Sourcebook*, 237, citing the "Black Rock Address," September 28, 1832.

13. Ibid.

14. Ibid., 238.

15. Ibid.

16. Ibid.

17. Daniel Parker, *Views on the Two Seeds Taken from Genesis* (Vandalia, IL: Robert Blackwell, 1826), 8.

18. Peter Cartwright, *The Autobiography of Peter Cartwright* (New York: Phillips and Hunt, 1856), 133–134.

19. Leonard, *Baptist Ways*, 267–268.

20. Ibid., 269–270.

21. Winthrop Hudson, ed., *Walter Rauschenbusch: Selected Writings* (New York: Paulist Press, 1984), 79.

## Chapter 3

1. Norman Maring and Winthrop Hudson, *A Baptist Manual of Polity and Practice*, rev. ed. (Valley Forge, PA: Judson, 1991), 198.

2. Ibid.

3. Ibid., 201–202.

4. Ibid., 202.

5. W. H. Brackney, "American Baptist Home Mission Society," in Bill J. Leonard, ed., *Dictionary of Baptists in America*, 23–24 (Downers Grove, IL: InterVarsity, 1994).

6. Deborah Vansau McCauley, *Appalachian Mountain Religion: A History* (Chicago: University of Illinois Press, 1955), 41.

7. Robert A. Baker, *The Southern Baptist Convention and Its People, 1607–1972* (Nashville: Broadman, 1974), 289.

8. Ibid., 398.

9. S. L. Still, "Woman's American Baptist Foreign Mission Society," in Leonard, *Dictionary of Baptists in America*, 292.

10. Baker, *The Southern Baptist Convention and Its People*, 298.

11. *Annual of the Northern Baptist Convention* (Nashville: Convention Press, 1908), 41.

12. Ibid., 90.

13. *Annual*, Southern Baptist Convention (Nashville, 1913), 22.

14. George W. Schroeder, *The Church Brotherhood Guidebook* (Nashville: Broadman, 1950), 36; and Bill J. Leonard, "A History of the Baptist Laymen's Movement," *Baptist History and Heritage* (January 1978): 35–44, 62.

15. *Annual of the Northern Baptist Convention*, 1921, 226–229.

16. Paul M. Nagano, "December 7, 1941: Pearl Harbor and War with Japan," *American Baptist Quarterly* 17 (June 1998): 95.

17. L. Russ Bush and Tom J. Nettles, *Baptists and the Bible* (Chicago: Moody Press, 1980), 433, citing John A. Broadus, *A Treatise on the Preparation and Delivery of Sermons* (New York: Hodder and Stoughton, 1898), 21.

18. Jeff Todd Titon, *Powerhouse for God: Speech, Chant, and Song in an Appalachian Baptist Church* (Austin: University of Texas Press, 1988), 305.

19. Stephen Shoemaker, *God's Stories: New Narratives from Sacred Texts* (Valley Forge, PA: Judson, 1998), xv–xvi.

20. Melva Wilson Costen, *African American Christian Worship* (Nashville: Abingdon, 1993), 104–105.

21. Glenn T. Miller, "Baptist World Outreach and U.S. Foreign Affairs," in James E. Wood, Jr., ed., *Baptists and the American Experience*, (Valley Forge, PA: Judson, 1976), 168.

22. Ibid.

23. Brenda M. Meehan, "A. C. Dixon: An Early Fundamentalist," *Foundations* (January–March 1967), 57.

24. James L. Thompson, Jr., "Southern Baptists and Postwar Disillusionment, 1918–1919," *Foundations* (April–June 1978), 114.

25. Harry Emerson Fosdick, *The Living of These Days* (San Francisco: Harper, 1956), 294.

26. Ibid.

27. "The World Disarmament Conference, A Petition," in Eldon Ernst, "Twentieth Century War and Peace," *Foundations* (October–December 1972), 310–311.

28. "International Affairs—War and Peace," in Ernst, "Twentieth-Century War and Peace," 310–311.

29. Ibid.

30. *Watchman-Examiner*, September 13, 1934; cited in William Loyd Allen, "How Baptists Assessed Hitler," *Peace Work* (May–August 1987), 12.

31. Official report of the Fifth Baptist World Congress, cited in Allen, "How Baptists Assessed Hitler," 12.

32. Ibid., 13.

33. Jitsuo Morikawa, "Toward an Asian American Theology," *American Baptist Quarterly* 12 (June, 1993), 182..

34. "International Affairs—War and Peace," 313.

35. Nagano, "December 7, 1941: Pearl Harbor and War with Japan," 98.

36. Ibid., 118.

37. Ibid., 261.

38. H. Shelton Smith, Robert T. Handy, and Lefferts A. Loetscher, eds., *American Christianity: An Historical Interpretation with Representative Documents* (New York: Charles Scribner's Sons, 1963), 2:255.

39. Ibid., 2:239.

40. Ibid., 2:245.

41. William Newton Clarke, *An Outline of Christian Theology* (New York: Charles Scribner's Sons, 1914), 5.

42. Smith, Handy, and Loetscher, *American Christianity*, 2:259.

43. Ibid., 2:256.

44. E. Glenn Hinson, "Baptist Contributions to Liberalism," *Baptist History and Heritage* 35 (Winter 2000): 39, citing William R. Hutchinson, *The Modernist Impulse in American Protestantism* (Cambridge: Harvard University Press, 1976), 114. The Disciples of Christ are an American denomination that grew out the Restorationist movement of the nineteenth century.

45. Winthrop S. Hudson, *Baptists in Transition: Individualism and Christian Responsibility* (Valley Forge, PA: Judson, 1979), 120.

46. Hinson, "Baptist Contributions to Liberalism," 39–40.

47. LeRoy Moore Jr., "Academic Freedom: A Chapter in the History of the Colgate Rochester Divinity School," *Foundations* (January–March 1967), 67.

48. Hinson, "Baptist Contributions to Liberalism," 43, citing William Newton Clarke, *An Outline of Christian Theology* (New York: Charles Scribner's Sons, 1898), 3.

49. Ibid., 47.

50. Ibid., 46.

51. G. T. Halbrooks, "Poteat, William Louis," in Leonard, *Dictionary of Baptists in America*, 223

52. Hinson, "Baptist Contributions to Liberalism," 48, citing Kenneth Cauthen, *The Impact of American Religious Liberalism* (New York: Harper and Row, 1962), 62. Cauthen's analysis of Baptist hesitancy regarding "creedalism" would be disputed by numerous conservative Baptists in both the twentieth and the twenty-first centuries.

53. George Marsden, *Fundamentalism and American Culture* (New York: Oxford University Press, 1980), 43–71.

54. W. A. Hoffecker, "Princeton Theology," in Daniel G. Reid, coordinating ed., *Dictionary of Christianity in America* (Downers Grove, IL: InterVarsity Press, 1990), 942.

55. Ibid., 159.

56. Earnest Sandeen, "The Baptists and Millenarianism," *Foundations* (January–March 1970), 21–22.

57. C. Allyn Russell, *Voices of American Fundamentalism* (Philadelphia: Westminster, 1976), 80; and Leonard, *Baptist Ways*, 400.

58. Ibid., 94. "Germanized" refers to liberal theology that many fundamentalists believed had been imported to the United States in ways that corrupted faith and doctrine.

59. *Watchman-Examiner*, May 20, 1920, 652.

60. Russell, *Voices of American Fundamentalism*, 127–128.

61. Ibid., 134.

62. Ibid., 162–163.

63. Ibid., 77.

64. Joseph D. Ban, "Two Views of One Age: Fosdick and Straton," *Foundations*14 (April–June 1971): 157; and Leonard, *Baptist Ways*, 400.

65. Russell, *Voices of American Fundamentalism*, 26,

66. Ibid., 29–31.

67. Ibid., 40.

68. Ibid., 93.

69. Norman H. Maring, *Baptists in New Jersey* (Valley Forge, PA: Judson, 1964), 332.

70. Ibid., 333–334.

71. Ibid., 569.

72. Harry Emerson Fosdick, "Shall the Fundamentalists Win?" in Smith, Handy, and Loetscher, *American Christianity*, 2:296.

**Chapter 4**

1. William L. Lumpkin, *Baptist Confessions of Faith* (Valley Forge, PA: Judson, 1974), 16. The survey of Baptist statements presented here is representative of major

and distinct doctrines but is not all-inclusive. Lumpkin's work surveys a variety of classic Baptist confessions of faith.

2. Ibid.

3. Ibid., 326.

4. Ibid., 16.

5. Ibid., 117.

6. Ibid., 156–158.

7. Ibid., 158.

8. John Clarke, *Ill Newes from New-England*, 1651, in H. Shelton Smith, Robert T. Handy, and Lefferts A. Loetscher, eds., *American Christianity: An Historical Interpretation with Representative Documents*, 167 (New York: Charles Scribner's Sons, 1960).

9. Lumpkin, *Baptist Confessions of Faith*, 162–163.

10. Ibid., 205.

11. Ibid., 226.

12. Ibid., 165.

13. Ibid., 165–166.

14. Ibid., 102.

15. Ibid., 122.

16. Ibid., 178.

17. Ibid., 244.

18. Ibid., 245.

19. Ibid., 248.

20. Ibid., 324.

21. Robison B. James, *The Unfettered Word* (Waco: Word Books, 1987); Duane A. Garrett and Richard R. Melick Jr., *Authority and Interpretation: A Baptist Perspective* (Grand Rapids: Baker Book House, 1987); and Robison B. James and David S. Dockery, *Beyond the Impasse?: Scripture, Interpretation, and Theology in Baptist Life* (Nashville: Broadman, 1992).

22. Lumpkin, *Baptist Confessions of Faith*, 209.

23. Ibid., 254–255.

24. Ibid., 264.

25. Ibid., 118.

26. Ibid., 226.

27. Ibid., 228.

28. Ibid., 264.

29. Ibid., 120.

30. Ibid.

31. Smith, Handy, and Loetscher, *American Christianity*, 167.

32. Obadiah Holmes, *Baptist Piety: The Last Will and Testament of Obadiah Holmes*, edited with historical introduction by Edwin S. Gaustad (Valley Forge: Judson, 1994), 91.

33. Lumpkin, *Baptist Confessions of Faith*, 119.

34. Ibid., 167.

35. Ibid.

36. Ibid., 291.

37. Ibid., 193.

38. Ibid., 137.

39. Ibid.

40. Ibid., 138.

41. Ibid., 120–121.

42. Ibid., 291–292.

43. Ibid., 292.

44. Ibid., 293.

45. Ibid., 183.

46. Ibid., 164.

47. Ibid., 120.

48. Ibid., 288.

49. Ibid., 138.

50. Ibid.

51. Ibid., 168.

52. Ibid., 288.

53. Ibid., 183.

54. Ibid., 122.

55. Ibid., 166.

56. Ibid., 167. The *Somerset Confession* (1655) also confirms that ministers were chosen from the membership of a specific church. No standard offices are set forth. Ministers were to be ordained with "fasting, prayer, and laying on of hands for the performance of several duties, whereunto they are called." See 212–213.

57. Ibid., 229, 231.

58. Ibid., 288–289.

59. Ibid., 290.

60. Ibid., 319.

61. Ibid., 319–320.

62. Ibid., 139–140.

63. Ibid., 135.

64. Ibid., 233.

65. Ibid., 331–332.

66. Ibid., 332.

67. Ibid., 347.

68. Ibid., 349.

69. Ibid., 351.

70. Benjamin Griffith, *An Essay on the Power of an Association*, 1749, in H. Leon McBeth, ed., *A Sourcebook for Baptist Heritage* (Nashville: Broadman, 1990), 146.

71. Lumpkin, *Baptist Confessions of Faith*, 361–362.

72. Ibid., 364.

73. *Constitution and Articles of Faith of the General Association of Regular Baptists* (Schaumburg, IL: GARBC), 2; see also Bill J. Leonard, "Types of Confessional Documents Among Baptists," *Review and Expositor* 76 (Winter 1979): 34.

74. *Constitution and Articles of Faith of the General Association of Regular Baptists*, 5.

75. Ibid.

76. Ibid., 8

77. McBeth, *A Sourcebook for Baptist Heritage*, 503.

78. Ibid., 514–515.

79. Ibid.

80. *The Baptist Faith and Message* (Nashville: LifeWay Christian Resources, 2001), 16–17.

## Chapter 5

1. Robert A. Baker, *The Southern Baptist Convention and Its People, 1607–1972* (Nashville: Broadman, 1974), 262.

2. Ibid., 266.

3. S. L. Still, "Woman's American Baptist Home Mission Society," in Bill J. Leonard, ed., *Dictionary of Baptists in America* (Downers Grove, IL: InterVarsity Press, 1994), 292–293.

4. Ibid., 292.

5. Norman Maring, *American Baptists Whence and Whither* (Valley Forge, PA: Judson, 1968), 75.

6. Ibid., 76.

7. W. H. Brackney, "American Baptist Churches in the USA," in Leonard, *Dictionary of Baptists in America*, 22.

8. Ibid.

9. Ibid.

10. Everett C. Goodwin, *Baptists in the Balance* (Valley Forge, PA: Judson, 1997), 391.

11. Baker, *The Southern Baptist Convention and Its People*, 383.

12. Don A. Sanford, *A Choosing People: The History of Seventh Day Baptists* (Nashville: Broadman, 1992), 150.

13. Ibid., 178–179.

14. Albert W. Wardin, ed., *Baptists Around the World: A Comprehensive Handbook* (Nashville: Broadman and Holman, 1995), 383.

15. Ibid., 384.

16. Sanford, *A Choosing People*, 225–230.

17. Baker, *The Southern Baptist Convention and Its People*, 159.

18. Ibid., 165.

19. Ibid., 167.

20. Ibid., 204–205.

21. J. William Jones, *Christ in the Camp or Religion in the Confederate Army* (Harrisonburg, VA: Sprinkle Publications, 1986.

22. Charles Reagan Wilson, *Baptized in Blood: the Religion of the Lost Cause, 1865–1920* (Athens: University of Georgia Press, 1980); Bill J. Leonard, *God's Last and Only Hope: The Fragmentation of the Southern Baptist Convention* (Grand Rapids: Eerdmans, 1990).

23. Frank S. Mead and Samuel Hill, eds., *Handbook of Denominations in the United States*, 9th ed., rev. (Nashville: Abingdon, 1992), 55.

24. Ibid., 51.

25. John G. Crowley, *Primitive Baptists of the Wiregrass South* (Gainesville: University Press of Florida, 1998), 60.

26. Wardin, *Baptists Around the World*, 422.

27. James L. Peacock and Reul W. Tyson Jr., *Pilgrims of Paradox: Calvinism and Experience Among the Primitive Baptists of the Blue Ridge* (Washington, DC: Smithsonian Institution Press, 1989), 97–98.

28. Howard Dorgan, *Giving Glory to God in Appalachia: Worship Practices of Six Baptist Subdenominations* (Knoxville: University of Tennessee Press, 1987), 10.

29. Bill J. Leonard, *Baptist Ways: A History* (Valley Forge, PA: Judson, 2003), 206–207; Howard Dorgan, "Old Time Baptists of Central Appalachia," in Bill J. Leonard, ed., *Appalachian Christianity: Profiles in Regional Pluralism* (Knoxville: University of Tennessee Press, 1999), 117–118.

30. Howard Dorgan, *In the Hands of a Happy God: Primitive Baptist Universalists of Central Appalachia* (Knoxville: University of Tennessee Press, 1997), 96. While this group is very small and has churches in Virginia, West Virginia, and North Carolina, it is a fascinating example of theological variety in Baptist life. Dorgan's book is the first full study of the little-known movement.

31. Howard Dorgan, *The Old Regular Baptists of Central Appalachia* (Knoxville: University of Tennessee Press, 1989), 5.

32. Dorgan, *Giving Glory to God in Appalachia*, 20.

33. Dorgan, *The Old Regular Baptists of Central Appalachia*, 36.

34. Ibid., 22, citing the articles of faith of the Mountain District Primitive Baptist Association and the Sardis Association of Old Regular Baptists.

35. Ibid., 25.

36. Ibid., 55–56.

37. Clifford A. Grammich Jr., *Local Baptists, Local Politics* (Knoxville: University of Tennessee Press, 1999), 79.

38. Mead and Hill, *Handbook of Denominations*, 57–58.

39. Dorgan, *Giving Glory to God in Appalachia*, 32.

40. Ibid.

41. Ibid., 34–35.

42. Ibid., 35.

43. Ibid., 36.

44. Wardin, *Baptists Around the World*, 424.

45. Ibid., 424–425.

46. Ibid., 427.

47. J. E. Johnson, "Baptist General Conference," in Leonard, *Dictionary of Baptists in America*, 47.

48. Ibid.

49. Mead and Hill, *Handbook of Denominations*, 41.

50. Wardin, *Baptists Around the World*, 378.

51. Ibid., 378.

52. Ibid., 371.

53. H. W. Pipkin, "German Baptist Churches of North America, General Conference of," in Leonard, *Dictionary of Baptists in America*, 131.

54. Wardin, *Baptists Around the World*, 381.

55. Ibid., 371, 381–382.

56. Ibid., 393.

57. "Cedarville University Partners with Southern Baptist Convention," *Maranatha Baptist Watchman*, March 2003, 6.

58. Ibid.

59. C. Allyn Russell, *Voices of American Fundamentalism: Seven Biological Studies* (Philadelphia: Westminster, 1976).

60. Wardin, *Baptists Around the World*, 404–406.

61. Ibid., 407.

62. Bill J. Leonard, "Independent Baptists: From Sectarian Minority to 'Moral Majority,'" *Church History* 56 (December 1987): 504–517.

63. Wardin, *Baptists Around the World*, *387*.

64. Ibid., 386–388.

65. Ibid., 379.

66. Ibid., 371, 379–380.

67. Ibid., 402.

68. H. Leon McBeth, ed., *A Sourcebook for Baptist Heritage* (Nashville: Broadman, 1990), 558.

69. Wardin, *Baptists Around the World*, 402.

70. Ibid., 402–403.

71. Ibid., 410.

72. Ibid., 411.

73. Ibid.

74. Leroy Fitts, *A History of Black Baptists* (Nashville: Broadman, 1985), 80.

75. Ibid., 82–83.

76. Ibid., 86–88.

77. Ibid., 92–93.

78. "History," National Baptist Convention, Web page.

79. Fitts, *A History of Black Baptists*, 103–104.

80. Wardin, *Baptists Around the World*, 416.

81. G. T. Halbrooks, "Alliance of Baptists," in Leonard, *Dictionary of Baptists in America*, 19.

82. Alan Neely, "The History of the Alliance of Baptists," in Walter B. Shurden, ed., *The Struggle for the Soul of the SBC* (Macon: Mercer University Press, 1993), 113.

83. Daniel Vestal, "The History of the Cooperative Baptist Fellowship," in Shurden, *The Struggle for the Soul of the SBC*, 264–265.

84. Ibid., 269 and 273.

## Chapter 6

1. William L. Lumpkin, *Baptist Confessions of Faith* (Valley Forge, PA: Judson, 1974), 122.

2. Ibid., 248.

3. Ibid., 361–362.

4. Ibid., 385.

5. *Articles of Faith*, First Baptist Church, Dallas, Texas, 1970.

6. William H. Brackney, *The Baptists* (Westport, CT: Praeger, 1994), 28.

7. Ibid.

8. Ibid., 29.

9. H. Shelton Smith, Robert T. Handy, and Lefferts A. Loetscher, eds., *American Christianity: An Interpretation with Representative Documents* (New York: Charles Scribner's Sons, 1963), 2:297–298.

10. L. Russ Bush and Tom J. Nettles, *Baptists and the Bible* (Chicago: Moody Press, 1980), 358.

11. Brackney, *The Baptists*, 31.

12. H. Leon McBeth, *A Sourcebook for Baptist Heritage* (Nashville: Broadman, 1990), 505.

13. Ibid.

14. *The Baptist Faith and Message* (Nashville: LifeWay Christian Resources, 2000), 7.

15. McBeth, *A Sourcebook for Baptist Heritage*, 500.

16. Ibid., 502.

17. Robert A. Baker, *The Southern Baptist Convention and Its People, 1607–1972* (Nashville: Broadman, 1974), 416.

18. David S. Dockery, "The Divine-Human Authorship of Inspired Scripture," in Duane A. Garrett and Richard R. Melick Jr., eds., *Authority and Interpretation: A Baptist Perspective* (Grand Rapids, MI: Baker Book House, 1987), 38–39. Dockery puts this statement in quotation but does not indicate the specific source, though he suggests several works that explore the topic; see 38n.

19. David S. Dockery, *The Doctrine of the Bible* (Nashville: Convention Press, 1991), 86–87.

20. L. Russ Bush and Tom J. Nettles, *Baptists and the Bible* (Chicago: Moody Bible Institute, 1980), 400.

21. Paige Patterson, "Beyond the Impasse: Fidelity to the God Who Speaks," in Robison B. James and David S. Dockery, eds., *Beyond the Impasse? Scripture, Interpretation, and Theology in Baptist Life* (Nashville: Broadman, 1992), 166.

22. Walter Harrelson, "Passing on the Biblical Tradition Intact: The Role of Historical Criticism, in James and Dockery, *Beyond the Impasse?*, 61.

23. C. Allyn Russell, *Voices of American Fundamentalism* (Philadelphia: Westminster Press, 1974), 26.

24. "Statement of Faith," Baptist Bible Fellowship International, bible.ca/cr-Baptists-BBFI.htm.

25. Ibid.

26. Daniel Featley, *The Dippers Dipt, or, the Anabaptists Duck'd and Plung'd over Head and Eares, at a Disputation at Southwark* (London: Nicholas Bourne and Richard Royston, 1646), n.p.

27. J. R. Graves, "A Statement of Landmark Principles, 1857," in McBeth, *A Sourcebook for Baptist Heritage*, 319.

28. Lumpkin, *Baptist Confessions of Faith*, 292.

29. Ibid., 292–293.

30. Ben Bogard, *The Baptist Way Book* (Texarkana: Bogard Press, 1946), cited in McBeth, *A Sourcebook for Baptist Heritage*, 560.

31. Henry Cook, *What Baptists Stand For* (London: Kingsgate, 1947), cited in Brian Stanley, "Planting Self-Governing Churches," *Baptist Quarterly* 34 (October 1992): 66.

32. Christine Leigh Heyrman, *Southern Cross: The Beginnings of the Bible Belt* (New York: Knopf, 1997), 97.

33. Ibid., 121–122.

34. Ibid., 55.

35. W. T. Whitley, *A History of British Baptists*, rev. ed. (London: Kingsgate, 1932), 86.

36. Walter Rauschenbusch, "Why I Am a Baptist," cited in J. M. Dawson, *Baptists and the American Republic* (Nashville: Broadman, 1956), 173.

### Chapter 7

1. Walter Rauschenbusch, *Christianity and the Social Crisis* (1907), cited in C. C. Goen, "Baptists and Church-State Issues in the Twentieth Century," *American Baptist Quarterly* 6 (December 1987): 227.

2. George W. Truett, "Baptists and Religious Liberty," in H. Leon McBeth, ed., *A Sourcebook for Baptist Heritage* (Nashville: Broadman, 1990), 469.

3. Goen, "Baptists and Church-State Issues," 249.

4. Thomas Helwys, *A Short Declaration of the Mystery of Iniquity*, edited and with an introduction by Richard Groves (Macon, GA: Mercer University Press, 1998), 37.

5. Roger Williams, *The Bloudy Tenant of Persecution*, cited in James M. Dawson, *Baptists and the American Republic* (Nashville: Broadman, 1956), 32.

6. William Henry Brackney, *The Baptists* (New York: Greenwood, 1988), 95.

7. *Backus Collection*, Andover-Newton Theological School, cited in Dawson, *Baptists and the American Republic*, 75.

8. William McLoughlin, *Soul Liberty: The Baptists' Struggle in New England, 1630–1833* (Hanover, NH: Brown University Press, 1991), 245–246.

9. McBeth, *A Sourcebook for Baptist Heritage* 180.

10. Walfred H. Peterson, "Liberty and Justice for All," in James E. Wood Jr., ed., *Baptists and the American Experience* (Valley Forge, PA: Judson, 1976), 97.

11. Walter Rauschenbusch, "The New Evangelism," *The Independent* 66 (January–June 1904): 1054–1059, republished in Winthrop S. Hudson, ed., *Walter Rauschenbusch: Selected Writings* (New York: Paulist Press, 1984), 187–188.

12. Dawson, *Baptists and the American Republic*, 193.

13. Keith Harper, *The Quality of Mercy: Southern Baptists and Social Christianity, 1890–1920* (Tuscaloosa: University of Alabama Press, 1996),

14. Paul Harvey, *Redeeming the South: Religious Cultures and Racial Identities Among Southern Baptists, 1865–1925* (Chapel Hill: University of North Carolina Press, 1997), 212.

15. Ibid., 214.

16. Ibid., 217.

17. *Syllabus of Errors* in *Documents of the Christian Church*, edited by Henry Bettenson (New York: Oxford University Press, 1963), 383–384.

18. J. Frank Norris, *Searchlight*, April 14, 1922; "Six Reasons Why Al Smith Should Not Be President," *Searchlight* (November 18, 1927; and Bill J. Leonard, *Baptist Ways: A History* (Valley Forge, PA: Judson, 2003), 404.

19. John Lee Eighmy, *Churches in Cultural Captivity* (Knoxville: University of Tennessee Press, 1972), 171.

20. Goen, "Baptists and Church-State Issues," 244. The speech was written in large part by Bill Moyers, at that time Lyndon Johnson's executive assistant and a Baptist seminary graduate.

21. "Why Did God Allow Kennedy's Death?" *Sword of the Lord*, January 24, 1964; "What Was Back of Kennedy's Murder?" *Sword of the Lord*, January 31, 1964; John R. Rice, "Senator Robert F. Kennedy's Death," *Sword of the Lord*, June 28, 1968; and Leonard, *Baptist Ways*, 405–406.

22. Oran P. Smith, *The Rise of Baptist Republicanism* (New York: New York University Press, 1997), 182.

23. American Baptist Association, Web page, "The Interactive Bible, False Doctrines."

24. Goen, "Baptists and Church-State Issues," 234–235.

25. "The Church and Public Policy: Actions," in Wood, *Baptists and the American Experience*, 257.

26. Stan L. Hastey, "Public Affairs, Baptist Joint Committee on," in *The Encyclopedia of Southern Baptists* (Nashville: Broadman, 1982), 4:2429–2430.

27. David T. Morgan, *The New Crusades, The New Holy Land: Conflict in the Southern Baptist Convention, 1969–1991* (Tuscaloosa: University of Alabama Press, 1996), 108–109.

28. Rdward L. Queen II, *In the South Baptists Are the Center of Gravity* (Brooklyn: Carlson Publishing, 1991), 105–106.

29. Goen, "Baptists and Church-State Issues," 246.

30. Eighmy, *Churches in Cultural Captivity*, 165–169. Eighmy provides a good summary of this issue as related to the SBC.

31. Goen, "Baptists and Church-State Issues," 239.

32. Ibid.

33. O. Carroll Arnold, "The Exercise of Religious Freedom," in Wood, *Baptists and the American Experience*, 220.

34. Goen, "Baptists and Church-State Issues," 240.

35. "American Baptist Policy Statement on Church and State," *American Baptist Quarterly* 6 (December 1987): 204.

36. Ibid., 205.

37. Ibid., 213.

38. Ibid., 211.

39. Jimmy Carter, *Living Faith* (New York: Times Books, 1996), 35.

40. Ibid., 30–31.

41. Samuel Hill and Dennis Owen, *The New Religious Political Right in America* (Nashville: Abingdon, 1982), 69.

42. James L. Guth, "The Politics of Preachers: Southern Baptist Ministers and Christian Right Activism," in David G. Bromley and Anson Shupe, eds., *New Christian Politics*, 236 (Macon: Mercer University Press, 1984); Hill and Owen suggest that "the greatest support" for the New Religious Political Right came from "independent Baptist Congregations." See *The New Religious Political Right in America*, 15.

43. Hill and Owen, *The New Religious Political Right in America*, 109.

44. CNN.Com/US, Web page, September 14, 2001.

45. Queen, *In the South the Baptists Are the Center of Gravity*, 110.

46. Hill and Owen, *The New Religious Political Right in America*, 182.

47. Ibid.

48. Ibid., 174.

49. Ibid., 184.

50. Brad Owens, "Patterson Thrusts Social Agenda into Fray," *Baptist Messenger*, June 26, 1986, 4.

51. Dan Martin, "Nominee Vows Pro-Life, Racial Justice Stands," *Baptist Standard*, September 14, 1988, 3.

52. Ibid.

53. Barry Hankins, *Uneasy in Zion: Southern Baptist Conservatives and American Culture* (Tuscaloosa: University of Alabama Press, 2002), 62.

54. Ibid., 64.

55. Ibid., 140–141.

56. Ibid., 118.

57. Ibid, 119.

58. Melissa Rogers, "Baptists and the Establishment Clause," in Everett C. Goodwin, ed., *Baptists in the Balance: The Tension Between Freedom and Responsibility*, 302 (Valley Forge, PA: Judson, 1997).

59. Baptist Joint Committee, Web page.

60. Ibid.

61. Brackney, *The Baptists*, 105; Hankins, *Uneasy in Zion*, 137.

## Chapter 8

1. Albert W. Wardin, ed., *Baptists Around the World: A Comprehensive Handbook* (Nashville: Broadman and Holman, 1995), 391.

2. Ibid., 378.

3. Ibid.., 382.

4. Ibid.., 392.

5. William Warren Sweet, *Religion on the American Frontier: The Baptists* (Chicago: University of Chicago Press, 1931), 320.

6. Ibid., 325.

7. Bill J. Leonard, *Baptist Ways: A History* (Valley Forge, PA: Judson, 2003), 186.

8. C. Eric Lincoln and Lawrence H. Mamiya, "The Black Baptists: The First Black Churches in America," in Everett C. Goodwin, ed., *Baptists in the Balance*, 100 (Valley Forge, PA: Judson, 1997).

9. Ibid., 101–102.

10. Ibid., citing Miles Mark Fisher, "What Is a Negro Baptist?" *Home Mission College Review* 1, no. 1 (May 1927).

11. Floyd T. Cunningham, "Wandering in the Wilderness: Black Baptist Thought After Emancipation," *American Baptist Quarterly* 5 (March 1986): 271.

12. Ibid.

13. Henry H. Tucker, "Are We Orthodox on the Race Question?" *Christian Index*, March 22, 1883, cited in H. Shelton Smith, *In His Image, But . . . Racism in Southern Religion, 1780–1910* (Durham: Duke University Press, 1972), 265.

14. Ibid.

15. Ibid.

16. Paul Harvey, *Redeeming the South: Religious Cultures and Racial Identities Among Southern Baptists, 1865–1925* (Chapel Hill: University of Chapel Hill Press, 1997), 227–228.

17. E. C. Morris, *Sermons, Addresses, and Reminiscences and Important Correspondence* (Nashville: National Baptist Publishing Board, 1901), 81, cited in Larry Frazier, "Sutton E. Grigg's *Imperium in Imperio* as Evidence of Black Baptist Radicalism," *Baptist History and Heritage* 35 (Spring 2000): 85.

18. Harvey, *Redeeming the South,* 229.

19. Ibid., 230–231.

20. Ibid., 231.

21. Rufus Perry, *The Cushite: Or, The Descendents of Ham, as found in the Sacred Scriptures and in the Writings of Ancient Historians and Poets from Noah to the Christian Era* (Springfield, MA: Willey, 1893), cited in Cunningham, "Wandering in the Wilderness," 273.

22. 1890 SBC *Proceedings,* viii, cited in Robert Norman Nash Jr., "The Influence of American Myth on Southern Baptist Foreign Missions, 1845–1945" (Ph.D. diss., Southern Baptist Theological Seminary, 1989), 169–170.

23. Nash, "The Influence of American Myth on Southern Baptist Missions," 171.

24. Charles Marsh, *God's Long Summer: Stories of Faith and Civil Rights* (Princeton, NJ: Princeton University Press, 1997), 89.

25. Ibid., 101.

26. Mark Newman, "Southern Baptists and Desegregation, 1945–1980," in Tony Badger, Walter Edgar, and Jan Nordby Gretlund, eds., *Southern Landscapes,* 183–184 (Tubingen: Stauffenburg-Verlag, 1996).

27. Ibid., 185.

28. D. E. Pitzer, "Jordan, Clarence," in Bill J. Leonard, ed., *Dictionary of Baptists in America,* 157–158 (Downes Grove, IL: Intervarsity Press, 1992).

29. Newman, "Southern Baptists and Desegregation," 190–191.

30. Ibid., 193–194.

31. Ibid., 200–201. Many who founded schools opposed "forced busing" to achieve racial balance or to respond to secularism in public schools.

32. Barry Hankins, *Uneasy in Zion: Southern Baptist Conservatives and American Culture* (Tuscaloosa: University of Alabama Press, 2002), 247.

33. Ibid.

34. Bill J. Leonard, "A Theology for Racism: Southern Fundamentalists and the Civil Rights Movement," in Badger, Edgar, and Gretlund, *Southern Landscapes,* 168.

35. Ibid., 169.

36. Ibid.

37. "American Baptist Association at Memphis," *Baptist Bible Tribune,* July 23, 1963, 3.

38. T. H. Masters, "I Examined my Conscience," *Fundamentalist,* July 1963, 1.

39. Noel Smith, "Martin Luther King," *Bible Baptist Tribune*, November 17, 1967.

40. Clay Cooper, "Church Found 'Meddling' in Civil Rights Crisis," *Fundamentalist*, November 1963, 5.

41. John R. Rice, "Sow to the Wind; Reap a Whirlwind," *Sword of the Lord*, September 24, 1965, 7.

42. Bob Spencer, "Dr. Martin Luther King Died by the Lawlessness He Encouraged," *Sword of the Lord*, June 14, 1968.

43. G. Archer Weniger, "Martin Luther King, Negro *Pro Communist*, Modernist," *Sword of the Lord*, November 9, 1962.

44. John R. Rice, *Sword of the Lord*, August 19, 1964, 3.

45. Andrew Manis, *Southern Civil Religions in Conflict: Civil Rights and the Culture Wars* (Mercer University Press, 2002), 34.

46. Ibid., 35.

47. Ibid., 36.

48. Ibid., 80.

49. Ibid., 30.

50. Ibid., 30–31.

51. Ibid., 32.

52. Ibid., 33.

53. Wallace C. Smith, "Progressive National Baptist Convention: The Roots of the Black Church," *American Baptist Quarterly* 19 (September 2000): 248.

54. Ibid., 254.

55. Ibid., 256–257.

56. John W. Kinney, "The National Baptist Convention of the United States of America: 'Give Us Free,'" *American Baptist Quarterly* 19 (September 2000): 239.

57. Ibid., 241.

58. Ibid.

59. Ibid., 241–242.

60. Ibid., 242–243.

61. Ibid., 243.

## Chapter 9

1. Donald G. Mathews, *Religion in the Old South* (Chicago: University of Chicago Press, 1977), 111.

2. Ibid., 113.

3. Carolyn D. Blevins, *Women's Place in Baptist Life* (Brentwood, TN: Baptist History and Heritage Society, 2003), 12. Other verses included Acts 2:14, Acts 21:9, and 1 Corinthians 11:5. Verses taken from the Revised English Bible.

4. Ibid.

5. Ibid.

6. Ibid., 11.

7. Ibid.

8. Ibid., 13.

9. James R. Lynch, "Baptist Women in Ministry Through 1920," *American Baptist Quarter* 13 (December 1994): 304.

10. Elder John Sparks, *The Roots of Appalachian Christianity* (Lexington: University of Kentucky Press, 2001), 31.

11. Lynch, "Baptist Women in Ministry Through 1920," 304.

12. Ibid., 305.

13. Christine Leigh Heyrman, *Southern Cross: The Beginnings of the Bible Belt* (New York: Knopf, 1997), 166.

14. Ibid., 177.

15. Ibid., 311.

16. Lynch, "Baptist Women in Ministry Through 1920," 307.

17. Ibid., 309. Lura Maines served the Cipio and North Bethel Free Will Baptist churches.

18. Ibid., 310.

19. Ibid., 310–311.

20. Dana L. Robert, *American Women in Mission* (Macon, GA: Mercer University Press, 1996), 37.

21. Ibid., 130.

22. Mary L. Mild, "'Whom Shall I Send?': An Overview of the American Baptist Women's Foreign Missionary Movement from 1873–1913," *American Baptist Quarterly* 12 (September 1993): 203.

23. Blevins, *Women's Place in Baptist Life*, 30.

24. Norman H. Maring, *Baptists in New Jersey* (Valley Forge, PA: Judson, 1964), 233.

25. Catherine Allen, *Century to Celebrate: History of the Woman's Missionary Union* (Birmingham, AL: Woman's Missionary Union, 1987), 31.

26. Ibid.

27. Joy A. Barnhardt and Luther E. Barnhardt III, "The Baptist General Conference Foreign Mission Advance: An Investigation Into the Causes of Its Emergence," *American Baptist Quarterly* 6 (September 1987); 175.

28. Allen, *Century to Celebrate*, 327.

29. Mary L. Mild, "'Whom Shall I Send?'" 201.

30. "Status of Women," American Baptist Convention, 1965, *American Baptist Quarterly* 5 (June–September 1986): 321.

31. Ibid.

32. "The Empowerment of Women in the American Baptist Churches," *American Baptist Quarterly* 5 (June–September 1986): 320.

33. Ibid., 320–321.

34. American Baptist Women in Ministry, Web page, www.abwim.org/statistics.

35. "Resolution on the Place of Women in Christian Service," June 1973, sbc.net.

36. "Resolution on Women," June 1980; "Resolution on the Role of Women," June 1981, sbc.net.

37. Libby Bellinger, "The History of Southern Baptist Women in Ministry," in Walter B. Shurden, ed., *The Struggle for the Soul of the SBC* (Macon, GA: Mercer University Press, 1993), 130–131.

38. Ibid., 132.

39. Ibid., 132–133.

40. "Resolution on Ordination and the Role of Women in Ministry," June 1984, sbc.net.

41. Walter B. Shurden, "A Chronology," in Shurden, *The Struggle for the Soul of the SBC*, xiii.

42. "Resolution on Ordination and the Role of Women in Ministry," June 1984, sbc.net.

43. Bellinger, "The History of Southern Baptist Women in Ministry," 135.

44. "The Church," *Baptist Faith and Message* (Nashville: Southern Baptist Convention, 2000), 13.

45. "Of the Church," in "Statement of Faith," Baptist Bible Fellowship International, bible.ca/cr-Baptist-BBFI.htm.

46. "Eve Is Again Listening to the Voice of the Serpent," Landmark Independent Baptist Church Homepage, users.aol.com/libcfl/woman.htm.

47. Mary R. Sawyer, "Black Religion and Social Change: Women in Leadership Roles," in Larry G. Murphy, ed., *Down by the Riverside: Readings in African American Religion*, 305 (New York: New York University Press, 2000).

48. Ibid., 308.

49. Ibid.

50. Mechal Sobel, *Trabelin' On: The Slave Journey to an Afro-Baptist Faith* (Westport, CT: Greenwood Press, 1979), 233, cited in C. Eric Lincoln and Lawrence H. Mamiya, "The Black Denominations and the Ordination of Women," in Larry G. Murphy, ed., *Down by the Riverside: Readings in African American Religion*, 368 (New York: New York University Press, 2000).

51. Waveny Ann Moore and Twila Decker, "Women's Role in Male-Led Church," *St Petersburg Times*, September 9, 1999.

52. Lincoln and Mamiya, "The Black Denominations and the Ordination of Women," 372.

53. Ibid.

## Chapter 10

1. Clifford Geertz, *The Interpretation of Cultures* (New York: Basic Books, 1973), 89.

2. Martin E. Marty, "The Protestant Experience and Perspective," in *American Religious Values and the Future of America*, 33 (Philadelphia: Fortress, 1978), citing Philip Bagby, *Culture and History: Prolegomena to the Comparative Study of Civilizations* (Berkeley: University of California Press, 1963), 84, 104–105.

3. H. Richard Niebuhr, *Christ and Culture* (New York: Harper, 1951), 1–44. Niebuhr also includes two other motifs: Christ and culture in paradox, and Christ above culture.

4. Some of these issues, especially race and women's roles in the churches, are discussed in earlier chapters.

5. Barry Hankins, *Uneasy in Babylon: Southern Baptist Conservatives and American Culture* (Tuscaloosa: University of Alabama Press, 2002), 42, citing James Davison Hunter, *Culture Wars: The Struggle to Define America* (New York: Basic Books, 1991), 44–45.

6. Andrew Manis, *Southern Civil Religions in Conflict: Civil Rights and the Culture Wars* (Macon, GA: Mercer University Press, 2002), 160, citing Hunter, *Culture Wars*, 42–45, 50.

7. Richard J. Hooker, ed., *The Carolina Backcountry on the Eve of the Revolution: The Journal and Other Writings of Charles Woodmason, Anglican Itinerant* (Chapel Hill: University of North Carolina Press, 1953), 109; John G. Crowley, *Primitive Baptists of the Wiregrass South* (Gainesville: University Press of Florida, 1998), 8.

8. David Stricklin, *A Genealogy of Dissent: Southern Baptist Protest in the Twentieth Century* (Lexington: University Press of Kentucky, 1999), 11.

9. Bill J. Leonard, "What Can the Baptist Tradition Contribute to Christian Higher Education?," in Richard T. Hughes and William B. Adrian, eds., *Models for Christian Higher Education*, 367–382 (Grand Rapids, MI: William B. Eerdmans Publishing Company, 1997). See also Bill J. Leonard, "Christian Identity and Academic Rigor: The Case of Samford University," in *Models for Christian Higher Education*, 383–401.

10. A. J. Barton, "The Baptist Stand on Prohibition," *Religious Herald*, January 19, 1933, 4; cited in George D. Kelsey, *Social Ethics Among Southern Baptists, 1917–1969* (Metuchen, NJ: Scarecrow Press, 1973), 132.

11. Kelsey, *Social Ethics Among Southern Baptists*, 132.

12. B. D. Poage, ed., *The Tobacco Church II: A Manual for Congregational Leaders* (Richmond, KY: Christian Church in Kentucky, Kentucky Appalachian Ministry, 1995), 102; Bennett Poage, "The Church and Family Farm Ministry in Central Appalachia," in Bill J. Leonard, ed., *Christianity in Appalachia: Profiles in Regional Pluralism*, 18–39 (Knoxville: University of Tennessee Press, 1999).

13. www.abc-usa.org, resolutions.

14. These practices were not uncommon to many Protestant communions in the twentieth century. Though less prevalent, they continue to characterize various twenty-first-century Baptist groups.

15. Don A. Sanford, *A Choosing People: The History of Seventh Day Baptists* (Nashville: Broadman, 1992), 339. American Baptist Churches, USA passed a similar resolution; see www.abc-usa.org, resolutions.

16. www.abc-usa.org, resolutions.

17. See www.truelovewaits.com.

18. www.abc-usa.org, resolutions.

19. 1 Timothy 3 states that "a bishop" (pastor) should be "husband of one wife" with the same admonition for deacons. That leads some Baptists to believe that those who have been divorced cannot be appointed to that office.

20. Certain exceptions illustrate the way in which divorce is affecting all segments of Baptist life, including conservative leaders. During the 1990s Charles Stanley, pastor of First Baptist Church, Atlanta, Georgia, and a popular preacher on a nationally syndicated television program, announced that he and his wife were getting a divorce. In spite of Stanley's own conservatism as a biblical inerrantist, he asked that the deacons of the church permit him to continue as pastor. They voted to do so, though not without controversy and the loss of some of the church's members.

21. "Resolution on Homosexuality," June 1976, sbc.net.

22. "Resolution on Homosexuality," June 1977, sbc.net.

23. "Resolution on Homosexuality," June 1988, sbc.net.

24. "Resolution on Homosexuality, Military Service and Civil Rights," June 1993, sbc.net.

25. "Resolution on Homosexual Marriage," June 1996, sbc.net. A similar resolution was approved in 2003.

26. The Baptist Peace Fellowship distributed brochures at its booth at CBF meetings regarding more-open responses to homosexuals in the church. Schools with open admissions policies included divinity schools at Duke, Emory, and Wake Forest Universities. The open admissions policy at Wake Forest University, Winston-Salem, North Carolina, became a particular focal point when the new school began in 1999.

27. "Rationale for Homosexuality Statement," November 15, 2000, cbfonline .org.

28. "The Cooperative Baptist Fellowship (CBF) and Homosexuality," religioustolerance.org; and Russell D. Moore, "Divided CBF Battles Over Homosexuality," cephasministry.com/baptists_battles_over_homosexuality.htm.

29. "American Baptist Resolution on Homosexuality," October 1992, abc-usa . org.

30. "General Board Receives Report from Commission on Denominational Unity," November 28, 1997, abc-usa.org.

31. "American Baptists Concerned for Sexual Minorities," rainbowbaptists.org.

32. Ibid.

33. "Homosexual Men Win Again," www.baptist

34. "The Teachings of Southern Baptists and Fred Phelps," *Soulforce*, soulforce.org, 3.

35. Ibid., 5.

36. Leaders of the Southern Baptist Convention have sought to distance themselves from Phelps's militant actions and rhetoric, while Soulforce, a group of "open and affirming" Baptists with particular connection to the Southern Baptist Convention, states: "Southern Baptist leaders may not say 'God Hates Fags,' as Fred Phelps does, but the effect is still the same. These hurtful and hateful messages make gay, lesbian, bisexual, and transgender people hate themselves and hate God." Debates continue as to the nature and rhetoric of opposition to and support for homosexuals in Baptist life.

37. Yonat Shimron, "North Carolina Baptists Expel Church for Baptizing Gays," *Religion News Service*, beliefnet.com.

38. Ibid.

39. Paul R. Dekar, *For the Healing of the Nations: Baptist Peacemakers* (Macon, GA: Smyth and Helwys, 1993), 1–2.

40. Vincent Harding, "Fighting for Freedom with Church Fans," in Larry G. Murphy, ed., *Down by the Riverside: Readings in African American Religion* (New York: New York University Press, 2000), 475.

41. Kimon Howland Sargeant, *Seeker Churches: Promoting Traditional Religion in a Nontraditional Way* (New Brunswick, NJ: Rutgers University Press, 2000), 4.

42. Ibid., 4–5.

43. Ibid., 5.

44. Ibid.

45. www. saddleback.com/flash/s.

46. Ibid.

47. The idea of intentional marketing techniques is what distinguishes megachurches from big traditional churches.

48. www.fellowship.com/Fcweb/about fellowship/press.

49. Ibid. Fellowship Church does not baptize children under the age of seven years.

50. James Carroll, "Warring with God," *Boston Globe*, October 21, 2003.

51. *Winston-Salem Journal*, June 16, 2002, A-18.

# SELECTED BIBLIOGRAPHY

Ammerman, Nancy Tatom. *Baptist Battles: Social Change and Religious Conflict in the Southern Baptist Convention*. New Brunswick, NJ: Rutgers University Press, 1990. (Survey of the sociological implications of the controversy over biblical inerrancy in the Southern Baptist Convention.)

Armstrong, O. K., and Marjorie Armstrong. *The Baptists in America*. Garden City, NY: Doubleday, 1979. (Popular history of Baptists, written primarily for church folk.)

Backus, Isaac. *Isaac Backus on Church, State, and Calvinism: Pamphlets, 1754–1789*. Edited by William McLoughlin. Cambridge: Belknap Press of Harvard University Press, 1968. (Documents detailing issues of religious liberty, church order, and theology.)

Baker, Robert. *The Southern Baptist Convention and Its People*. Nashville: Broadman, 1972. (Standard historical text on the SBC.)

Banks, William L. *A History of Black Baptists in the United States*. Philadelphia: Continental, 1987. (Survey of diverse African American denominations and mission activities.

Begaye, Russell. "The Story of Indian Southern Baptists." *Baptist History and Heritage* 18 (July 1983): 30–39. (Early details of the growth of Baptist influence among Native Americans.)

Benedict, David. *A General History of the Baptist Denomination in America*. New York: Colby, 1848. (Classic nineteenth-century history of Baptists in the United States.)

Brackney, William. *The Baptists*. New York: Greenwood, 1988. (Distinctive doctrines of the Baptists and brief biographical sketches of Baptist leaders, male and female.)

————, ed. *Baptist in Life and Thought, 1600–1980*. Valley Forge, PA: Judson, 1983. (Collection of primary sources from Baptist history.)

Brumberg, Joan Jacobs. *Mission for Life: The Story of the Family of Adoniram Judson, the Dramatic Events of the First American Foreign Mission, and the Course of Evangelical Religion in the Nineteenth Century*. New York: Free Press, 1980. (Survey of the lives of various Judsons and examination of their impact on American evangelical life, with particular attention to the role of women in the family and on the mission field.)

Combs, James O., ed. *Roots and Origins of Baptist Fundamentalism*. Springfield, MO: Baptist Bible Tribune, 1984. (Baptist fundamentalist examination of the history of their tradition.)

Copeland, E. Luther. *The Southern Baptist Convention and the Judgment of History: The Taint of an Original Sin*. Lanham, MD: University Press of America, 1995. (Exploration of the controversy in the SBC from a "moderate" perspective, by a former SBC missionary.)

Dawson, J. M. *Baptists and the American Republic*. Nashville: Broadman, 1956. (Classic history of church/state issues among the Baptists, by a director of the Baptist Joint Committee on Public Affairs.)

Deweese, Charles W. "The Role of Circular Letters in Baptist Associations in America, 1707–1799." *Quarterly Review* 37 (October–December 1976): 52–57. (Examination of an important medium for communicating Baptist doctrine and practice in early America.)

Dorgan, Howard. *Giving Glory to God in Appalachia: Worship Practices of Six Baptist Subdenominations*. Knoxville: University of Tennessee Press, 1987. (Account of specific Baptist denominations located in central Appalachia.)

————. *In the Hands of a Happy God: Primitive Baptist Universalists of Central Appalachia*. Knoxville: University of Tennessee Press, 1997. (History of a little-known segment of Primitive Baptist life, a group that carries Calvinism full circle to assert that all are ultimately "elected" to salvation.)

Estep, William R. *Whole Gospel, Whole World: The Foreign Mission Board of the Southern Baptist Convention, 1845–1995*. Nashville: Broadman and Holman, 1994. (History of the SBC mission board, providing information about mission fields and missionary leaders.)

Fitts, Leroy. *A History of Black Baptists*. Nashville: Broadman, 1985. (Basic history of African American institutions and activities in America.)

Fletcher, Jesse C. *The Southern Baptist Convention: A Sesquicentennial History*. Nashville: Broadman and Holman, 1994. (Recent history of the SBC.)

Freeman, Curtis W., James Wm. McClendon Jr., and C. Rosalee Velloso da Silva. *Baptist Roots*. Valley Forge, PA: Judson, 1999. (Collection of source materials from Baptist men and women worldwide.)

Gardner, Robert G. *Baptists in Early America: A Statistical History, 1639–1790*. Atlanta: Georgia Baptist Historical Society, 1983. (Invaluable resource that provides actual statistics of Baptist churches and associations in the initial period of Baptist life in America.)

Gaustad, Edwin S., ed. *Baptist Piety: The Last Will and Testament of Obadiah Holmes*. Valley Forge, PA: Judson, 1994. (Introduction and primary source that offers insight into colonial Baptist life and persecution.)

———. *Liberty of Conscience: Roger Williams in America*. Grand Rapids, MI: Eerdmans, 1991. (Classic survey of the life and work of Roger Williams.)

Goodwin, Everett C., ed. *Baptists in the Balance*. Valley Forge, PA: Judson, 1997. (Collection of essays detailing elements of Baptist life from a variety of Baptist scholars representing various groups.)

Grammich, Clifford A. Jr. *Local Baptists, Local Politics*. Knoxville: University of Tennessee Press, 1999. (Statistical analysis of the role of Baptists in certain segments of the South.)

Hankins, Barry. *Uneasy in Zion: Southern Baptist Conservatives and American Culture*. Tuscaloosa: University of Alabama Press, 2002. (Survey of various issues and attitudes present among SBC conservatives after their movement gained control of the convention system, including religious liberty, homosexuality, women in ministry, and other culture-war issues.)

Harvey, Paul. *Redeeming the South: Religious Cultures and Racial Identities Among Southern Baptists, 1865–1925*. Chapel Hill: University of North Carolina Press, 1997. (Thorough study of both white and black Baptists from the end of the Civil War to the early twentieth century.)

Heyrman, Christine Leigh. *Southern Cross: The Beginnings of the Bible Belt*. New York: Knopf, 1997. (Discussion of Baptist life, particularly shifts in the "women's sphere" during the revival movements of the nineteenth century; helpful in understanding changes in Baptist identity.)

James, Robison B., ed. *The Unfettered Word: Southern Baptists Confront the Authority-Inerrancy Question*. Waco, TX: Word, 1987. (An effort to present the varying positions regarding biblical inerrancy in Baptist life.)

Knight, Richard. *History of the General or Six Principle Baptists in Europe and America*. New York: Arno Press, 1980. (Standard history of the Six Principle Baptists.)

Laws, Curtis L. "Fundamentalism Is Very Much Alive." *Watchman Examiner*, July 28, 1921. (Examination of early issues in the growth of American fundamentalism.)

Leonard, Bill J. *Baptist Ways: A History*. Valley Forge, PA: Judson, 2003. (Survey of Baptist history worldwide.)

———. "Getting Saved in America: Conversion Event in a Pluralistic Culture." *Review and Expositor* 82 (Winter 1985): 111–128. [Survey of changes in the morphology (process) of salvation from Jonathan Edwards to Billy Graham.]

———. *God's Last and Only Hope: The Fragmentation of the Southern Baptist Convention*. Grand Rapids, MI: Eerdmans, 1990. (Social history of the SBC and the development of its denominational identity after the Civil War.)

————. "Independent Baptists from Sectarian Minority to 'Moral Majority.'" *Church History* 56 (December 1987): 504–517. (Brief history of the Independent Baptist movement and its relationship to American culture.)

————. "A Theology for Racism: Southern Fundamentalists and the Civil Rights Movement." In Tony J. Badger, ed., *Southern Landscapes*. Tubingen: Stauffenburg, 1996. (Examination of the actual statements and ideology of Independent Baptist leaders in the latter twentieth century.)

Lumpkin, William L. *Baptist Confessions of Faith*. Valley Forge, PA: Judson, 1974. (Collection of classic Baptist confessions with commentary.)

Maring, Norman, and Winthrop Hudson. *A Baptist Manual of Polity and Practice*. Rev. ed. Valley Forge, PA: Judson, 1991. (Systematic explanation of distinctive Baptist organizational activities and ministries.)

Martin, Sandy D. "The Baptist Foreign Mission Convention, 1880–1894." *Baptist History and Heritage* 16 (October 1981): 12–25. (Examination of the role of black Baptists in shaping the modern missions movement and the growth of a consciousness regarding African "roots.")

————. *Black Baptists and African Missions*. Macon, GA: Mercer University Press, 1989. (The beginning of Baptist denominationalism among African American Baptists.)

McBeth, H. Leon. *The Baptist Heritage*. Nashville: Broadman, 1987. (Survey text related to Baptists worldwide.)

————, ed. *A Sourcebook for Baptist Heritage*. Nashville: Broadman, 1990. (One of the most thorough collections of Baptist sources; parallels his survey text.)

McCauley, Deborah Vansau. *Appalachian Mountain Religion: A History*. Chicago: University of Illinois Press, 1995. (Examination of "indigenous" mountain churches, with particular attention to Baptists and Holiness communions.)

McLoughlin, William. *Soul Liberty: The Baptists' Struggle in New England, 1630–1833*. Hanover, NH: University Press of New England, 1991. (Various sources and commentary regarding the faith and practice of early Baptists from the colonial through the national periods.)

Moore, David O. "The Withdrawal of Blacks from Southern Baptist Churches Following Emancipation." *Baptist History and Heritage* 16 (July 1981): 12–18. (Exploration of the reasons for the segregating of churches and the development of distinct Baptist denominations among African American Christians.)

Morris, Elias C. *Sermons, Addresses, and Reminiscences, and Important Correspondence*. 1901. Reprint. New York: Arno Press, 1980. (Fine primary-source collection of documents that detail African American Baptist issues and approaches, compiled by a leader among early-twentieth-century African American Baptists.)

Newman, Mark. *Getting Right with God: Southern Baptists and Segregation, 1945–1995*. Tuscaloosa: University of Alabama Press, 2001. (Survey of racial issues within and alongside the SBC to the latter twentieth century.)

Pitts, Walter F. *The Old Ship of Zion: The Afro-Baptist Ritual in the African Diaspora*. New York: Oxford University Press, 1993. (Superb examination of the development of Baptist identity out of slave society and experience.)

Rauschenbusch, Walter. *Christianity and the Social Crisis*. New York: Harper and Row, 1964. (One of many works written by the teacher sometimes known as the founder of the Social Gospel.)

Robert, Dana L. *American Women in Mission: A Social History of Their Thought and Practice*. Macon, GA: Mercer University Press, 1996. (Fine survey of the work of American women in the mission movement, of which Baptist women make up a significant portion.)

Russell, C. Allyn. *Voices of American Fundamentalism*. Philadelphia: Westminster, 1976. (Seven biographies of early fundamentalist leaders, most of whom are Baptist or have Baptist connections.)

Sanford, Don A. *A Choosing People: The History of Seventh Day Baptists*. Nashville: Broadman, 1992. (Standard history of Seventh Day Baptists.)

Shurden, Walter B. *Associationalism Among Baptists in America, 1707–1814*. New York: Arno Press, 1980. (Account of the development of the earliest Baptist associations and the varied rationales for these church connections that form the basis of Baptist denominationalism.)

————. *Baptist Identity: Four Fragile Freedoms*. Macon, GA: Smyth and Helwys, 1993. (Brief and helpful survey of the essentials of Baptist identity.)

Smith, Oran P. *The Rise of Baptist Republicanism*. New York: New York University Press, 1997. (Exploration of the growth of Baptist political conservatism in the United States.)

Smith, Wallace E. "Progressive National Baptist Convention: The Roots of the Black Church." *American Baptist Quarterly* 19 (September 2000): 245–259. (Brief history of the beginnings of an important black denomination.)

Sparks, John. *The Roots of Appalachian Christianity*. Lexington: University of Kentucky Press, 2002. (A study that uses the life and work of colonial preacher Shubal Stearns as a focus for understanding Baptists in Appalachia, by an elder among the United Baptists.)

Sweet, William Warren. *The Baptists, 1783–1830*. Chicago: University of Chicago Press, 1931. (Classic collection of primary sources from church records and other documents.)

Torbet, Robert. *A Social History of the Philadelphia Baptist Association: 1707–1940*. Philadelphia: Westbrook, 1944. (Survey of the founding and work of America's oldest Baptist association.)

Wardin, Albert W., ed. *Baptists Around the World: A Comprehensive Handbook*. Nashville: Broadman and Holman, 1995. (Survey of Baptist groups throughout the world, including statistics and basic beliefs country by country.)

Washington, James Melvin. *Frustrated Fellowship: The Black Baptist Quest for Social Power*. Macon, GA: Mercer University Press, 1986. (Study of the development of black Baptist denominations.)

Williams, A. D. *Benoni Stenson and the General Baptists*. Owensville, IN: General Baptist Publishing House, 1892. (Nineteenth-century history of the renewal of the General Baptists in America.)

Wood, James E., ed. *Baptists and the American Experience*. Valley Forge, PA: Judson, 1976. (Collection of articles that detail Baptist history and practice at the time of the American bicentennial.)

# INDEX